Regression Analysis with Python

Learn the art of regression analysis with Python

Luca Massaron

Alberto Boschetti

BIRMINGHAM - MUMBAI

Regression Analysis with Python

First published: February 2016

Production reference: 1250216

Published by Packt Publishing Ltd.
Livery Place
35 Livery Street
Birmingham B3 2PB, UK.

ISBN 978-1-78528-631-5

www.packtpub.com

Credits

Authors
Luca Massaron
Alberto Boschetti

Reviewers
Giuliano Janson
Zacharias Voulgaris

Commissioning Editor
Kunal Parikh

Acquisition Editor
Sonali Vernekar

Content Development Editor
Siddhesh Salvi

Technical Editor
Shivani Kiran Mistry

Copy Editor
Stephen Copestake

Project Coordinator
Nidhi Joshi

Proofreader
Safis Editing

Indexer
Mariammal Chettiyar

Graphics
Disha Haria

Production Coordinator
Nilesh Mohite

Cover Work
Nilesh Mohite

About the Authors

Luca Massaron is a data scientist and a marketing research director who is specialized in multivariate statistical analysis, machine learning, and customer insight with over a decade of experience in solving real-world problems and in generating value for stakeholders by applying reasoning, statistics, data mining, and algorithms. From being a pioneer of Web audience analysis in Italy to achieving the rank of a top ten Kaggler, he has always been very passionate about everything regarding data and its analysis and also about demonstrating the potential of data-driven knowledge discovery to both experts and non-experts. Favoring simplicity over unnecessary sophistication, he believes that a lot can be achieved in data science just by doing the essentials.

I would like to thank Yukiko and Amelia for their support, help, and loving patience.

Alberto Boschetti is a data scientist, with an expertise in signal processing and statistics. He holds a Ph.D. in telecommunication engineering and currently lives and works in London. In his work projects, he faces daily challenges that span from natural language processing (NLP) and machine learning to distributed processing. He is very passionate about his job and always tries to stay updated about the latest developments in data science technologies, attending meet-ups, conferences, and other events.

I would like to thank my family, my friends and my colleagues. Also, big thanks to the Open Source community.

About the Reviewers

Giuliano Janson's professional experiences have centered on advanced analytics and applied machine learning in healthcare. His work is primarily focused on extracting information from large, dirty, and noisy data utilizing machine learning, stats, Monte Carlo simulation, and data visualization to identify business opportunities and help leadership make data-driven decisions through actionable analytics.

> I'd like to thank my wife, Magda, and my two beautiful children, Alex and Emily, for all the love they share.

Zacharias Voulgaris is a data scientist and technical author specializing in data science books. He has an engineering and management background, with post-graduate studies in information systems and machine learning. Zacharias has worked as a research fellow in Georgia Tech, investigating and applying machine learning technologies to real-world problems, as an SEO manager in an e-marketing company in Europe, as a program manager in Microsoft, and as a data scientist in US Bank and G2 Web Services.

Dr. Voulgaris has also authored technical books, the most notable of which is *Data Scientist: The Definitive Guide to Becoming a Data Scientist, Technics Publications*, and is currently working on *Julia for Data Science, Manning Publications*. He has also written a number of data science-related articles on blogs and participates in various data science/machine learning meet-up groups. Finally, he has provided technical editorial aid in the book *Python Data Science Essentials, Packt Publishing*, by the same authors as this book.

> I would like to express my gratitude to the authors of the book for giving me the opportunity to contribute to this project. Also, I'd like to thank Bastiaan Sjardin for introducing me to them and to the world of technical editing.

www.PacktPub.com

eBooks, discount offers, and more

Did you know that Packt offers eBook versions of every book published, with PDF and ePub files available? You can upgrade to the eBook version at www.PacktPub.com and as a print book customer, you are entitled to a discount on the eBook copy. Get in touch with us at customercare@packtpub.com for more details.

At www.PacktPub.com, you can also read a collection of free technical articles, sign up for a range of free newsletters and receive exclusive discounts and offers on Packt books and eBooks.

https://www2.packtpub.com/books/subscription/packtlib

Do you need instant solutions to your IT questions? PacktLib is Packt's online digital book library. Here, you can search, access, and read Packt's entire library of books.

Why subscribe?

- Fully searchable across every book published by Packt
- Copy and paste, print, and bookmark content
- On demand and accessible via a web browser

Table of Contents

Preface

"Frustra fit per plura, quod potest fieri per pauciora.

(It is pointless to do with more what can be done with fewer)"

William of Ockham (1285-1347)

Linear models have been known to scholars and practitioners and studied by them for a long time now. Before they were adopted into data science and placed into the syllabi of numerous boot camps and in the early chapters of many practical how-to-do books, they have been a prominent and relevant element of the body of knowledge of statistics, economics, and of many other respectable quantitative fields of study.

Consequently, there is a vast availability of monographs, book chapters, and papers about linear regression, logistic regression (its classification variant), and the different types of generalized linear models; models where the original linear regression paradigm is adapted in its formulation in order to solve more complex problems.

Yet, in spite of such an embarrassment of riches, we have never encountered any book that really explains the speed and ease of implementation of such linear models when, as a developer or a data scientist, you have to quickly create an application or API whose response cannot be defined programmatically but it does have to learn from data.

Of course we are very well aware of the limitations of linear models (being simple unfortunately has some drawbacks) and we also know how there is no fixed solution for any data science problem; however, our experience in the field has told us that the following advantages of a linear model cannot be easily ignored:

- It's easy to explain how it works to yourself, to the management, or to anyone
- It's flexible in respect of your data problem, since it can handle numeric and probability estimates, ranking, and classification up to a large number of classes
- It's fast to train, no matter what the amount of data you have to process
- It's fast and easy to implement in any production environment
- It's scalable to real-time response toward users

If for you, as it is daily for us, it is paramount to deliver value from data in a fast and tangible way, just follow us and discover how far linear model can help you get to.

What this book covers

Chapter 1, Regression – The Workhorse of Data Science, introduces why regression is indeed useful for data science, how to quickly set up Python for data science and provides an overview of the packages used throughout the book with the help of examples. At the end of this chapter, we will be able to run all the examples contained in the following chapters. You will have clear ideas and motivations why regression analysis is not just an underrated technique taken from statistics but a powerful and effective data science algorithm.

Chapter 2, Approaching Simple Linear Regression, presents the simple linear regression by first describing a regression problem, where to fit a regressor, and then giving some intuitions underneath the math formulation of its algorithm. Then, you will learn how to tune the model for higher performances and understand every parameter of it, deeply. Finally, the engine under the hood the gradient descent will be described.

Chapter 3, Multiple Regression in Action, extends the simple linear regression to extract predictive information from more than a feature and create models that can solve real-life prediction tasks. The stochastic gradient descent technique, explained in the previous chapter, will be powered up to cope with a matrix of features and to complete the overview, you will be shown multi-collinearity, interactions, and polynomial regression topics.

Chapter 4, Logistic Regression, continues laying down the foundations of your knowledge of linear model. Starting from the necessary mathematical definitions, it demonstrates how to furthermore extend the linear regression to classification problems, both binary and multiclass.

Chapter 5, Data Preparation, discusses about the data feeding the model, describing what can be done to prepare the data in the best way and how to deal with unusual situations, especially when data is missing and outliers are present.

Chapter 6, Achieving Generalization, will introduce you to the key data science recipes for testing your model thoroughly, tune it at its best, make it parsimonious, and to put it against real fresh data, before proceeding to more complex techniques.

Chapter 7, Online and Batch Learning, illustrates the best practices to train classifiers on Big Data; it first focuses on batch learning and its limitations and then introduces online learning. Finally, you will be showed an example of Big Data, combining the benefits of online learning and the power of the hashing trick.

Chapter 8, Advanced Regression Methods, introduces some advanced methods for regression. Without getting too deep into their mathematical formulation, but always keeping an eye on practical applications, we will discuss the ideas underneath Least Angle Regression, Bayesian Regression, and stochastic gradient descent with hinge loss, and also touch upon bagging and boosting techniques.

Chapter 9, Real-world Applications for Regression Models, comprises of four practical examples of real-world data science problems solved by linear models. The ultimate goal is to demonstrate how to approach such problems and how develop the reasoning around their resolution, so that they can be used as blueprints for similar challenges you'll encounter.

What you need for this book

The execution of the code examples provided in this book requires an installation of Python 3.4.3 or newer on Mac OS X, Linux, or Microsoft Windows.

The code presented throughout the book will also make frequent use of Python's essential libraries for scientific and statistical computing such as SciPy, NumPy, Scikit-learn, Statsmodels, to a minor extent, matplotlib, and pandas.

Apart from taking advantage of Scientific distributions (such as Anaconda from Continuum Analytics) that can save you a lot of time from the time-consuming operations in order to create a working environment, we also suggest you to adopt Jupyter and its IPython Notebooks, as a more productive and scientific-friendly way to code your linear models in Python.

The first chapter will provide you with the step-by-step instructions and some useful tips to set up your Python environment, these core libraries and all the necessary tools.

Who this book is for

First, this book is addressed to Python developers with at least a basic understanding of data science, statistics, and math. Though the book doesn't require a previous background in data science or statistics, it can well address data scientists of any seniority who intend to learn how to best do regression analysis on a dataset. We imagine that you want to put intelligence in your data products but you don't want to depend on any black box. Therefore, you prefer a technique which is simple, understandable, and yet effective to be production grade. Through the book, we will provide you with the knowledge to use Python for building fast and better linear models and to deploy the resulting models in Python or in any computer language you prefer.

Conventions

In this book, you will find a number of text styles that distinguish between different kinds of information. Here are some examples of these styles and an explanation of their meaning.

Code words in text, database table names, folder names, filenames, file extensions, pathnames, dummy URLs, user input, and Twitter handles are shown as follows: "When inspecting the linear model, first check the `coef_` attribute."

A block of code is set as follows:

```
from sklearn import datasets
iris = datasets.load_iris()
```

Since we will be using IPython Notebooks along most of the examples, expect to have always an input (marked as In:) and often an output (marked Out:) from the cell containing the block of code. On your computer you have just to input the code after the In: and check if results correspond to the Out: content:

```
In: clf.fit(X, y)
Out: SVC(C=1.0, cache_size=200, class_weight=None, coef0=0.0,
     degree=3, gamma=0.0, kernel='rbf', max_iter=-1, probability=False,
     random_state=None, shrinking=True, tol=0.001, verbose=False)
```

When a command should be given in the terminal command line, you'll find the command with the prefix `$>`, otherwise, if it's for the Python REPL it will be preceded by `>>>`:

```
$>python
>>> import sys
```

```
>>> print sys.version_info
```

New terms and **important words** are shown in bold. Words that you see on the screen, for example, in menus or dialog boxes, appear in the text like this: "Go to the **Databases** section and create a new database using the UTF collation."

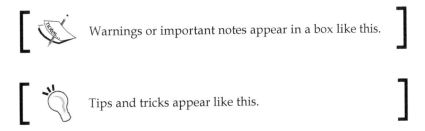

Warnings or important notes appear in a box like this.

Tips and tricks appear like this.

Reader feedback

Feedback from our readers is always welcome. Let us know what you think about this book — what you liked or disliked. Reader feedback is important for us as it helps us develop titles that you will really get the most out of.

To send us general feedback, simply e-mail `feedback@packtpub.com`, and mention the book's title in the subject of your message.

If there is a topic that you have expertise in and you are interested in either writing or contributing to a book, see our author guide at `www.packtpub.com/authors`.

Customer support

Now that you are the proud owner of a Packt book, we have a number of things to help you to get the most from your purchase.

Downloading the example code

You can download the example code files for this book from your account at http://www.packtpub.com. If you purchased this book elsewhere, you can visit http://www.packtpub.com/support and register to have the files e-mailed directly to you.

You can download the code files by following these steps:

1. Log in or register to our website using your e-mail address and password.
2. Hover the mouse pointer on the **SUPPORT** tab at the top.
3. Click on **Code Downloads & Errata**.
4. Enter the name of the book in the **Search** box.
5. Select the book for which you're looking to download the code files.
6. Choose from the drop-down menu where you purchased this book from.
7. Click on **Code Download**.

Once the file is downloaded, please make sure that you unzip or extract the folder using the latest version of:

- WinRAR / 7-Zip for Windows
- Zipeg / iZip / UnRarX for Mac
- 7-Zip / PeaZip for Linux

Downloading the color images of this book

We also provide you with a PDF file that has color images of the screenshots/diagrams used in this book. The color images will help you better understand the changes in the output. You can download this file from https://www.packtpub.com/sites/default/files/downloads/RegressionAnalysisWithPython_ColorImages.pdf.

Errata

Although we have taken every care to ensure the accuracy of our content, mistakes do happen. If you find a mistake in one of our books—maybe a mistake in the text or the code—we would be grateful if you could report this to us. By doing so, you can save other readers from frustration and help us improve subsequent versions of this book. If you find any errata, please report them by visiting http://www.packtpub.com/submit-errata, selecting your book, clicking on the **Errata Submission Form** link, and entering the details of your errata. Once your errata are verified, your submission will be accepted and the errata will be uploaded to our website or added to any list of existing errata under the Errata section of that title.

To view the previously submitted errata, go to https://www.packtpub.com/books/content/support and enter the name of the book in the search field. The required information will appear under the **Errata** section.

Piracy

Piracy of copyrighted material on the Internet is an ongoing problem across all media. At Packt, we take the protection of our copyright and licenses very seriously. If you come across any illegal copies of our works in any form on the Internet, please provide us with the location address or website name immediately so that we can pursue a remedy.

Please contact us at copyright@packtpub.com with a link to the suspected pirated material.

We appreciate your help in protecting our authors and our ability to bring you valuable content.

Questions

If you have a problem with any aspect of this book, you can contact us at questions@packtpub.com, and we will do our best to address the problem.

1
Regression – The Workhorse of Data Science

Welcome to this presentation on the workhorse of data science, linear regression, and its related family of linear models.

Nowadays, interconnectivity and data explosion are realities that open a world of new opportunities for every business that can read and interpret data in real time. Everything is facilitating the production and diffusion of data: the omnipresent Internet diffused both at home and at work, an army of electronic devices in the pockets of large portions of the population, and the pervasive presence of software producing data about every process and event. So much data is generated daily that humans cannot deal with it because of its volume, velocity, and variety. Thus, machine learning and AI are on the rise.

Coming from a long and glorious past in the field of statistics and econometrics, linear regression, and its derived methods, can provide you with a simple, reliable, and effective tool to learn from data and act on it. If carefully trained with the right data, linear methods can compete well against the most complex and fresh AI technologies, offering you unbeatable ease of implementation and scalability for increasingly large problems.

In this chapter, we will explain:

- Why linear models can be helpful as models to be evaluated in a data science pipeline or as a shortcut for the immediate development of a scalable minimum viable product
- Some quick indications for installing Python and setting it up for data science tasks
- The necessary modules for implementing linear models in Python

Regression analysis and data science

Imagine you are a developer hastily working on a very cool application that is going to serve thousands of customers using your company's website everyday. Using the available information about customers in your data warehouse, your application is expected to promptly provide a pretty smart and not-so-obvious answer. The answer unfortunately cannot easily be programmatically predefined, and thus will require you to adopt a *learning-from-data* approach, typical of data science or predictive analytics.

In this day and age, such applications are quite frequently found assisting numerous successful ventures on the Web, for instance:

- In the advertising business, an application delivering targeted advertisements

- In e-commerce, a batch application filtering customers to make more relevant commercial offers or an online app recommending products to buy on the basis of ephemeral data such as navigation records

- In the credit or insurance business, an application selecting whether to proceed with online inquiries from users, basing its judgment on their credit rating and past relationship with the company

There are numerous other possible examples, given the constantly growing number of use cases about machine learning applied to business problems. The core idea of all these applications is that you don't need to program how your application should behave, but you just set some desired behaviors by providing useful examples. The application will learn by itself what to do in any circumstance.

After you are clear about the purpose of your application and decide to use the learning-from-data approach, you are confident that you don't have to reinvent the wheel. Therefore, you jump into reading tutorials and documentation about data science and machine learning solutions applied to problems similar to yours (they could be papers, online blogs, or books talking about data science, machine learning, statistical learning, and predictive analytics).

After reading a few pages, you will surely be exposed to the wonders of many complex machine learning algorithms you likely have never heard of before.

However, you start being puzzled. It isn't simply because of the underlying complex mathematics; it is mostly because of the large amount of possible solutions based on very different techniques. You also often notice the complete lack of any discussion about how to deploy such algorithms in a production environment and whether they would scale up to real-time server requests.

At this point, you are completely unsure where should you start. This is when this book will come to your rescue.

Let's start from the beginning.

Exploring the promise of data science

Given a more interconnected world and the growing availability of data, data science has become quite a hot topic in recent years.

In the past, analytical solutions had strong constrains: the availability of data. Useful data was generally scarce and always costly to obtain and store. Given the current data explosion, now abundant and cheaper information at hand makes learning from data a reality, thus opening the doors to a wide range of predictive applications that were simply impractical before.

In addition, being in an interconnected world, most of your customers are now reachable (and susceptible of being influenced) through the Internet or through mobile devices. This simply means that being smart in developing automated solutions based on data and its predictive powers can directly and almost instantaneously affect how your business works and performs. Being able to reach your customers instantly everywhere, 24 hours a day, 365 days a year, enables your company to turn data into profits, if you know the right things to be done. In the 21ˢᵗ century, *data is the new oil of the digital economy,* as a memorable and still undisputed article on Wired stated not too long ago (`http://www.wired.com/insights/2014/07/data-new-oil-digital-economy/`).However, as with oil, data has to be extracted, refined, and distributed.

Being at the intersection of substantive expertise (knowing how to do business and make profits), machine learning (learning from data), and hacking skills (integrating various systems and data sources), data science promises to find the mix of tools to leverage your available data and turn it into profits.

However, there's another side to the coin.

The challenge

Unfortunately, there are quite a few challenging issues in applying data science to a business problem:

* Being able to process unstructured data or data that has been modeled for completely different purposes
* Figuring out how to extract such data from heterogeneous sources and integrate it in a timely manner

- Learning (from data) some effective general rules allowing you to correctly predict your problem

- Understanding what has been learned and being able to effectively communicate your solution to a non-technical managerial audience

- Scaling to real-time predictions given big data inputs

The first two points are mainly problems that require data manipulation skills, but from the third point onwards, we really need a data science approach to solve the problem.

The data science approach, based on machine learning, requires careful testing of different algorithms, estimating their predictive capabilities with respect to the problem, and finally selecting the best one to implement. This is exactly what the science in *data science* means: coming up with various different hypotheses and experimenting with them to find the one that best fits the problem and allows generalization of the results.

Unfortunately, there is no white unicorn in data science; there is no single hypothesis that can successfully fit all the available problems. In other words, we say that there is *no free lunch* (the name of a famous theorem from the optimization domain), meaning that there are no algorithms or procedures in data science that can always assure you the best results; each algorithm can be less or more successful, depending on the problem.

Data comes in all shapes and forms and reflects the complexity of the world we live in. The existing algorithms should have certain sophistication in order to deal with the complexity of the world, but don't forget that they are just models. Models are nothing but simplifications and approximations of the system of rules and laws we want to successfully represent and replicate for predictive reasons since *you can control only what you can measure*, as Lord Kelvin said. An approximation should be evaluated based on its effectiveness, and the efficacy of learning algorithms applied to real problems is dictated by so many factors (type of problem, data quality, data quantity, and so on) that you really cannot tell in advance what will work and what won't. Under such premises, you always want to test the simpler solutions first, and follow the principle of *Occam's razor* as much as possible, favoring simpler models against more complex ones when their performances are comparable.

Sometimes, even when the situation allows the introduction of more complex and more performant models, other factors may still favor the adoption of simpler yet less performant solutions. In fact, the best model is not always necessarily the most performant one. Depending on the problem and the context of application, issues such as ease of implementation in production systems, scalability to growing volumes of data, and performance in live settings, may deeply redefine how important the role of predictive performance is in the choice of the best solution.

In such situations, it is still advisable to use simpler, well-tuned models or easily explainable ones, if they provide an acceptable solution to the problem.

The linear models

In your initial overview of the problem of what machine learning algorithm to use, you may have also stumbled upon linear models, namely linear regression and logistic regression. They both have been presented as basic tools, building blocks of a more sophisticated knowledge that you should achieve before hoping to obtain the best results.

Linear models have been known and studied by scholars and practitioners for a long time. Before being promptly adopted into data science, linear models were always among the basic statistical models to start with in predictive analytics and data mining. They also have been a prominent and relevant tool part of the body of knowledge of statistics, economics, and many other quantitative subjects.

By a simple check (via a query from an online bookstore, from a library, or just from Google Books – `https://books.google.com/`), you will discover there is quite a vast availability of publications about linear regression. There is also quite an abundance of publications about logistic regression, and about other different variants of the regression algorithm, the so-called generalized linear models, adapted in their formulation to face and solve more complex problems.

As practitioners ourselves, we are well aware of the limits of linear models. However, we cannot ignore their strong positive key points: simplicity and efficacy. We also cannot ignore that linear models are indeed among the most used learning algorithms in applied data science, making them real workhorses in data analysis (in business as well as in many scientific domains).

Far from being the best tool at hand, they are always a good starting point in a data science path of discovery because they don't require hacking with too many parameters and they are very fast to train. Thus, linear models can point out the predictive power of your data at hand, identify the most important variables, and allow you to quickly test useful transformations of your data before applying more complex algorithms.

In the course of this book, you will learn how to build prototypes based on linear regression models, keeping your data treatment and handling pipeline prompt for possible development reiterations of the initial linear model into more powerful and complex ones, such as neural networks or support vector machines.

Moreover, you will learn that you maybe don't even need more complex models, sometimes. If you are really working with lots of data, after having certain volumes of input data feed into a model, using simple or complex algorithms won't matter all that much anymore. They will all perform to the best of their capabilities.

The capability of big data to make even simpler models as effective as a complex one has been pointed out by a famous paper co-authored by Alon Halevy, Peter Norvig, and Fernando Pereira from Google about *The Unreasonable Effectiveness of Data* (http://static.googleusercontent.com/media/research.google.com/it//pubs/archive/35179.pdf). Before that, the idea was already been known because of a less popular scientific paper by Microsoft researchers, Michele Banko and Eric Brill, *Scaling to Very Very Large Corpora for Natural Language Disambiguation* (http://ucrel.lancs.ac.uk/acl/P/P01/P01-1005.pdf).

In simple and short words, the algorithm with more data wins most of the time over other algorithms (no matter their complexity); in such a case, it could well be a linear model.

However, linear models can be also helpful downstream in the data science process and not just upstream. As they are fast to train, they are also fast to be deployed and you do not need coding complex algorithms to do so, allowing you to write the solution in any script or programming language you like, from SQL to JavaScript, from Python to C/C++.

Given their ease of implementation, it is not even unusual that, after building complex solutions using neural networks or ensembles, such solutions are reverse-engineered to find a way to make them available in production as a linear model and achieve a simpler and scalable implementation.

What you are going to find in the book

In the following pages, the book will explain algorithms as well as their implementation in Python to solve practical real-world problems.

Linear models can be counted among supervised algorithms, which are those algorithms that can formulate predictions on numbers and classes if previously given some correct examples to learn from. Thanks to a series of examples, you will immediately distinguish if a problem could be tractable using this algorithm or not.

Given the statistical origins of the linear models family, we cannot neglect starting from a statistical perspective. After contextualizing the usage of linear models, we will provide all the essential elements for understanding on what statistical basis and for what purpose the algorithm has been created. We will use Python to evaluate the statistical outputs of a linear model, providing information about the different statistical tests used.

The data science approach is quite practical (to solve a problem for its business impact), and many limitations of the statistical versions of linear models actually do not apply. However, knowing how the R-squared coefficient works or being able to evaluate the residuals of a regression or highlighting the collinearity of its predictors, can provide you with more means to obtain good results from your work in regression modeling.

Starting from regression models involving a single predictive variable, we will move on to consider multiple variables, and from predicting just numbers we will progress to estimating the probability of there being a certain class among two or many.

We will particularly emphasize how to prepare data, both the target variable (a number or a class) to be predicted and the predictors; variables contributing to a correct prediction. No matter what your data is made of, numbers, nouns, text, images, or sounds, we will provide you with the method to correctly prepare your data and transform it in such a way that your models will perform the best.

You will also be introduced to the scientific methodology at the very foundations of data science, which will help you understand why the data science approach is not just simply theoretical but also quite practical, since it allows obtaining models that can really work when applied to real-world problems.

The last pages of the book will cover some of the more advanced techniques for handling big data and complexity in models. We will also provide you with a few examples from relevant business domains and offer plenty of details about how to proceed to build a linear model, validate it, and later on implement it into a production environment.

Python for data science

Given the availability of many useful packages for creating linear models and given the fact that it is a programming language quite popular among developers, Python is our language of choice for all the code presented in this book.

Created in 1991 as a general-purpose, interpreted, object-oriented language, Python has slowly and steadily conquered the scientific community and grown into a mature ecosystem of specialized packages for data processing and analysis. It allows you to perform uncountable and fast experiments, easy theory development, and prompt deployments of scientific applications.

As a developer, you will find using Python interesting for various reasons:

- It offers a large, mature system of packages for data analysis and machine learning. It guarantees that you will get all that you need in the course of a data analysis, and sometimes even more.

- It is very versatile. No matter what your programming background or style is (object-oriented or procedural), you will enjoy programming with Python.

- If you don't know it yet, but you know other languages well such as C/C++ or Java, it is very simple to learn and use. After you grasp the basics, there's no better way to learn more than by immediately starting to code.

- It is cross-platform; your solutions will work perfectly and smoothly on Windows, Linux, and Mac OS systems. You won't have to worry about portability.

- Although interpreted, it is undoubtedly fast compared to other mainstream data analysis languages such as R and MATLAB (though it is not comparable to C, Java, and the newly emerged Julia language).

- There are packages that allow you to call other platforms, such as R and Julia, outsourcing some of the computations to them and improving your script performance. Moreover, there are also static compilers such as Cython or just-in-time compilers such as PyPy that can transform Python code into C for higher performance.

- It can work better than other platforms with in-memory data because of its minimal memory footprint and excellent memory management. The memory garbage collector will often save the day when you load, transform, dice, slice, save, or discard data using the various iterations and reiterations of data wrangling.

Installing Python

As a first step, we are going to create a fully working data science environment you can use to replicate and test the examples in the book and prototype your own models.

No matter in what language you are going to develop your application, Python will provide an easy way to access your data, build your model from it, and extract the right parameters you need to make predictions in a production environment.

Python is an open source, object-oriented, cross-platform programming language that, compared with its direct competitors (for instance, C/C++ and Java), produces very concise and very readable code. It allows you to build a working software prototype in a very short time, to maintain it easily, and to scale it to larger quantities of data. It has become the most used language in the data scientist's toolbox because it is a general-purpose language made very flexible thanks to a large variety of available packages that can easily and rapidly help you solve a wide spectrum of both common and niche problems.

Choosing between Python 2 and Python 3

Before starting, it is important to know that there are two main branches of Python: version 2 and 3. Since many core functionalities have changed, scripts built for one versions are often incompatible (they won't work without raising errors and warnings) with the other one. Although the third version is the newest, the older one is still the most used version in the scientific area, and the default version for many operating systems (mainly for compatibility in upgrades). When version 3 was released in 2008, most scientific packages weren't ready, so the scientific community was stuck with the previous version. Fortunately, since then, almost all packages have been updated, leaving just a few orphans of Python 3 compatibility (see http://py3readiness.org/ for a compatibility overview).

In this book, which should address a large audience of developers, we agreed that it would have been better to work with Python 3 rather than the older version. Python 3 is the future of Python; in fact, it is the only version that will be further developed and improved by the Python foundation. It will be the default version of the future. If you are currently working with version 2 and you prefer to keep on working with it, we suggest you to run these following few lines of code at the beginning every time you start the interpreter. By doing so, you'll render Python 2 capable of executing most version 3 code with minimal or no problems at all (the code will patch just a few basic incompatibilities, after installing the future package using the command pip install future, and let you safely run all the code in this book):

```
from __future__ import unicode_literals
# to make all string literals into unicode strings
from __future__ import print_function # To print multiple strings
from six import reraise as raise_ # Raising exceptions with a
traceback
from __future__ import division # True division
from __future__ import absolute_import # Flexible Imports
```

The `from __future__ import` commands should always occur at the beginning of your script or you may experience Python reporting an error.

Step-by-step installation

If you have never used Python (but that doesn't mean that you may not already have it installed on your machine), you need to first download the installer from the main website of the project, `https://www.python.org/downloads/` (remember, we are using version 3), and then install it on your local machine.

This section provides you with full control over what can be installed on your machine. This is very useful when you are going to use Python as both your prototyping and production language. Furthermore, it could help you keep track of the versions of packages you are using. Anyway, please be warned that a step-by-step installation really takes time and effort. Instead, installing a ready-made scientific distribution will lessen the burden of installation procedures and may well facilitate initial learning because it can save you quite a lot of time, though it will install a large number of packages (that for the most part you may never use) on your computer all at once. Therefore, if you want to start immediately and don't need to control your installation, just skip this part and proceed to the next section about scientific distributions.

As Python is a multiplatform programming language, you'll find installers for computers that either run on Windows or Linux/Unix-like operating systems. Please remember that some Linux distributions (such as Ubuntu) already have Python packed in the repository, which makes the installation process even easier:

1. Open a Python shell, type `python` in the terminal or click on the Python **IDLE** icon. Then, to test the installation, run the following code in the Python interactive shell or REPL:

```
>>> import sys
>>> print (sys.version)
```

 Downloading the example code

You can download the example code files for all Packt books you have purchased from your account at `http://www.packtpub.com`. If you purchased this book elsewhere, you can visit `http://www.packtpub.com/support` and register to have the files e-mailed directly to you.

```
Python 3.5.0 Shell                                              _ □ ×
File  Edit  Shell  Debug  Options  Window  Help
Python 3.5.0 (v3.5.0:374f501f4567, Sep 13 2015, 02:16:59) [MSC v.1900 32 bit (
Intel)] on win32
Type "copyright", "credits" or "license()" for more information.
>>> import sys
>>> print (sys.version)
3.5.0 (v3.5.0:374f501f4567, Sep 13 2015, 02:16:59) [MSC v.1900 32 bit (Intel)]
>>>
                                                              Ln: 6 Col: 4
```

If a syntax error is raised, it means that you are running Python 2 instead of Python 3. Otherwise, if you don't experience an error and you read that your Python version is 3.x (at the time of writing this book, the latest version was 3.5.0), then congratulations on running the version of Python we elected for this book.

To clarify, when a command is given in the terminal command line, we prefix the command with $>. Otherwise, if it's for the Python REPL, it's preceded by >>>.

Installing packages

Depending on your system and past installations, Python may not come bundled with all you need, unless you have installed a distribution (which, on the other hand, is usually stuffed with much more than you may need).

To install any packages you need, you can use the commands pip or easy_install; however, easy_install is going to be dropped in the future and pip has important advantages over it. It is preferable to install everything using pip because:

- It is the preferred package manager for Python 3 and, starting with Python 2.7.9 and Python 3.4, it is included by default with the Python binary installers
- It provides an uninstall functionality
- It rolls back and leaves your system clear if, for whatever reason, the package installation fails

The command `pip` runs on the command line and makes the process of installing, upgrading, and removing Python packages simply a breeze.

As we mentioned, if you're running at least Python 2.7.9 or Python 3.4 the `pip` command should already be there. To verify which tools have been installed on your local machine, directly test with the following command if any error is raised:

```
$> pip -V
```

In some Linux and Mac installations, the command is present as `pip3` (more likely if you have both Python 2 and 3 on your machine), so, if you received an error when looking for `pip`, also try running the following:

```
$> pip3 -V
```

Alternatively, you can also test if the old command `easy_install` is available:

```
$> easy_install --version
```

 Using `easy_install` in spite of pip's advantages makes sense if you are working on Windows because `pip` will not install binary packages (it will try to build them); therefore, if you are experiencing unexpected difficulties installing a package, `easy_install` can save your day.

If your test ends with an error, you really need to install `pip` from scratch (and in doing so, also `easy_install` at the same time).

To install `pip`, simply follow the instructions given at `https://pip.pypa.io/en/stable/installing/`. The safest way is to download the `get-pi.py` script from `https://bootstrap.pypa.io/get-pip.py` and then run it using the following:

```
$> python get-pip.py
```

By the way, the script will also install the setup tool from `https://pypi.python.org/pypi/setuptools`, which contains `easy_install`.

As an alternative, if you are running a Debian/Ubuntu Unix-like system, then a fast shortcut would be to install everything using `apt-get`:

```
$> sudo apt-get install python3-pip
```

After checking this basic requirement, you're now ready to install all the packages you need to run the examples provided in this book. To install a generic package, `<pk>`, you just need to run the following command:

```
$> pip install <pk>
```

Alternatively, if you prefer to use `easy_install`, you can also run the following command:

```
$> easy_install <pk>
```

After that, the `<pk>`package and all its dependencies will be downloaded and installed.

If you are not sure whether a library has been installed or not, just try to import a module inside it. If the Python interpreter raises an `Import Error` error, it can be concluded that the package has not been installed.

Let's take an example. This is what happens when the NumPy library has been installed:

```
>>> import numpy
```

This is what happens if it is not installed:

```
>>> import numpy
Traceback (most recent call last):
File "<stdin>", line 1, in <module>
ImportError: No module named numpy
```

In the latter case, before importing it, you'll need to install it through `pip` or `easy_install`.

Take care that you don't confuse packages with modules. With `pip`, you install a package; in Python, you import a module. Sometimes, the package and the module have the same name, but in many cases they don't match. For example, the `sklearn` module is included in the package named `Scikit-learn`.

Package upgrades

More often than not, you will find yourself in a situation where you have to upgrade a package because the new version either is required by a dependency or has additional features that you would like to use. To do so, first check the version of the library you have installed by glancing at the `__version__` attribute, as shown in the following example using the NumPy package:

```
>>> import numpy
>>> numpy.__version__  # 2 underscores before and after
'1.9.2'
```

Now, if you want to update it to a newer release, say the 1.10.1 version, you can run the following command from the command line:

```
$> pip install -U numpy==1.10.1
```

Alternatively, but we do not recommend it unless it proves necessary, you can also use the following command:

```
$> easy_install --upgrade numpy==1.10.1
```

Finally, if you are just interested in upgrading it to the latest available version, simply run the following command:

```
$> pip install -U numpy
```

You can alternatively also run the `easy_install` alternative:

```
$> easy_install --upgrade numpy
```

Scientific distributions

As you've read so far, creating a working environment is a time-consuming operation for a data scientist. You first need to install Python and then, one by one, you can install all the libraries that you will need (sometimes, the installation procedures may not go as smoothly as you'd hoped for earlier).

If you want to save time and effort and want to ensure that you have a working Python environment that is ready to use, you can just download, install, and use a scientific Python distribution. Apart from Python itself, distributions also include a variety of preinstalled packages, and sometimes they even have additional tools and an IDE set up for your usage. A few of them are very well known among data scientists and, in the sections that follow, you will find some of the key features for two of these packages that we found most useful and practical.

To immediately focus on the contents of the book, we suggest that you first download and install a scientific distribution, such as Anaconda (which is the most complete one around, in our opinion). Then, after practicing the examples in the book, we suggest you to decide to fully uninstall the distribution and set up Python alone, which can be accompanied by just the packages you need for your projects.

Again, if possible, download and install the version containing Python 3.

The first package that we would recommend you try is Anaconda (`https://www.continuum.io/downloads`), which is a Python distribution offered by Continuum Analytics that includes nearly 200 packages, including NumPy, SciPy, Pandas, IPython, Matplotlib, Scikit-learn, and Statsmodels. It's a cross-platform distribution that can be installed on machines with other existing Python distributions and versions, and its base version is free. Additional add-ons that contain advanced features are charged separately. Anaconda introduces conda, a binary package manager, as a command-line tool to manage your package installations. As stated on its website, Anaconda's goal is to provide enterprise-ready Python distribution for large-scale processing, predictive analytics, and scientific computing.

As a second suggestion, if you are working on Windows, WinPython (`http://winpython.sourceforge.net`) could be a quite interesting alternative (sorry, no Linux or MacOS versions). WinPython is also a free, open source Python distribution maintained by the community. It is designed with scientists in mind, and it includes many essential packages such as NumPy, SciPy, Matplotlib, and IPython (the same as Anaconda's). It also includes Spyder as an IDE, which can be helpful if you have experience using the MATLAB language and interface. A crucial advantage is that it is portable (you can put it into any directory, or even on a USB flash drive, without the need for any administrative elevation). Using WinPython, you can have different versions present on your computer, move a version from a Windows computer to another, and you can easily replace an older version with a newer one just by replacing its directory. When you run WinPython or its shell, it will automatically set all the environment variables necessary for running Python as it were regularly installed and registered on your system.

Finally, another good choice for a distribution that works on Windows could be Python(x,y). Python(x,y) (`http://python-xy.github.io`) is a free, open source Python distribution maintained by the scientific community. It includes a number of packages, such as NumPy, SciPy, NetworkX, IPython, and Scikit-learn. It also features Spyder, the interactive development environment inspired by the MATLAB IDE.

Introducing Jupyter or IPython

IPython was initiated in 2001 as a free project by Fernando Perez. It addressed a lack in the Python stack for scientific investigations. The author felt that Python lacked a user programming interface that could incorporate the scientific approach (mainly meaning experimenting and interactively discovering) in the process of software development.

A scientific approach implies fast experimentation with different hypotheses in a reproducible fashion (as do data exploration and analysis tasks in data science), and when using IPython you will be able to more naturally implement an explorative, iterative, trial-and-error research strategy in your code writing.

Recently, a large part of the IPython project has been moved to a new one called **Jupyter** (http://jupyter.org):

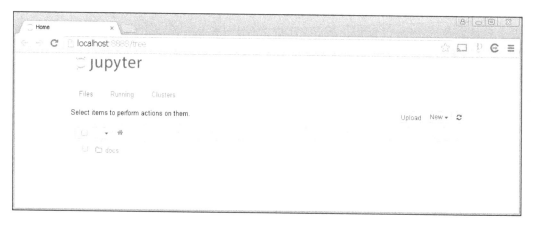

This new project extends the potential usability of the original IPython interface to a wide range of programming languages such as the following:

- R (https://github.com/IRkernel/IRkernel)
- Julia (https://github.com/JuliaLang/IJulia.jl)
- Scala (https://github.com/mattpap/IScala)

For a complete list of available kernels, please visit: https://github.com/ipython/ipython/wiki/IPython-kernels-for-other-languages.

You can use the same IPython-like interface and interactive programming style no matter what language you are developing in, thanks to the powerful idea of kernels, which are programs that run the user's code, as communicated by the frontend interface; they then provide feedback on the results of the executed code to the interface itself.

IPython (Python is the zero kernel, the original starting point) can be simply described as a tool for interactive tasks operable by a console or by a web-based notebook, which offers special commands that help developers to better understand and build the code currently being written.

Contrary to an IDE interface, which is built around the idea of writing a script, running it afterwards, and finally evaluating its results, IPython lets you write your code in chunks, run each of them sequentially, and evaluate the results of each one separately, examining both textual and graphic outputs. Besides graphical integration, it provides further help, thanks to customizable commands, a rich history (in the JSON format), and computational parallelism for enhanced performance when dealing with heavy numeric computations.

In IPython, you can easily combine code, comments, formulas, charts and interactive plots, and rich media such as images and videos, making it a complete scientific sketchpad for all your experimentations and their results together. Moreover, IPython allows reproducible research, allowing any data analysis and model building to be recreated easily under different circumstances:

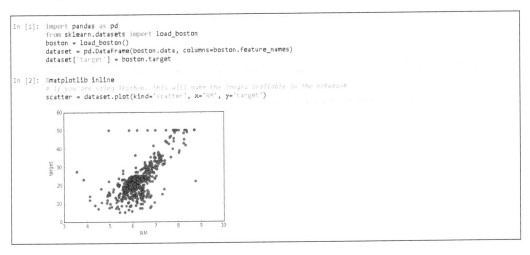

IPython works on your favorite browser (which could be Explorer, Firefox, or Chrome, for instance) and when started presents a cell waiting for code to written in. Each block of code enclosed in a cell can be run and its results are reported in the space just after the cell. Plots can be represented in the notebook (inline plot) or in a separate window. In our example, we decided to plot our chart inline.

Notes can be written easily using the Markdown language, a very easy and accessible markup language (http://daringfireball.net/projects/markdown).

Such an approach is also particularly fruitful for tasks involving developing code based on data, since it automatically accomplishes the often-neglected duty of documenting and illustrating how data analysis has been done, as well as its premises, assumptions, and intermediate/final results. If part of your job is also to present your work and attract internal or external stakeholders to the project, IPython can really perform the magic of storytelling for you with little additional effort. On the web page `https://github.com/ipython/ipython/wiki/A-gallery-of-interesting-IPython-Notebooks`, there are many examples, some of which you may find inspiring for your work as we did.

Actually, we have to confess that keeping a clean, up-to-date IPython Notebook has saved us uncountable times when meetings with managers/stakeholders have suddenly popped up, requiring us to hastily present the state of our work.

As an additional resource, IPython offers you a complete library of many magic commands that allow you to execute some useful actions such as measuring the time it takes for a command to execute, or creating a text file with the output of a cell. We distinguish between line magic and cell magic, depending on whether they operate a single line of code or the code contained in an entire cell. For instance, the magic command `%timeit` measures the time it takes to execute the command on the same line of the line magic, whereas `%%time` is a cell magic that measures the execution time of an entire cell.

If you want to explore more about magic commands, just type `%quickref` into an IPython cell and run it: a complete guide will appear to illustrate all available commands.

In short, IPython lets you:

- See intermediate (debugging) results for each step of the analysis
- Run only some sections (or cells) of the code
- Store intermediate results in JSON format and have the ability to version-control them
- Present your work (this will be a combination of text, code, and images), share it via the IPython Notebook Viewer service (`http://nbviewer.ipython.org/`), and easily export it into HTML, PDF, or even slide shows

IPython is our favored choice throughout this book, and it is used to clearly and effectively illustrate operations with scripts and data and their consequent results.

For a complete treatise on the full range of IPython functionalities, please refer to the two Packt Publishing books *IPython Interactive Computing and Visualization Cookbook, Cyrille Rossant, Packt Publishing*, September 25 2014, and *Learning IPython for Interactive Computing and Data Visualization, Cyrille Rossant, Packt Publishing*, April 25 2013.

For our illustrative purposes, just consider that every IPython block of instructions has a numbered input statement and an output one, so you will find the code presented in this book structured in two blocks, at least when the output is not at all trivial; otherwise just expect only the input part:

```
In:  <the code you have to enter>
Out: <the output you should get>
```

Please notice that we do not number the inputs or the outputs.

Though we strongly recommend using IPython, if you are using a REPL approach or an IDE interface, you can use the same instructions and expect identical results (but for print formats and extensions of the returned results).

Python packages and functions for linear models

Linear models diffuse in many different scientific and business applications and can be found, under different functions, in quite a number of different Python packages. We have selected a few for use in this book. Among them, Statsmodels is our choice for illustrating the statistical properties of models, and Scikit-learn is instead the package we recommend for easily and seamlessly preparing data, building models, and deploying them. We will present models built with Statsmodels exclusively to illustrate the statistical properties of the linear models, resorting to Scikit-learn to demonstrate how to approach modeling from a data science point of view.

NumPy

NumPy, which is Travis Oliphant's creation, is at the core of every analytical solution in the Python language. It provides the user with multidimensional arrays, along with a large set of functions to operate multiple mathematical operations on these arrays. Arrays are blocks of data arranged along multiple dimensions and that implement mathematical vectors and matrices. Arrays are useful not just for storing data, but also for fast matrix operations (vectorization), which are indispensable when you wish to solve ad hoc data science problems.

In the book, we are primarily going to use the module `linalg` from NumPy; being a collection of linear algebra functions, it will provide help in explaining the nuts and bolts of the algorithm:

- Website: `http://www.numpy.org/`
- Import conventions: `import numpy as np`
- Version at the time of print: `1.9.2`
- Suggested install command: `pip install numpy`

> As a convention largely adopted by the Python community, when importing NumPy, it is suggested that you alias it as np:
>
> `import numpy as np`
>
> There are importing conventions also for other Python features that we will be using in the code presented in this book.

SciPy

An original project by Travis Oliphant, Pearu Peterson, and Eric Jones, SciPy completes NumPy's functionalities, offering a larger variety of scientific algorithms for linear algebra, sparse matrices, signal and image processing, optimization, fast Fourier transformation, and much more.

The `scipy.optimize` package provides several commonly used optimization algorithms, used to detail how a linear model can be estimated using different optimization approaches:

- Website: `http://www.scipy.org/`
- Import conventions: `import scipy as sp`
- Version at time of print: `0.16.0`
- Suggested install command: `pip install scipy`

Statsmodels

Previously part of Scikit, Statsmodels has been thought to be a complement to SciPy statistical functions. It features generalized linear models, discrete choice models, time series analysis, and a series of descriptive statistics as well as parametric and nonparametric tests.

In Statsmodels, we will use the `statsmodels.api` and `statsmodels.formula.api` modules, which provide functions for fitting linear models by providing both input matrices and formula's specifications:

- Website: `http:/statsmodels.sourceforge.net/`
- Import conventions: `import statsmodels.api as sm` and `import statsmodels.formula.api as smf`
- Version at the time of print: `0.6.1`
- Suggested install command: `pip install statsmodels`

Scikit-learn

Started as part of the **SciPy Toolkits (SciKits)**, Scikit-learn is the core of data science operations on Python. It offers all that you may need in terms of data preprocessing, supervised and unsupervised learning, model selection, validation, and error metrics. Expect us to talk at length about this package throughout the book.

Scikit-learn started in 2007 as a Google Summer of Code project by David Cournapeau. Since 2013, it has been taken over by the researchers at INRA (French Institute for Research in Computer Science and Automation).

Scikit-learn offers modules for data processing (`sklearn.preprocessing`, `sklearn.feature_extraction`), model selection, and validation (`sklearn.cross_validation`, `sklearn.grid_search`, and `sklearn.metrics`) and a complete set of methods (`sklearn.linear_model`) in which the target value, being both a number or a probability, is expected to be a linear combination of the input variables:

- Website: `http://scikit-learn.org/stable/`
- Import conventions: None; modules are usually imported separately
- Version at the time of print: `0.16.1`
- Suggested install command: `pip install scikit-learn`

 Note that the imported module is named `sklearn`.

Summary

In this chapter, we glanced at the usefulness of linear models under the data science perspective and we introduced some basic concepts of the data science approach that will be explained in more detail later and will be applied to linear models. We have also provided detailed instructions on how to set up the Python environment; these will be used throughout the book to present examples and provide useful code snippets for the fast development of machine learning hypotheses.

In the next chapter, we will begin presenting linear regression from its statistical foundations. Starting from the idea of correlation, we will build up the simple linear regression (using just one predictor) and provide the algorithm's formulations.

2

Approaching Simple Linear Regression

Having set up all your working tools (directly installing Python and IPython or using a scientific distribution), you are now ready to start using linear models to incorporate new abilities into the software you plan to build, especially predictive capabilities. Up to now, you have developed software solutions based on certain specifications you defined (or specifications that others have handed to you). Your approach has always been to tailor the response of the program to particular inputs, by writing code carefully mapping every single situation to a specific, predetermined response. Reflecting on it, by doing so you were just incorporating practices that you (or others) have learned from experience.

However, the world is complex, and sometimes your experience is not enough to make your software smart enough to make a difference in a fairly competitive business or in challenging problems with many different and mutable facets.

In this chapter, we will start exploring an approach that is different from manual programming. We are going to present an approach that enables the software to self-learn the correct answers to particular inputs, provided you can define the problem in terms of data and target response and that you can incorporate in the processes some of your domain expertise—for instance, choosing the right features for prediction. Therefore, your experience will go on being critical when it comes to creating your software, though in the form of learning from data. In fact, your software will be learning from data accordingly to your specifications. We are also going to illustrate how it is possible to achieve this by resorting to one of the simplest methods for deriving knowledge from data: linear models.

Specifically, in this chapter, we are going to discuss the following topics:

- Understanding what problems machine learning can solve
- What problems a regression model can solve
- The strengths and weaknesses of correlation
- How correlations extends to a simple regression model
- The when, what, and why of a regression model
- The essential mathematics behind gradient descent

In the process, we will be using some statistical terminology and concepts in order to provide you with the prospect of linear regression in the larger frame of statistics, though our approach will remain practical, offering you the tools and hints to start building linear models using Python and thus enrich your software development.

Defining a regression problem

Thanks to machine learning algorithms, deriving knowledge from data is possible. Machine learning has solid roots in years of research: it has really been a long journey since the end of the fifties, when Arthur Samuel clarified machine learning as being a "field of study that gives computers the ability to learn without being explicitly programmed."

The data explosion (the availability of previously unrecorded amounts of data) has enabled the widespread usage of both recent and classic machine learning techniques and made them high-performance techniques. If nowadays you can talk by voice to your mobile phone and expect it to answer properly to you, acting as your secretary (such as Siri or Google Now), it is uniquely because of machine learning. The same holds true for every application based on machine learning such as face recognition, search engines, spam filters, recommender systems for books/music/movies, handwriting recognition, and automatic language translation.

Some other actual usages of machine learning algorithms are somewhat less obvious, but nevertheless important and profitable, such as credit rating and fraud detection, algorithmic trading, advertising profiling on the Web, and health diagnostics.

Generally speaking, machine learning algorithms can learn in three ways:

- **Supervised learning**: This is when we present labeled examples to learn from. For instance, when we want to be able to predict the selling price of a house in advance in a real estate market, we can get the historical prices of houses and have a supervised learning algorithm successfully figure out how to associate the prices to the house characteristics.

- **Unsupervised learning**: This is when we present examples without any hint, leaving it to the algorithm to create a label. For instance, when we need to figure out how the groups inside a customer database can be partitioned into similar segments based on their characteristics and behaviors.

- **Reinforcement learning**: This is when we present examples without labels, as in unsupervised learning, but get feedback from the environment as to whether label guessing is correct or not. For instance, when we need software to act successfully in a competitive setting, such as a videogame or the stock market, we can use reinforcement learning. In this case, the software will then start acting in the setting and it will learn directly from its errors until it finds a set of rules that ensure its success.

Linear models and supervised learning

Unsupervised learning has important applications in robotic vision and automatic feature creation, and reinforcement learning is critical for developing autonomous AI (for instance, in robotics, but also in creating intelligent software agents); however, supervised learning is most important in data science because it allows us to accomplish something the human race has aspired to for ages: prediction.

Prediction has applications in business and for general usefulness, enabling us to take the best course of action since we know from predictions the likely outcome of a situation. Prediction can make us successful in our decisions and actions, and since ancient times has been associated with magic or great wisdom.

Supervised learning is no magic at all, though it may look like sorcery to some people, as Sir Arthur Charles Clarke stated, "any sufficiently advanced technology is indistinguishable from magic." Supervised learning, based on human achievements in mathematics and statistics, helps to leverage human experience and observations and turn them into precise predictions in a way that no human mind could. However, supervised learning can predict only in certain favorable conditions. It is paramount to have examples from the past at hand from which we can extract rules and hints that can support wrapping up a highly likely prediction given certain premises.

In one way or another, no matter the exact formulation of the machine learning algorithm, the idea is that you can tell the outcome because there have been certain premises in the observed past that led to particular conclusions.

In mathematical formalism, we call the outcome we want to predict the response or target variable and we usually label it using the lower case letter y.

The premises are instead called the **predictive variables**, or simply attributes or features, and they are labeled as a lowercase x if there is a single one and by an uppercase X if there are many. Using the uppercase letter X we intend to use matrix notation, since we can also treat the y as a response vector (technically a column vector) and the X as a matrix containing all values of the feature vectors, each arranged into a separate column of the matrix.

It is also important to always keep a note of the dimensions of X and y; thus, by convention, we can call n the number of observations and p the number of variables. Consequently our X will be a matrix of size (n, p), and our y will always be a vector of size n.

Throughout the book, we will also have recourse to statistical notation, which is actually a bit more explicit and verbose. A statistical formula tries to give an idea of all the predictors involved in the formula (we will show an example of this later) whereas matrix notation is more implicit.

We can affirm that, when we are learning to predict from data in a supervised way, we are actually building a function that can answer the question about how X can imply y.

Using these new matrix symbolic notations, we can define a function, a functional mapping that can translate X values into y without error or with an acceptable margin of error. We can affirm that all our work will be to determinate a function of the following kind:

$$y = h(X)$$

When the function is specified, and we have in mind a certain algorithm with certain parameters and an X matrix made up of certain data, conventionally we can refer to it as a hypothesis. The term is suitable because we can intend our function as a ready hypothesis, set with all its parameters, to be tested if working more or less well in predicting our target y.

Before talking about the function (the supervised algorithm that does all the magic), we should first spend some time reasoning about what feeds the algorithm itself. We have already introduced the matrix X, the predictive variables, and the vector y, the target answer variable; now it is time to explain how we can extract them from our data and what exactly their role is in a learning algorithm.

Reflecting on predictive variables

Reflecting on the role of your predictive variable in a supervised algorithm, there are a few caveats that you have to keep in mind throughout our illustrations in the book, and yes, they are very important and decisive.

To store the predictive variables, we use a matrix, usually called the X matrix:

$$X = \begin{bmatrix} x_1 \\ x_2 \\ . \\ . \\ . \\ x_n \end{bmatrix}$$

In this example, our X is made up of only one variable and it contains n cases (or observations).

> If you would like to know when to use a variable or feature, just consider that in machine learning *feature* and *attribute* are terms that are favored over *variable*, which has a definitively statistical flavor hinting at something that varies. Depending on the context and audience, you can effectively use one or the other.

In Python code, you can build a one-column matrix structure by typing:

```
In: import numpy as np
    vector = np.array([1,2,3,4,5])
    row_vector = vector.reshape((5,1))
    column_vector = vector.reshape((1,5))
    single_feature_matrix = vector.reshape((1,5))
```

Using the NumPy `array` we can quickly derive a vector and a matrix. If you start from a Python list, you will get a vector (which is neither a row nor a column vector, actually). By using the `reshape` method, you can transform it into a row or column vector, based on your specifications.

Real-world data usually need matrices that are more complex, and real-world matrices comprise uncountable different data columns (the variety element of big data). Most likely, a standard X matrix will have more columns, so the notation we will be referring to is:

$$X = \begin{bmatrix} x_{1,1} & x_{1,2} & - & x_{1,p} \\ x_{2,1} & x_{2,2} & - & x_{2,p} \\ & & . \\ & & . \\ & & . \\ x_{n,1} & x_{n,2} & - & x_{n,p} \end{bmatrix}$$

Now, our matrix has more variables, all p variables, so its size is n x p. In Python, there are two methods to make up such a data matrix:

```
In:  multiple_feature_matrix =
   np.array([[1,2,3,4,5],[6,7,8,9,10],[11,12,13,14,15]])
```

You just have to transform with the `array` function a list of lists, where each internal list is a row matrix; or you create a vector with your data and then reshape it in the shape of your desired matrix:

```
In: multiple_feature_matrix = \
np.array([[1,2,3,4,5],[6,7,8,9,10],[11,12,13,14,15]])
```

In NumPy there are also special functions for rapidly creating matrices of ones and zeros. As an argument, just specify the intended (x, y) shape in a tuple:

```
all_zeros = np.zeros((5,3))
all_ones = np.ones((5,3))
```

The information present in the set of observations from the past, that we are using as X, can deeply affect how we are going to build the link between our X and the y.

In fact, usually it is the case that we do not know the full range of possible associations between X and y because:

- We have just observed a certain X, so our experience of y for a given X is biased, and this is a sampling bias because, as in a lottery, we have drawn only certain numbers in a game and not all the available ones

- We never observed certain (X, y) associations (please note the formulation in a tuple, indicating the interconnection between X and y), because they never happened before, but that does not exclude them from happening in the future (and incidentally we are striving to forecast the future)

There is little to do with the second problem, (we can extrapolate the future only through the directions pointed out by the past), but you can actually check how recent the data you are using is. If you are trying to forecast in a context that is very susceptible to changes and mutable from day to day, you have to keep in mind that your data could quickly become outdated and you may be unable to guess new trends. An example of a mutable context where we constantly need to update models is the advertising sector (where the competitive scenery is frail and continually changing). Consequently, you continually need to gather fresher data that could allow you to build a much more effective supervised algorithm.

As for the first problem, you can solve it using more and more cases from different sources. The more you sample, the more likely your drawn set of X will resemble a complete set of possible and true associations of X with y. This is understandable via an important idea in probability and statistics: the law of large numbers.

The law of large numbers suggests that, as the number of your experiments grows, so the likelihood that the average of their results will represent the true value (that the experiments themselves are trying to figure out) will increase.

Supervised algorithms learn from large samples of historical data, called **batches**, fetched all at once from large data repositories, such as databases or data lakes. Alternatively, they also could pick the examples that are most useful for their learning by themselves and ignore the bulk of the data (this is called **active learning** and it is a kind of semi-supervised learning that we won't discuss here).

If our environment is fast-paced, they also could just stream data as it is available, continuously adapting to any new association between the predictive variables and the response (this is called online learning and we will discuss it in *Chapter 7, Online and Batch Learning*).

Another important aspect of the X matrix of predictors to be considered is that up to now we assumed that we could deterministically derive the response y using the information in the matrix X. Unfortunately this is not always so in the real world and it is not rare that you actually try to figure out your response y using a completely wrong set of predictive X. In such cases, you have to figure out that you are actually wasting your time in trying to fit something working between your X and y and that you should look for some different X (again more data in the sense of more variables).

According to the model used, having more variables and cases is usually beneficial under different points of view. More cases reduces the possibility of learning from a biased and limited set of observations. Many algorithms can better estimate their internal parameters (and produce more accurate predictions) if trained using large sets of observations. Also, having more variables at hand can be beneficial, but in the sense that it increases the chance of having explicative features to be used for machine learning. Many algorithms are in fact sensitive to redundant information and noise present in features, consequently requiring some feature selection to reduce the predictors involved in the model. This is quite the case with linear regression, which can surely take advantage of more cases for its training, but it should also receive a parsimonious and efficient set of features to perform at its best. Another important aspect to know about the X matrix is that it should be made up solely of numbers. Therefore, it really matters what you are working with. You can work with the following:

- Physical measurements, which are always OK because they are naturally numbers (for example, height)

- Human measurements, which are a bit less OK, but are still fine when they have a certain order (that is, all numbers that we give as scores based on our judgment) and so they can be converted into rank numbers (such as 1, 2, and 3 for the first, second, and third values, and so on)

We call such values quantitative measurements. We expect quantitative measurement to be continuous and that means a quantitative variable can take any real positive or negative number as a valid value. Human measurements are usually only positive, starting from zero or one, so it is just a fair approximation to consider them quantitative.

For physical measurements, in statistics, we distinguish between interval and ratio variables. The difference is that ratio variables have a natural zero whereas in interval data the zero is an arbitrary one. A good example is temperature; in fact, unless you use the Kelvin scale, whose zero is an absolute one, both Fahrenheit and Celsius have arbitrary scales. The main implication is about the ratios (if the zero is arbitrary, the ratio is also arbitrary).

Human measurements that are numerical are called **ordinal variables**. Unlike interval data, ordinal data does not have a natural zero. Moreover, the interval between each value on an interval scale is equal and regular; however, in an ordinal scale, though the distance between the values is the same, their real distance could be very different. Let's think of a scale made of three textual values: good, average, and bad. Next, let's say that we arbitrarily decide that good is 3, average is 2, and bad is 1. We call this arbitrary assignment of values ordinal encoding. Now, from a mathematical point of view, though the interval between 3 and 2 in respect of the interval from 2 to 1 is the same (that is, one point), are we really sure that the real distance between good and average is the same as that from average and bad? For instance, in terms of customer satisfaction, does it costs the same effort going from an evaluation of bad to one of average and from one of average to one of excellent?

Qualitative measurements (for example, a value judgment such as good, average, or bad, or an attribute such as being colored red, green, or blue) need some work to be done, some clever data manipulation, but they can still be part of our X matrix using the right transformation. Even more unstructured qualitative information (such as text, sound, or a drawing) can be transformed and reduced to a pool of numbers and can be ingested into an X matrix.

Qualitative variables can be stored as numbers into single-value vectors or they can have a vector for each class. In such a case, we are talking about binary variables (also called dummy variables in statistical language).

We are going to discuss in greater detail how to transform the data at hand, especially if its type is qualitative, into an input matrix suitable for supervised learning in *Chapter 5, Data Preparation*.

As a starting point before working on the data itself, it is necessary to question the following:

- The quality of the data—that is, whether the data available can really represent the right information pool for extracting X-y rules
- The quantity of data—that is, checking how much data is available, keeping in mind that, for building robust machine learning solutions, it is safer to have a large variety of variables and cases (at least when you're dealing with thousands of examples)
- The extension of data in time—that is, checking how much time the data spans in the past (since we are learning from the past)

Reflecting on response variables

Reflecting on the role of the response variable, our attention should be first drawn to what type of variable we are going to predict, because that will distinguish the type of supervised problem to be solved.

If our response variable is a quantitative one, a numeric value, our problem will be a regression one. Ordinal variables can be solved as a regression problem, especially if they take many different distinct values. The output of a regression supervised algorithm is a value that can be directly used and compared with other predicted values and with the real response values used for learning.

For instance, as an example of a regression problem, in the real estate business a regression model could predict the value of a house just from some information about its location and its characteristics, allowing an immediate discovery of market prices that are too cheap or too expensive by using the model's predictions as an indicator of a fair fact-based estimation (if we can reconstruct the price by a model, it is surely well justified by the value of the measurable characteristics we used as our predictors).

If our response variable is a qualitative one, our problem is one of classification. If we have to guess between just two classes, our problem is called **a binary classification**; otherwise, if more classes are involved, it is a called a multi-label classification problem.

For instance, if we want to guess the winner in a game between two football teams, we have a binary classification problem because we just need to know if the first team will win or not (the two classes are *team wins, team loses*). A multi-label classification could instead be used to predict which football team among a certain number will win (so in our prediction, the classes to be guessed are the teams).

Ordinal variables, if they do not take many distinct values, can be solved as a multi-label classification problem. For instance, if you have to guess the final ranking of a team in a football championship, you could try to predict its final position in the leader board as a class. Consequently, in this ordinal problem you have to guess many classes corresponding to different positions in the championship: class 1 could represent the first position, class 2 the second position, and so on. In conclusion, you could figure the final ranking of a team as the positional class whose likelihood of winning is the greatest.

As for the output, classification algorithms can provide both classification into a precise class and an estimate of the probability of being part of any of the classes at hand.

Continuing with examples from the real estate business, a classification model could predict if a house could be a bargain or if it could increase its value given its location and its characteristics, thus allowing a careful investment selection.

The most noticeable problem with response variables is their exactness. Measurement errors in regression problems and misclassification in classification ones can damage the ability of your model to perform well on real data by providing inaccurate information to be learned. In addition, biased information (such as when you provide cases of a certain class and not from all those available) can hurt the capacity of your model to predict in real-life situations because it will lead the model to look at data from a non-realistic point of view. Inaccuracies in the response variable are more difficult and more dangerous for your model than problems with your features.

For single predictors, the outcome variable y is also a vector. In NumPy, you just set it up as a generic vector or as a column vector:

```
In: y = np.array([1,2,3,4,5]).reshape((5,1))
```

The family of linear models

The family of linear models is so named because the function that specifies the relationship between the X, the predictors, and the y, the target, is a linear combination of the X values. A linear combination is just a sum where each addendum value is modified by a weight. Therefore, a linear model is simply a smarter form of a summation.

Of course there is a trick in this summation that makes the predictors perform like they do while predicting the answer value. As we mentioned before, the predictors should tell us something, they should give us some hint about the answer variable; otherwise any machine learning algorithm won't work properly. We can predict our response because the information about the answer is already somewhere inside the features, maybe scattered, twisted, or transformed, but it is just there. Machine learning just gathers and reconstructs such information.

In linear models, such inner information is rendered obvious and extracted by the weights used for the summation. If you actually manage to have some meaningful predictors, the weights will just do all the heavy work to extract it and transform it into a proper and exact answer.

Since the X matrix is a numeric one, the sum of its elements will result in a number itself. Linear models are consequently the right tool for solving any regression problem, but they are not limited to just guessing real numbers. By a transformation of the response variable, they can be enabled to predict counts (positive integer numbers) and probabilities relative to being part of a certain group or class (or not).

In statistics, the linear model family is called the **generalized linear model (GLM)**. By means of special link functions, proper transformation of the answer variable, proper constraints on the weights and different optimization procedures (the learning procedures), GLM can solve a very wide range of different problems. In this book, our treatise won't extend beyond what is necessary to the statistical field. However, we will propose a couple of models of the larger family of the GLM, namely linear regression and logistic regression; both methods are appropriate to solve the two most basic problems in data science: regression and classification.

Because linear regression does not require any particular transformation of the answer variable and because it is conceptually the real foundation of linear models, we will start by understanding how it works. To make things easier, we will start from the case of a linear model using just a single predictor variable, a so-called **simple linear regression**. The predictive power of a simple linear regression is very limited in comparison with its multiple form, where many predictors at once contribute to the model. However, it is much easier to understand and figure out its functioning.

Preparing to discover simple linear regression

We provide some practical examples in Python throughout the book and do not leave explanations about the various regression models at a purely theoretical level. Instead, we will explore together some example datasets, and systematically illustrate to you the commands necessary to achieve a working regression model, interpret its structure, and deploy a predicting application.

 A dataset is a data structure containing predictive variables and sometimes response ones. For machine learning purposes, it can be structured or semi-structured into a matrix form, in the shape of a table with rows and columns.

For the initial presentation of the linear regression in its simple version (using only one predictive variable to forecast the response variable), we have chosen a couple of datasets relative to real estate evaluation.

Real estate is quite an interesting topic for an automatic predictive model since there is quite a lot of freely available data from censuses and, being an open market, even more data can be scraped from websites monitoring the market and its offers. Moreover, because the renting or buying of a house is quite an important economic decision for many individuals, online services that help to gather and digest the large amounts of available information are indeed a good business model idea.

The first dataset is quite a historical one. Taken from the paper by Harrison, D. and Rubinfeld, D.L. *Hedonic Housing Prices and the Demand for Clean Air* (J. Environ. Economics & Management, vol.5, 81-102, 1978), the dataset can be found in many analysis packages and is present at the UCI Machine Learning Repository (`https://archive.ics.uci.edu/ml/datasets/Housing`).

The dataset is made up of 506 census tracts of Boston from the 1970 census and it features 21 variables regarding various aspects that could impact real estate value. The target variable is the median monetary value of the houses, expressed in thousands of USD. Among the available features, there are some fairly obvious ones such as the number of rooms, the age of the buildings, and the crime levels in the neighborhood, and some others that are a bit less obvious, such as the pollution concentration, the availability of nearby schools, the access to highways, and the distance from employment centers.

The second dataset from the Carnegie Mellon University Statlib repository (`https://archive.ics.uci.edu/ml/datasets/Housing`) contains 20,640 observations derived from the 1990 US Census. Each observation is a series of statistics (9 predictive variables) regarding a block group — that is, approximately 1,425 individuals living in a geographically compact area. The target variable is an indicator of the house value of that block (technically it is the natural logarithm of the median house value at the time of the census). The predictor variables are basically median income.

The dataset has been used in Pace and Barry (1997), *Sparse Spatial Autoregressions, Statistics and Probability Letters,* (`http://www.spatial-statistics.com/pace_manuscripts/spletters_ms_dir/statistics_prob_lets/pdf/fin_stat_letters.pdf`), a paper on regression analysis including spatial variables (information about places including their position or their nearness to other places in the analysis). The idea behind the dataset is that variations of house values can be explained by exogenous variables (that is, external to the house itself) representing population, the density of buildings, and the population's affluence aggregated by area.

The code for downloading the data is as follows:

```
In: from sklearn.datasets import fetch_california_housing
    from sklearn.datasets import load_boston
    boston = load_boston()
    california = fetch_california_housing()
```

 As the Boston dataset is already included in the Scikit-learn package, the California one has to be downloaded from the Statlib datasets archive and it is necessary for you to have an Internet connection. It will also take some time, depending on your speed of connection.

We will be exclusively using the Boston dataset in this and the following chapters, but you can explore the California one and try to replicate the analysis done on the Boston one. Please remember to use the preceding code snippet before running any other code or you won't have the `boston` and `california` variables available for analysis.

Starting from the basics

We will start exploring the first dataset, the Boston dataset, but before delving into numbers, we will upload a series of helpful packages that will be used during the rest of the chapter:

```
In: import numpy as np
    import pandas as pd
    import matplotlib.pyplot as plt
    import matplotlib as mpl
```

If you are working from an IPython Notebook, running the following command in a cell will instruct the Notebook to represent any graphic output in the Notebook itself (otherwise, if you are not working on IPython, just ignore the command because it won't work in IDEs such as Python's IDLE or Spyder):

```
In: %matplotlib inline
    # If you are using IPython, this will make the images available in
    the Notebook
```

To immediately select the variables that we need, we just frame all the data available into a Pandas data structure, `DataFrame`.

Inspired by a similar data structure present in the R statistical language, a `DataFrame` renders data vectors of different types easy to handle under the same dataset variable, offering at the same time much convenient functionality for handling missing values and manipulating data:

```
In: dataset = pd.DataFrame(boston.data,
columns=boston.feature_names)
  dataset['target'] = boston.target
```

At this point, we are ready to build our first regression model, learning directly from the data present in our Pandas DataFrame.

As we mentioned, linear regression is just a simple summation, but it is indeed not the simplest model possible. The simplest is the statistical mean. In fact, you can simply guess by always using the same constant number, and the mean very well absolves such a role because it is a powerful descriptive number for data summary.

The mean works very well with normally distributed data but often it is quite suitable even for different distributions. A normally distributed curve is a distribution of data that is symmetric and has certain characteristics regarding its shape (a certain height and spread).

The characteristics of a normal distribution are defined by formulas and there are appropriate statistical tests to find out if your variable is normal or not, since many other distributions resemble the bell shape of the normal one and many different normal distributions are generated by different mean and variance parameters.

The key to understanding if a distribution is normal is the **probability density function (PDF)**, a function describing the probability of values in the distribution.

In the case of a normal distribution, the PDF is as follows:

$$f\left(x \mid \mu, \sigma\right) = \frac{1}{\sigma\sqrt{2\pi}} e^{-\frac{(x-\mu)^2}{2\sigma^2}}$$

In such a formulation, the symbol μ represents the mean (which coincides with the median and the mode) and the symbol σ is the variance. Based on different means and variances, we can calculate different value distributions, as the following code demonstrates and visualizes:

```
In: import matplotlib.pyplot as plt
import numpy as np
import matplotlib.mlab as mlab
```

```
import math
x = np.linspace(-4,4,100)
for mean, variance in [(0,0.7),(0,1),(1,1.5),(-2,0.5)]:
    plt.plot(x,mlab.normpdf(x,mean,variance))
plt.show()
```

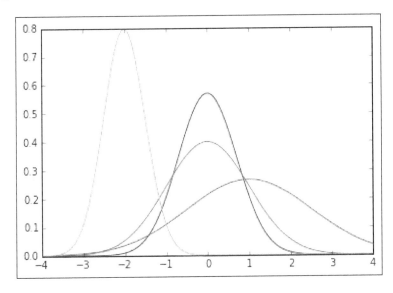

Because of its properties, the normal distribution is a fundamental distribution in statistics since all statistical models involve working on normal variables. In particular, when the mean is zero and the variance is one (unit variance), the normal distribution, called a standard normal distribution under such conditions, has even more favorable characteristics for statistical models.

Anyway, in the real world, normally distributed variables are instead rare. Consequently, it is important to verify that the actual distribution we are working on is not so far from an ideal normal one or it will pose problems in your expected results. Normally distributed variables are an important requirement for statistical models (such as mean and, in certain aspects, linear regression). On the contrary, machine learning models do not depend on any previous assumption about how your data should be distributed. But, as a matter of fact, even machine learning models work well if data has certain characteristics, so working with a normally distributed variable is preferable to other distributions. Throughout the book, we will provide warnings about what to look for and check when building and applying machine learning solutions.

For the calculation of a mean, relevant problems can arise if the distribution is not symmetric and there are extreme cases. In such an occurrence, the extreme cases will tend to draw the mean estimate towards them, which consequently won't match with the bulk of the data. Let's then calculate the mean of the value of the 506 tracts in Boston:

```
In: mean_expected_value = dataset['target'].mean()
```

In this case, we calculated the mean using a method available in the Pandas DataFrame; however, the NumPy function mean can be also called to calculate a mean from an array of data:

```
In: np.mean(dataset['target'])
```

In terms of a mathematical formulation, we can express this simple solution as follows:

$$y = \bar{x}$$

We can now evaluate the results by measuring the error produced in predicting the real y values by this rule. Statistics suggest that, to measure the difference between the prediction and the real value, we should square the differences and then sum them all. This is called **the squared sum of errors**:

```
In: Squared_errors = pd.Series(mean_expected_value -\
                        dataset['target'])**2
  SSE = np.sum(Squared_errors)
  print ('Sum of Squared Errors (SSE): %01.f' % SSE)
```

Now that we have calculated it, we can visualize it as a distribution of errors:

```
In: density_plot = Squared_errors.plot('hist')
```

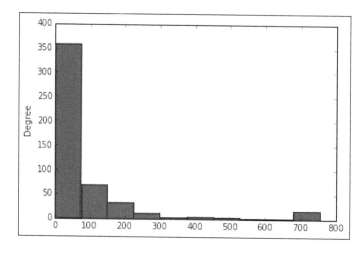

The plot shows how frequent certain errors are in respect of their values. Therefore, you will immediately notice that most errors are around zero (there is a high density around that value). Such a situation can be considered a good one, since in most cases the mean is a good approximation, but some errors are really very far from the zero and they can attain considerable values (don't forget that the errors are squared, anyway, so the effect is emphasized). When trying to figure out such values, your approach will surely lead to a relevant error and we should find a way to minimize it using a more sophisticated approach.

A measure of linear relationship

Evidently, the mean is not a good representative of certain values, but it is certainly a good baseline to start from. Certainly, an important problem with the mean is its being fixed, whereas the target variable is changeable. However, if we assume that the target variable changes because of the effect of some other variable we are measuring, then we can adjust the mean with respect to the variations in cause.

One improvement on our previous approach could be to build a mean conditional on certain values of another variable (or even more than one) actually related to our target, whose variation is somehow similar to the variation of the target one.

Intuitively, if we know the dynamics we want to predict with our model, we can try to look for variables that we know can impact the answer values.

In the real estate business, we actually know that usually the larger a house is, the more expensive it is; however, this rule is just part of the story and the price is affected by many other considerations. For the moment, we will keep it simple and just assume that an extension to a house is a factor that positively affects the price, and consequently, more space equals more costs when building the house (more land, more construction materials, more work, and consequently a higher price).

Now, we have a variable that we know should change with our target and we just need to measure it and extend our initial formula based on constant values with something else.

In statistics, there is a measure that helps to measure how (in the sense of how much and in what direction) two variables relate to each other: **correlation**.

In correlation, a few steps are to be considered. First, your variables have to be standardized (or your result won't be a correlation but a covariation, a measure of association that is affected by the scale of the variables you are working with).

In statistical Z score standardization, you subtract from each variable its mean and then you divide the result by the standard deviation. The resulting transformed variable will have a mean of 0 and a standard deviation of 1 (or unit variance, since variance is the squared standard deviation).

The formula for standardizing a variable is as follows:

$$x = \frac{x - \bar{x}}{\sigma x}$$

This can be achieved in Python using a simple function:

```
In: def standardize(x):
        return (x-np.mean(x))/np.std(x)
```

After standardizing, you compare the squared difference of each variable with its own mean. If the two differences agree in sign, their multiplication will become positive (evidence that they have the same directionality); however, if they differ, the multiplication will turn negative. By summing all the multiplications between the squared differences, and dividing them by the number of observations, you will finally get the correlation which will be a number ranging from -1 to 1.

The absolute value of the correlation will provide you with the intensity of the relation between the two variables compared, 1 being a sign of a perfect match and zero a sign of complete independence between them (they have no relation between them). The sign instead will hint at the proportionality; positive is direct (when one grows the other does the same), negative is indirect (when one grows, the other shrinks).

Covariance can be expressed as follows:

$$cov(x_i, y) = \frac{1}{n} * \sum (x_i - \bar{x}_i) * (y - \bar{y})$$

Whereas, Pearson's correlation can be expressed as follows:

$$r = \frac{1}{n} * \frac{\sum (x_i - \bar{x}_i) * (y - \bar{y})}{\sigma_{x_i} * \sigma_y}$$

Let's check these two formulations directly on Python. As you may have noticed, Pearson's correlation is really covariance calculated on standardized variables, so we define the `correlation` function as a wrapper of both the `covariance` and `standardize` ones (you can find all these functions ready to be imported from `Scipy`; we are actually recreating them here just to help you understand how they work):

```
In:
def covariance(variable_1, variable_2, bias=0):
     observations = float(len(variable_1))
    return np.sum((variable_1 - np.mean(variable_1)) * \
    (variable_2 - np.mean(variable_2)))/(observations-min(bias,1))

  def standardize(variable):
     return (variable - np.mean(variable)) / np.std(variable)

  def correlation(var1,var2,bias=0):
     return covariance(standardize(var1), standardize(var2),bias)

  from scipy.stats.stats import pearsonr
  print ('Our correlation estimation: %0.5f' %
  (correlation(dataset['RM'], dataset['target'])))
  print ('Correlation from Scipy pearsonr estimation: %0.5f' %
  pearsonr(dataset['RM'], dataset['target'])[0])
```

```
Out: Our correlation estimation: 0.69536
    Correlation from Scipy pearsonr estimation: 0.69536
```

Our correlation estimation for the relation between the value of the target variable and the average number of rooms in houses in the area is 0.695, which is positive and remarkably strong, since the maximum positive score of a correlation is 1.0.

 As a way to estimate if a correlation is relevant or not, just square it; the result will represent the percentage of the variance shared by the two variables.

Let's graph what happens when we correlate two variables. Using a **scatterplot**, we can easily visualize the two involved variables. A scatterplot is a graph where the values of two variables are treated as Cartesian coordinates; thus, for every (x, y) value a point is represented in the graph:

```
In: x_range = [dataset['RM'].min(),dataset['RM'].max()]
    y_range = [dataset['target'].min(),dataset['target'].max()]
    scatter_plot = dataset.plot(kind='scatter', x='RM', y='target',\
    xlim=x_range, ylim=y_range)
    meanY = scatter_plot.plot(x_range, [dataset['target'].mean(),\
dataset['target'].mean()], '--' , color='red', linewidth=1)
    meanX = scatter_plot.plot([dataset['RM'].mean(),\
    dataset['RM'].mean()], y_range, '--', color='red', linewidth=1)
```

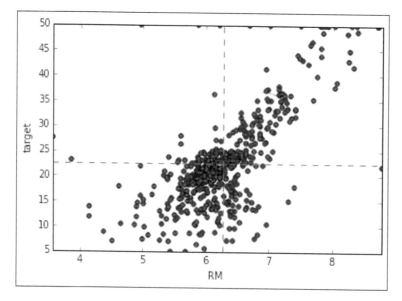

The scatterplot also plots the average value for both the target and the predictor variables as dashed lines. This divides the plot into four quadrants. If we compare it with the previous covariance and correlation formulas, we can understand why the correlation value was close to 1: in the bottom-right and in top-left quadrants, there are just a few mismatching points where one of variables is above its average and the other is below its own.

A perfect match (correlation values of 1 or -1) is possible only when the points are in a straight line (and all points are therefore concentrated in the right-uppermost and left-lowermost quadrants). Thus, correlation is a measure of linear association, of how close to a straight line your points are. Ideally, having all your points on a single line favors a perfect mapping of your predictor variable to your target.

Extending to linear regression

Linear regression tries to fit a line through a given set of points, choosing the best fit. The best fit is the line that minimizes the summed squared difference between the value dictated by the line for a certain value of x and its corresponding y values. (It is optimizing the same squared error that we met before when checking how good a mean was as a predictor.)

Since linear regression is a line; in bi-dimensional space (x, y), it takes the form of the classical formula of a line in a Cartesian plane: $y = mx + q$, where m is the angular coefficient (expressing the angle between the line and the x axis) and q is the intercept between the line and the x axis.

Formally, machine learning indicates the correct expression for a linear regression as follows:

$$y = \beta X + \beta_0$$

Here, again, X is a matrix of the predictors, β is a matrix of coefficients, and β_0 is a constant value called the **bias** (it is the same as the Cartesian formulation, only the notation is different).

We can better understand its functioning mechanism by seeing it in action with Python, first using the `StatsModels` package, then using the Scikit-learn one.

Regressing with Statsmodels

Statsmodels is a package designed with statistical analysis in mind; therefore, its function offers quite a rich output of statistical checks and information. Scalability is not an issue for the package; therefore, it is really a good starting point for learning, but is certainly not the optimal solution if you have to crunch quite large datasets (or even big data) because of its optimization algorithm.

There are two different methods (two modules) to work out a linear regression with Statsmodels:

- `statsmodels.api`: This works with distinct predictor and answer variables and requires you to define any transformation of the variables on the predictor variable, including adding the intercept
- `statsmodels.formula.api`: This works in a similar way to R, allowing you to specify a functional form (the formula of the summation of the predictors)

We will illustrate our example using the `statsModels.api`; however, we will also show you an alternative method with `statsmodels.formula.api`.

As a first step, let's upload both the modules of Statsmodels, naming them as conventionally indicated in the package documentation:

```
In: import statsmodels.api as sm
    import statsmodels.formula.api as smf
```

As a second step, it is necessary to define the y and X variables:

```
In: y = dataset['target']
    X = dataset['RM']
    X = sm.add_constant(X)
```

The X variable needs to be extended by a constant value (); the bias will be calculated accordingly. In fact, as you remember, the formula of a linear regression is as follows:

$$y = \beta X + \beta_0$$

However, using `StatsModels.api`, the formula actually becomes the following:

$$y = \beta X$$

This can be interpreted as a combination of the variables in X, multiplied by its corresponding β value.

Consequently, the predictor X now contains both the predictive variable and a unit constant. Also, β is no longer a single coefficient, but a vector of coefficients.

Let's have a visual confirmation of this by requiring the first values of the Pandas DataFrame using the `head` method:

```
In: X.head()
```

	const	RM
0	1	6.575
1	1	6.421
2	1	7.185
3	1	6.998
4	1	7.147

At this point, we just need to set the initialization of the linear regression calculation:

```
In: linear_regression = sm.OLS(y,X)
```

Also, we need to ask for the estimation of the regression coefficients, the β vector:

```
In: fitted_model = linear_regression.fit()
```

If we had wanted to manage the same result using the `StatsModels.formula.api`, we should have typed the following:

```
In: linear_regression = smf.ols(formula='target ~ RM', data=dataset)
    fitted_model = linear_regression.fit()
```

The previous two code lines simultaneously comprise both steps seen together, without requiring any particular variable preparation since the bias is automatically incorporated. In fact, the specification about how the linear regression should work is incorporated into the string `target ~ RM`, where the variable name left of the tilde (~) indicates the answer variable, the variable name (or names, in the case of a multiple regression analysis) on the right being for the predictor.

Actually, `smf.ols` expects quite a different input compared to `sm.OLS`, because it can accept our entire original dataset (it selects what variables are to be used by using the provided formula), whereas `sm.OLS` expects a matrix containing just the features to be used for prediction. Consequently, some caution has to be exercised when using two such different approaches.

A summary (a method of the fitted model) can quickly tell you everything that you need to know about regression analysis. In case you have tried `statsmodesl.formula.api`, we also re-initialize the linear regression using the `StatsModels.api` since they are not working on the same X and our following code relies on `sm.OLS` specifications:

```
In: linear_regression = sm.OLS(y,X)
    fitted_model = linear_regression.fit()
    fitted_model.summary()
```

OLS Regression Results

Dep. Variable:	target	R-squared:	0.484
Model:	OLS	Adj. R-squared:	0.483
Method:	Least Squares	F-statistic:	471.8
Date:	Sat, 28 Nov 2015	Prob (F-statistic):	2.49e-74
Time:	21:02:32	Log-Likelihood:	-1673.1
No. Observations:	506	AIC:	3350.
Df Residuals:	504	BIC:	3359.
Df Model:	1		
Covariance Type:	nonrobust		

	coef	std err	t	P>|t|	[95.0% Conf. Int.]
const	-34.6706	2.650	-13.084	0.000	-39.877 -29.465
RM	9.1021	0.419	21.722	0.000	8.279 9.925

Omnibus:	102.585	Durbin-Watson:	0.684
Prob(Omnibus):	0.000	Jarque-Bera (JB):	612.449
Skew:	0.726	Prob(JB):	1.02e-133
Kurtosis:	8.190	Cond. No.	58.4

You will receive quite a long series of tables containing many statistical tests and information. Though quite daunting at the beginning, you actually do not need all these outputs, unless the purpose of your analysis is a statistical one. Data science is mainly concerned with real models working on predicting real data, not on formally correct specifications of statistical problems. Nevertheless, some of these outputs are still useful for successful model building and we are going to provide you with an insight into the main figures.

Before explaining the outputs, we first need to extract two elements from the fitted model: the coefficients and the predictions calculated on the data on which we built the model. They both are going to come in very handy during the following explanations:

```
In: print (fitted_model.params)
   betas = np.array(fitted_model.params)
   fitted_values = fitted_model.predict(X)
```

The coefficient of determination

Let's start from the first table of results. The first table is divided into two columns. The first one contains a description of the fitted model:

- **Dep. Variable**: It just reminds you what the target variable was
- **Model**: Another reminder of the model that you have fitted, the OLS is ordinary least squares, another way to refer to linear regression
- **Method**: The parameters fitting method (in this case least squares, the classical computation method)
- **No. Observations**: The number of observations that have been used
- **DF Residuals**: The degrees of freedom of the residuals, which is the number of observations minus the number of parameters

- **DF Model**: The number of estimated parameters in the model (excluding the constant term from the count)

The second table gives a more interesting picture, focusing how good the fit of the linear regression model is and pointing out any possible problems with the model:

- **R-squared**: This is the coefficient of determination, a measure of how well the regression does with respect to a simple mean.

- **Adj. R-squared**: This is the coefficient of determination adjusted based on the number of parameters in a model and the number of observations that helped build it.

- **F-statistic**: This is a measure telling you if, from a statistical point of view, all your coefficients, apart from the bias and taken together, are different from zero. In simple words, it tells you if your regression is really better than a simple average.

- **Prob (F-statistic)**: This is the probability that you got that F-statistic just by lucky chance due to the observations that you have used (such a probability is actually called the **p-value** of F-statistic). If it is low enough you can be confident that your regression is really better than a simple mean. Usually in statistics and science a test probability has to be equal or lower than 0.05 (a conventional criterion of statistical significance) for having such a confidence.

- **AIC**: This is the **Akaike Information Criterion**. AIC is a score that evaluates the model based on the number of observations and the complexity of the model itself. The lesser the AIC score, the better. It is very useful for comparing different models and for statistical variable selection.

- **BIC**: This is the **Bayesian Information Criterion**. It works as AIC, but it presents a higher penalty for models with more parameters.

Most of these statistics make sense when we are dealing with more than one predictor variable, so they will be discussed in the next chapter. Thus, for the moment, as we are working with a simple linear regression, the two measures that are worth examining closely are F-statistic and R-squared. F-statistic is actually a test that doesn't tell you too much if you have enough observations and you can count on a minimally correlated predictor variable. Usually it shouldn't be much of a concern in a data science project.

R-squared is instead much more interesting because it tells you how much better your regression model is in comparison to a single mean. It does so by providing you with a percentage of the unexplained variance of a mean as a predictor that actually your model was able to explain.

If you want to compute the measure yourself, you just have to calculate the sum of squared errors of the mean of the target variable. That's your baseline of unexplained variance (the variability in house prices that in our example we want to explain by a model). If from that baseline you subtract the sum of squared errors of your regression model, you will get the residual sum of squared errors, which can be compared using a division with your baseline:

```
In: mean_sum_squared_errors = np.sum((dataset['target']-\
    dataset['target'].mean())**2)

    regr_sum_squared_errors = np.sum((dataset['target']-\
    fitted_values)**2)

    (mean_sum_squared_errors-\
    regr_sum_squared_errors) / mean_sum_squared_errors
```

Out: 0.48352545599133412

 When working with floats, rounding errors are possible, so don't be afraid if some of the lesser decimals don't match in your calculations; if they match the 8th decimal, you can be quite confident that the result is the same.

Ideally, if you can reduce your sum of squared errors of the regression to zero, you will get the maximum percentage of explained variance—that is, a score of 1.

The R-squared measure is also comparable with the percentage that you obtain squaring the correlation between your predictor and the target variable.

In our example, it is 0.484, which actually is exactly our R-squared correlation:

```
In: (pearsonr(dataset['RM'], dataset['target'])[0])**2
```

Out: 0.4835254559913339

As we have seen, R-squared is perfectly aligned with the squared errors that the linear regression is trying to minimize; thus, a better R-squared means a better model. However, there are some problems with the measure (and with linear regression itself, actually) when working with more predictors at once. Again, we have to wait until we model more predictors at once; therefore, just for a simple linear regression, a better R-squared should hint at a better model.

Meaning and significance of coefficients

The second output table informs us about the coefficients and provides us with a series of tests. These tests can make us confident that we have not been fooled by a few extreme observations in the foundations of our analysis or by some other problem:

- **coef**: The estimated coefficient
- **std err**: The standard error of the estimate of the coefficient; the larger it is, the more uncertain the estimation of the coefficient
- **t**: The t-statistic value, a measure indicating whether the coefficient true value is different from zero
- **P > |t|**: The p-value indicating the probability that the coefficient is different from zero just by chance
- **[95.0% Conf. Interval]**: The lower and upper values of the coefficient, considering 95% of all the chances of having different observations and so different estimated coefficients

From a data science viewpoint, t-tests and confidence bounds are not very useful because we are mostly interested in verifying whether our regression is working while predicting answer variables. Consequently, we will focus just on the `coef` value (the estimated coefficients) and on their standard error.

The coefficients are the most important output that we can obtain from our regression model because they allow us to re-create the weighted summation that can predict our outcomes.

In our example, our coefficients are *−34.6706* for the bias (also called the **intercept**, recalling the formula for a line in a Cartesian space) and *9.1021* for the RM variable. Recalling our formula, we can plug in the numbers we obtained:

$$y = \beta X + \beta_0$$

Now, if you replace the betas and X with the estimated coefficients, and the variables' names with *−34.6706* and *9.1021*, everything becomes the following:

$$y = 9.1021 * x_{RM} - 34.6706$$

Now, if you know the average number of rooms in an area of Boston, you can make a quick estimate of the expected value. For instance, x_{RM} is 4.55:

```
In: 9.1021*4.55-34.6706
```

```
Out: 6.743955
```

We have to notice two points here. First, in such a formulation, the beta of each variable becomes its *unit change* measure, which corresponds to the change the outcome will undergo if the variable increases by one unit. In our case, our average room space becomes 5.55:

```
In: 9.1021*5.55-34.6706
```

```
Out: 15.846055
```

The increase for a unit change in x_{RM} corresponds to a change in the outcome equivalent to β_{RM}. The other point to be noticed is that, if our average room space becomes 1 or 2, our estimated value will turn negative, which is completely unrealistic. This is because the mapping between predictor and the target variable happened in a delimited bound of values of the predictor:

```
In: (np.min(dataset['RM']),np.max(dataset['RM']))
Out: (3.5609999999999999, 8.7799999999999994)
```

Whenever we try to estimate our answer values using an x (or a set of X) that is outside the boundaries we used for fitting the model, we risk a response that has not been optimized at all by the linear regression calculations. Expressed in another way, linear regression can learn what it sees, and, unless there is a clear linear functional form between the predictor and the target (they can be truly expressed as a line), you risk weird estimations when your predictors have an unusual value. In other words, a linear regression can always work within the range of values it learned from (this is called **interpolation**) but can provide correct values for its learning boundaries (a different predictive activity called **extrapolation**) only in certain conditions.

 As we previously mentioned, the number of observations used for fitting the model is of paramount importance to obtain a robust and reliable linear regression model. The more observations, the less likely the model is to be surprised by unusual values when running in production.

Standard errors instead are very important because they signal a weak or unclear relationship between the predictor and the answer. You can notice this by dividing the standard error by its beta. If the ratio is 0.5 or even larger, then it's a clear sign that the model has little confidence that it provided you with the right coefficient estimates. Having more cases is always the solution because it can reduce the standard errors of the coefficients and improve our estimates; however, there are also other methods to reduce errors, such as removing the redundant variance present among the features by a principal component analysis or selecting a parsimonious set of predictors by greedy selections. All these topics will be discussed when we work with multiple predictors; at this point in the book, we will illustrate the remedies to such a problem.

Evaluating the fitted values

The last table deals with an analysis of the residuals of the regression. The residuals are the difference between the target values and the predicted fitted values:

- **Skewness**: This is a measure of the symmetry of the residuals around the mean. For symmetric distributed residuals, the value should be around zero. A positive value indicates a long tail to the right; a negative value a long tail to the left.

- **Kurtosis**: This is a measure of the shape of the distribution of the residuals. A bell-shaped distribution has a zero measure. A negative value points to a too flat distribution; a positive one has too great a peak.

- **Omnibus D'Angostino's test**: This is a combined statistical test for skewness and kurtosis.

- **Prob(Omnibus)**: This is the Omnibus statistic turned into a probability.

- **Jarque-Bera**: This is another test of skewness and kurtosis.

- **Prob (JB)**: This is the JB statistic turned into a probability.

- **Durbin-Watson**: This is a test for the presence of correlation among the residuals (relevant during analysis of time-based data).

- **Cond. No**: This is a test for multicollinearity (we will deal with the concept of multicollinearity when working with many predictors).

A close analysis of residuals is quite relevant in statistical practice since it can highlight the presence of serious problems with regression analysis. When working with a single variable it is interesting to visually check its residuals to figure out if there are strange cases or if the residuals don't distribute randomly. In particular, it is important to keep an eye out for any of these three problems showing up:

1. Values too far from the average. Large standardized residuals hint at a serious difficulty when modeling such observations. Also, in the process of learning these values, the regression coefficients may have been distorted.

2. Different variance in respect of the value of the predictor. If the linear regression is an average conditioned on the predictor, dishomogeneous variance points out that the regression is not working properly when the predictor has certain values.

3. Strange shapes in the cloud of residual points may indicate that you need a more complex model for the data you are analyzing.

In our case, we can easily compute the residuals by subtracting the fitted values from the answer variable and then plotting the resulting standardized residuals in a graph:

```
In: residuals = dataset['target']-fitted_values
    normalized_residuals = standardize(residuals)
```

```
In: residual_scatter_plot = plt.plot(dataset['RM'], normalized_
residuals,'bp')
```

```
mean_residual = plt.plot([int(x_range[0]),round(x_range[1],0)], [0,0],
'-', color='red', linewidth=2)
```

```
upper_bound = plt.plot([int(x_range[0]),round(x_range[1],0)], [3,3], '--
', color='red', linewidth=1)
```

```
lower_bound = plt.plot([int(x_range[0]),round(x_range[1],0)], [-3,-3],
'--', color='red', linewidth=1)
```

```
plt.grid()
```

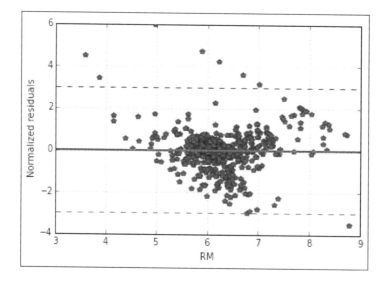

The resulting scatterplot indicates that the residuals show some of the problems we previously indicated as a warning that something is not going well with your regression analysis. First, there are a few points lying outside the band delimited by the two dotted lines at normalized residual values −3 and +3 (a range that should hypothetically cover 99.7% of values if the residuals have a normal distribution). These are surely influential points with large errors and they can actually make the entire linear regression under-perform. We will talk about possible solutions to this problem when we discuss outliers in the next chapter.

Then, the cloud of points is not at all randomly scattered, showing different variances at different values of the predictor variable (the **abscissa axis**) and you can spot unexpected patterns (points in a straight line, or the core points placed in a kind of U shape).

We are not at all surprised; the average number of rooms is likely a good predictor but it is not the only cause, or it has to be rethought as a direct cause (the number of rooms indicates a larger house, but what if the rooms are smaller than average?). This leads us to discuss whether a strong correlation really makes a variable a good working candidate for a linear relationship.

Correlation is not causation

Actually, seeing a correlation between your predictor and your target variable, and managing to model it successfully using a linear regression, doesn't really mean that there is a causal relation between the two (though your regression may work very well, and even optimally).

Though using a data science approach, instead of a statistical one, will guarantee a certain efficacy in your model, it is easy to fall into some mistakes when having no clue why your target variable is correlated with a predictor.

We will tell you about six different reasons, and offer a cautionary word to help you handle such predictors without difficulty:

- **Direct causation**: x causes y; for instance, in the real estate business the value is directly proportional to the size of the house in square meters.
- **Reciprocal effects**: x causes y but it is also influenced by y. This is quite typical of many macro-economic dynamics where the effect of a policy augments or diminishes its effects. As an example in real estate, high crime rates in an area can lower its prices but lower prices mean that the area could quickly become even more degraded and dangerous.
- **Spurious causation**: This happens when the real cause is actually z, which causes both x and y; consequently it is just a fallacious illusion that x implies y because it is z behind the scenes. For instance, the presence of expensive art shops and galleries may seem to correlate with house prices; in reality, both are determined by the presence of affluent residents.
- **Indirect causation**: x in reality is not causing y but it is causing something else, which then causes y. A good municipality investing in infrastructures after higher taxes can indirectly affect house prices because the area becomes more comfortable to live in, thus attracting more demand. Higher taxes, and thus more investments, indirectly affect house prices.
- **Conditional effect**: x causes y in respect of the values of another variable z; for instance, when z has certain values x is not influencing y but, when z takes particular values, the x starts impacting y. We also call this situation interaction. For instance the presence of schools in an area can become an attractor when the crime rate is low, so it affects house prices only when there is little criminality.

- **Random effect**: Any recorded correlation between x and y has been due to a lucky sampling selection; in reality there is no relationship with y at all.

The ideal case is when you have a direct causation; then, you will have a predictor in your model that will always provide you with the best values to derive your responses.

In the other cases, it is likely that the imperfect cause-effect relationship with the target variable will lead to more noisy estimates, especially in production when you will have to work with data not seen before by the model.

Reciprocal effects are more typical of econometric models. They require special types of regression analysis. Including them in your regression analysis may improve your model; however, their role may be underestimated.

Spurious and indirect causes will add some noise to your x and y relationship; this could bring noisier estimates (larger standard errors). Often, the solution is to get more observations for your analysis.

Conditional effects, if not caught, can limit your model's ability to produce accurate estimates. If you are not aware of any of them, given your domain knowledge of the problem, it is a good step to check for any of them using some automatic procedure to test possible interactions between the variables.

Random effects are the worst possible thing that could happen to your model, but they are easily avoided if you follow the data science procedure that we will be describing in *Chapter 6, Achieving Generalization*, when we deal with all the actions necessary to validate your model's results.

Predicting with a regression model

When we plug the coefficients into the regression formula, predicting is just a matter of applying new data to the vector of coefficients by a matrix multiplication.

First, you can rely on the fitted model by providing it with an array containing new cases. In the following example, you can see how, given the Xp variable with a single new case, this is easily predicted using the `predict` method on the fitted model:

```
In: RM = 5
    Xp = np.array([1,RM])
    print ("Our model predicts if RM = %01.f the answer value \
    is %0.1f" % (RM, fitted_model.predict(Xp)))

Out:  Our model predicts if RM = 5 the answer value is 10.8
```

A nice usage of the `predict` method is to project the fitted predictions on our previous scatterplot to allow us to visualize the price dynamics in respect of our predictor, the average number of rooms:

```
In: x_range = [dataset['RM'].min(),dataset['RM'].max()]

    y_range = [dataset['target'].min(),dataset['target'].max()]

    scatter_plot = dataset.plot(kind='scatter', x='RM', y='target',\
    xlim=x_range, ylim=y_range)

    meanY = scatter_plot.plot(x_range,\
    [dataset['target'].mean(),dataset['target'].mean()], '--',\
    color='red', linewidth=1)

    meanX =scatter_plot.plot([dataset['RM'].mean(),\
    dataset['RM'].mean()], y_range, '--', color='red', linewidth=1)

    regression_line = scatter_plot.plot(dataset['RM'], fitted_values,\
    '-', color='orange', linewidth=1)
```

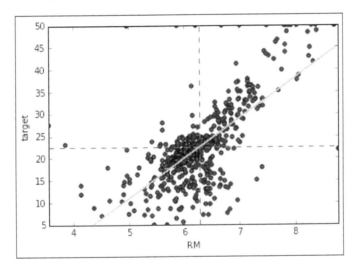

Using the previous code snippet, we will obtain the preceding graphical representation of the regression line containing a further indication of how such a line crosses the cloud of data points. For instance, thanks to this graphical display, we can notice that the regression line exactly passes at the intersection of the *x* and *y* averages.

Besides the `predict` method, generating the predictions is quite easy by just using the `dot` function in `NumPy`. After preparing an *X* matrix containing both the variable data and the bias (a column of ones) and the coefficient vectors, all you have to do is to multiply the matrix by the vector. The result will itself be a vector of length equal to the number of observations:

```
In: predictions_by_dot_product = np.dot(X,betas)
  print ("Using the prediction method: %s" % fitted_values[:10])
  print ("Using betas and a dot product: %s" %
predictions_by_dot_product[:10])
```

```
Out: Using the prediction method: [ 25.17574577  23.77402099  30.72803225
29.02593787  30.38215211
   23.85593997  20.05125842  21.50759586  16.5833549   19.97844155]
Using betas and a dot product: [ 25.17574577  23.77402099  30.72803225
29.02593787  30.38215211
   23.85593997  20.05125842  21.50759586  16.5833549   19.97844155]
```

A comparison of the results obtained by the `predict` method and this simple multiplication will reveal a perfect match. Because predicting from a linear regression is simple, if necessary you could even implement this multiplication on your application in a language different from Python. In such a case, you will just need to find a matrix calculation library or program a function by yourself. To our knowledge, you can easily write such a function even in the SQL script language.

Regressing with Scikit-learn

As we have seen while working with the `StatsModels` package, a linear model can be built using a more oriented machine learning package such as Scikit-learn. Using the `linear_model` module, we can set a linear regression model specifying that the predictors shouldn't be normalized and that our model should have a bias:

```
In: from sklearn import linear_model
  linear_regression = \
  linear_model.LinearRegression(normalize=False,\
  fit_intercept=True)
```

Data preparation, instead, requires counting the observations and carefully preparing the predictor array to specify its two dimensions (if left as a vector, the fitting procedure will raise an error):

```
In: observations = len(dataset)
X = dataset['RM'].values.reshape((observations,1))
# X should be always a matrix, never a vector
y = dataset['target'].values # y can be a vector
```

After completing all the previous steps, we can fit the model using the `fit` method:

```
In: linear_regression.fit(X,y)
```

A very convenient feature of the Scikit-learn package is that all the models, no matter their type of complexity, share the same methods. The `fit` method is always used for fitting and it expects an *X* and a *y* (when the model is a supervised one). Instead, the two common methods for making an exact prediction (always for regression) and its probability (when the model is probabilistic) are `predict` and `predict_proba`, respectively.

After fitting the model, we can inspect the vector of the coefficients and the bias constant:

```
In: print (linear_regression.coef_)
   print (linear_regression.intercept_)
```

```
Out: [ 9.10210898]
      -34.6706207764
```

Using the `predict` method and slicing the first 10 elements of the resulting list, we output the first 10 predicted values:

```
In: print (linear_regression.predict(X)[:10])
```

```
Out: [ 25.17574577  23.77402099  30.72803225  29.02593787  30.38215211
   23.85593997  20.05125842  21.50759586  16.5833549   19.97844155]
```

As previously seen, if we prepare a new matrix and we add a constant, we can calculate the results by ourselves using a simple matrix–vector multiplication:

```
In: Xp = np.column_stack((X,np.ones(observations)))
   v_coef = list(linear_regression.coef_) +\
   [linear_regression.intercept_]
```

As expected, the result of the product provides us with the same estimates as the `predict` method:

```
In: np.dot(Xp,v_coef)[:10]
```

```
Out: array([ 25.17574577,  23.77402099,  30.72803225,  29.02593787,
         30.38215211,  23.85593997,  20.05125842,  21.50759586,
         16.5833549 ,  19.97844155])
```

At this point, it would be natural to question the usage of such a `linear_model` module. Compared with the previous functions offered by Statsmodels, Scikit-learn seems to offer little statistical output, and one seemingly with many linear regression features stripped out. In reality, it offers exactly what is needed in data science and it is perfectly fast-performing when dealing with large datasets.

If you are working on IPython, just try the following simple test to generate a large dataset and check the performance of the two versions of linear regression:

```
In: from sklearn.datasets import make_regression
    HX, Hy = make_regression(n_samples=10000000, n_features=1,\
    n_targets=1, random_state=101)
```

After generating ten million observations of a single variable, start by measuring using the `%%time` magic function for IPython. This magic function automatically computes how long it takes to complete the calculations in the IPython cell:

```
In: %%time
    sk_linear_regression = linear_model.LinearRegression(\
    normalize=False,fit_intercept=True)
    sk_linear_regression.fit(HX,Hy)
```

```
Out: Wall time: 647 ms
```

Now, it is the turn of the Statsmodels package:

```
In: %%time
    sm_linear_regression = sm.OLS(Hy,sm.add_constant(HX))
    sm_linear_regression.fit()
```

```
Out: Wall time: 2.13 s
```

Though a single variable is involved in the model, Statsmodels's default algorithms prove to be three times slower than Scikit-learn. We will repeat this test in the next chapter, too, when using more predictive variables in one go and other different `fit` methods.

Minimizing the cost function

At the core of linear regression, there is the search for a line's equation that it is able to minimize the sum of the squared errors of the difference between the line's y values and the original ones. As a reminder, let's say our regression function is called h, and its predictions h(X), as in this formulation:

$$y \approx h(X) = \beta X + \beta_0$$

Consequently, our cost function to be minimized is as follows:

$$\frac{1}{2n} * \sum (h(X) - y)^2$$

There are quite a few methods to minimize it, some performing better than others in the presence of large quantities of data. Among the better performers, the most important ones are **Pseudoinverse** (you can find this in books on statistics), **QR factorization**, and **gradient descent**.

Explaining the reason for using squared errors

Looking under the hood of a linear regression analysis, at first it could be puzzling to realize that we are striving to minimize the squared differences between our estimates and the data from which we are building the model. Squared differences are not as intuitively explainable as absolute differences (the difference without a sign).

For instance, if you have to predict a monetary value, such as the price of a stock or the return from an advertising activity, you are more interested in knowing your absolute error, not your R-squared one, which could be perceived as misleading (since with squares larger losses are emphasized).

As we mentioned before, linear regression takes its steps from the statistical knowledge domain, and there are actually quite a few reasons in statistics that make minimizing a squared error preferable to minimizing an absolute one.

Unfortunately, such reasons are quite complex and too technical and consequently beyond the real scope of this book; however, from a high-level point of view, a good and reasonable explanation is that squaring nicely achieves two very important objectives:

- It removes negative values; therefore opposite errors won't reciprocally cancel each other when summed
- It emphasizes larger differences, because as they are squared they will proportionally increase the sum of the errors compared to a simple sum of absolute values

Minimizing the squared differences with an estimator leads us to use the mean (as we suggested before as a basic model, without providing any justification for it).

Let's just check together using Python, without developing all the formulations. Let's define an x vector of values:

```
In: import numpy as np
  x = np.array([9.5, 8.5, 8.0, 7.0, 6.0])
```

Let's also define a function returning the cost function as squared differences:

```
In: def squared_cost(v,e):
       return np.sum((v-e)**2)
```

Using the `fmin` minimization procedure offered by the `scipy` package, we try to figure out, for a vector (which will be our x vector of values), the value that makes the least squared summation:

```
In: from scipy.optimize import fmin
  xopt = fmin(squared_cost, x0=0, xtol=1e-8, args=(x,))


Out: Optimization terminated successfully.
        Current function value: 7.300000
        Iterations: 44
        Function evaluations: 88
```

We just output our best e value and verify if it actually is the mean of the x vector:

```
In: print ('The result of optimization is %0.1f' % (xopt[0]))
  print ('The mean is %0.1f' % (np.mean(x)))


Out: The result of optimization is 78.0
       The mean is 78.0
```

If instead we try to figure out what minimizes the sum of absolute errors:

```
In: def absolute_cost(v,e):
        return np.sum(np.abs(v-e))


In: xopt = fmin(absolute_cost, x0=0, xtol=1e-8, args=(x,))


Out: Optimization terminated successfully.
        Current function value: 5.000000
           Iterations: 44
           Function evaluations: 88


In: print ('The result of optimization is %0.1f' % (xopt[0]))
```

```
print ('The median is %0.1f' % (np.median(x)))
```

```
Out: The result of optimization is 8.0
    The median is 8.0
```

We will find out that it is the median, not the mean. Unfortunately, the median does not have the same statistical properties as the mean.

Pseudoinverse and other optimization methods

There is an analytical formula for solving a regression analysis and getting a vector of coefficients out of data, minimizing the cost function:

$$w = (X^T X)^{-1} X^T y$$

Demonstrating this equation goes beyond the practical scope of this book, but we can test it using the power of Python coding.

We can therefore directly solve for this by using `np.linalg.inv` from NumPy to obtain the inverse of a matrix, or alternative methods such as solving for w in linear equations that are called normal equations:

$$(X^T X)^{-1} * w = X^T y$$

Here the function `np.linalg.solve` can do all the calculations for us:

```
In: observations = len(dataset)
  X  = dataset['RM'].values.reshape((observations,1))
  # X should be always a matrix, never a vector
  Xb = np.column_stack((X,np.ones(observations))) # We add the bias
  y  = dataset['target'].values # y can be a vector

  def matrix_inverse(X,y, pseudo=False):
    if pseudo:
        return np.dot(np.linalg.pinv(np.dot(X.T,X)),np.dot(X.T,y))
    else:
        return np.dot(np.linalg.inv(np.dot(X.T, X)),np.dot(X.T,y))

  def normal_equations(X,y):
```

```
        return np.linalg.solve(np.dot(X.T,X), np.dot(X.T,y))
```

```
  print (matrix_inverse(Xb, y))
  print (matrix_inverse(Xb, y, pseudo=True))
  print (normal_equations(Xb, y))
```

Out:
```
  [  9.10210898 -34.67062078]
  [  9.10210898 -34.67062078]
  [  9.10210898 -34.67062078]
```

The only problem in solving a linear regression using these approaches is complexity, possibly some loss in accuracy of the computation when directly calculating the inverse using np.linalg.inv, and, naturally, the fact that the X^TX multiplication has to be invertible (sometimes it isn't when using multiple variables that are strongly related to each other).

Even using another algorithm (QR factorization, a core algorithm in Statsmodels that can overcome some previously quoted numeric misbehaviors), the worst performance can be estimated to be $O(n^3)$; that is, cubic complexity.

Using Pseudoinverse (in NumPy, np.linalg.pinv) can help achieve a $O(n^m)$ complexity where m is estimated to be <2.37 (approximately quadratic, then).

This can really be a great limitation in being able to quickly estimate linear regression analysis. In fact, if you are working with 10^3 observations, a feasible number of observations in statistical analysis, it will take at worst 10^9 computations; however, when working with data science projects, which easily reach 10^6 observations, the number of computations required to find the solution to a regression problem may rocket to 10^{18}.

Gradient descent at work

As an alternative to the usual classical optimization algorithms, the gradient descent technique is able to minimize the cost function of a linear regression analysis using far fewer computations. Gradient descent complexity ranks in the order $O(n*p)$, thus making learning regression coefficients feasible even in the occurrence of a large n (which stands for the number of observations) and a large p (number of variables).

The method works by leveraging a simple heuristic that gradually converges on the optimal solution starting from a random one. Explaining it simply, it resembles walking blind in the mountains. If you want to descend to the lowest valley, even if you don't know and can't see the path, you can proceed approximately by going downhill for a while, then stopping, then going downhill again and so on, always aiming at each stage for where the surface descends until you arrive at a point when you cannot descend anymore. Hopefully, at that point you will have reached your destination.

In such a situation, your only risk is happening on an intermediate valley (where there is a wood or a lake, for instance) and mistaking it for your desired arrival because the land stops descending there.

In an optimization process, such a situation is defined as a local minimum (whereas your target is a global minimum instead, the best minimum possible) and it is a possible outcome of your journey downhill depending on the function you are working on minimizing. The good news is, in any case, that the error function of the linear model family is a bowl-shaped one (technically our cost function is a concave one) and it is unlikely that you can get caught anywhere if you descend properly.

The necessary steps to work out a gradient-descent-based solution are easily described, given our cost function for a set of coefficients (the vector w):

$$J(w) = \frac{1}{2n} \sum (Xw - y)^2$$

We first start by choosing a random initialization for w, by choosing some random numbers (taken from a standardized normal curve, for instance, having a zero mean and unit variance).

Then we start reiterating an update of the values of w (opportunely using the gradient descent computations) until the marginal improvement from the previous $J(w)$ is small enough to let us figure out that we have finally reached an optimum minimum.

We can opportunely update our coefficients, one by one, by subtracting from each of them a portion alpha (α, the learning rate) of the partial derivative of the cost function:

$$w_j = w_j - \alpha * \frac{\partial}{\partial w} J(w)$$

Here, in our formula, w_j is to be intended as a single coefficient (we are iterating over them). After resolving the partial derivative, the final resolution form is as follows:

$$w_j = w_j - \alpha * \frac{1}{n} \sum (Xw - y) * x_j$$

Simplifying everything, our gradient for the coefficient of x is just the average of our predicted values multiplied by their respective x value.

Alpha, called the **learning rate**, is very important in the process, because, if it is too large, it may cause the optimization to detour and fail. You have to think of each gradient as a jump or as a run in a direction. If you fully take it, you may happen to pass over the optimum minimum and end up in another rising slope. Too many consecutive long steps may even force you to climb up the cost slope, worsening your initial position (given by a cost function that is its summed square, the loss of an overall score of fitness).

Using a small alpha, gradient descent won't jump beyond the solution but it may take a much longer time to reach the desired minimum. How to choose the right alpha is a matter of trial and error; anyway, starting from an alpha such as 0.01 is never a bad choice, based on our experience in many optimization problems.

Naturally, the gradient, given the same alpha, will in any case produce shorter steps as you approach the solution. Visualizing the steps in a graph can really give you a hint about whether gradient descent is working out a solution or not.

Though quite conceptually simple (it is based on an intuition that we have surely applied ourselves to move step-by-step, directing where we can optimize our result), gradient descent is very effective and indeed scalable when working with real data. Such interesting characteristics have elevated it to the core optimization algorithm in machine learning; it is not limited to just the linear model family, but it can also be extended, for instance, to neural networks for the process of back propagation, which updates all the weights of the neural net in order to minimize training errors. Surprisingly, gradient descent is also at the core of another complex machine learning algorithm, gradient boosting tree ensembles, where we have an iterative process minimizing the errors using a simpler learning algorithm (a so-called **weak learner** because it is limited by a high bias) to progress towards optimization.

Here is a first implementation in Python. We will slightly modify it in the next chapter to make it work efficiently with more predictors than one:

```
In: observations = len(dataset)
   X   = dataset['RM'].values.reshape((observations,1))
   # X should be always a matrix, never a vector
   X = np.column_stack((X,np.ones(observations))) # We add the bias
   y   = dataset['target'].values # y can be a vector
```

Now, after defining the response variable, selecting our predictor (the RM feature, the average number of rooms per dwelling), and adding a bias (the constant number 1), we are ready in the following code to define all the functions in our optimization process:

```
In: import random

    def random_w( p ):
        return np.array([np.random.normal() for j in range(p)])


    def hypothesis(X,w):
        return np.dot(X,w)


    def loss(X,w,y):
        return hypothesis(X,w) - y


    def squared_loss(X,w,y):
        return loss(X,w,y)**2


    def gradient(X,w,y):
        gradients = list()
        n = float(len( y ))
        for j in range(len(w)):
            gradients.append(np.sum(loss(X,w,y) * X[:,j]) / n)
        return gradients


    def update(X,w,y, alpha=0.01):
        return [t - alpha*g for t, g in zip(w, gradient(X,w,y))]


    def optimize(X,y, alpha=0.01, eta = 10**-12, iterations = 1000):
        w = random_w(X.shape[1])
        path = list()
        for k in range(iterations):
            SSL = np.sum(squared_loss(X,w,y))
            new_w = update(X,w,y, alpha=alpha)
            new_SSL = np.sum(squared_loss(X,new_w,y))
            w = new_w
            if k>=5 and (new_SSL - SSL <= eta and \
        new_SSL - SSL >= -eta):
                path.append(new_SSL)
                return w, path
```

```
        if k % (iterations / 20) == 0:

            path.append(new_SSL)
    return w, path
```

After finally defining all the functions necessary for gradient descent to work, we can start optimizing it for a solution to our single regression problem:

```
IN: alpha = 0.048

  w, path = optimize(X,y,alpha, eta = 10**-12, iterations = 25000)
  print ("These are our final coefficients: %s" % w)
  print ("Obtained walking on this path of squared loss %s" % path)


Out: These are our final coefficients: [9.1021032698295059,\
    -34.670584445862119]

  Obtained walking on this path of squared loss [369171.02494038735,
23714.645148620271, 22452.194702610999, 22154.055704515144,
22083.647505550518, 22067.019977742671, 22063.093237887566,
22062.165903044533, 22061.946904602359, 22061.895186155631,
22061.882972380481, 22061.880087987909, 22061.879406812728,
22061.879245947097, 22061.879207957238, 22061.879198985589,
22061.879196866852, 22061.879196366495, 22061.879196248334,
22061.879196220427, 22061.879196220034]
```

Scikit-learn `linear_regression` (and other linear models present in the linear methods module) are actually powered by gradient descent, making Scikit-learn our favorite choice when working in data science projects with large and big data.

Summary

In this chapter, we introduced linear regression as a supervised machine learning algorithm. We explained its functional form, its relationship with the statistical measures of mean and correlation, and we tried to build a simple linear regression model on the Boston house prices data. After doing that we finally glanced at how regression works under the hood by proposing its key mathematical formulations and their translation into Python code.

In the next chapter, we will continue our discourse about linear regression, extending our predictors to multiple variables and carrying on our explanation where we left it suspended during our initial illustration with a single variable. We will also point out the most useful transformations you can apply to data to make it suitable for processing by a linear regression algorithm.

Multiple Regression in Action

In the previous chapter, we introduced linear regression as a supervised method for machine learning rooted in statistics. Such a method forecasts numeric values using a combination of predictors, which can be continuous numeric values or binary variables, given the assumption that the data we have at hand displays a certain relation (a linear one, measurable by a correlation) with the target variable. To smoothly introduce many concepts and easily explain how the method works, we limited our example models to just a single predictor variable, leaving to it all the burden of modeling the response.

However, in real-world applications, there may be some very important causes determining the events you want to model but it is indeed rare that a single variable could take the stage alone and make a working predictive model. The world is complex (and indeed interrelated in a mix of causes and effects) and often it cannot be easily explained without considering various causes, influencers, and hints. Usually more variables have to work together to achieve better and reliable results from a prediction.

Such an intuition decisively affects the complexity of our model, which from this point forth will no longer be easily represented on a two-dimensional plot. Given multiple predictors, each of them will constitute a dimension of its own and we will have to consider that our predictors are not just related to the response but also related among themselves (sometimes very strictly), a characteristic of data called **multicollinearity**.

Before starting, we'd like to write just a few words on the selection of topics we are going to deal with. Though in the statistical literature there is a large number of publications and books devoted to regression assumptions and diagnostics, you'll hardly find anything here because we will leave out such topics. We will be limiting ourselves to discussing problems and aspects that could affect the results of a regression model, on the basis of a practical data science approach, not a purely statistical one.

Given such premises, in this chapter we are going to:

- Extend the procedures for a single regression to a multiple one, keeping an eye on possible sources of trouble such as multicollinearity

- Understand the importance of each term in your linear model equation

- Make your variables work together and increase your ability to predict using interactions between variables

- Leverage polynomial expansions to increase the fit of your linear model with non-linear functions

Using multiple features

To recap the tools seen in the previous chapter, we reload all the packages and the Boston dataset:

```
In: import numpy as np
    import pandas as pd
    import matplotlib.pyplot as plt
    import matplotlib as mpl
    from sklearn.datasets import load_boston
    from sklearn import linear_model
```

If you are working on the code in an IPython Notebook (as we strongly suggest), the following magic command will allow you to visualize plots directly on the interface:

```
In: %matplotlib inline
```

We are still using the Boston dataset, a dataset that tries to explain different house prices in the Boston of the 70s, given a series of statistics aggregated at the census zone level:

```
In: boston = load_boston()
    dataset = pd.DataFrame(boston.data, columns=boston.feature_names)
    dataset['target'] = boston.target
```

We will always work by keeping with us a series of informative variables, the number of observation and variable names, the input data matrix, and the response vector at hand:

```
In: observations = len(dataset)
    variables = dataset.columns[:-1]
    X = dataset.ix[:,:-1]
    y = dataset['target'].values
```

Model building with Statsmodels

As a first step toward extending to more predictors the previously done analysis with Statsmodels, let's reload the necessary modules from the package (one working with matrices and the other with formulas):

```
In: import statsmodels.api as sm
    import statsmodels.formula.api as smf
```

Let's also prepare a suitable input matrix, naming it Xc after having it incremented by an extra column containing the bias vector (a constant variable having the unit value):

```
In: Xc = sm.add_constant(X)
    linear_regression = sm.OLS(y,Xc)
    fitted_model = linear_regression.fit()
```

After having fitted the preceding specified model, let's immediately ask for a summary:

```
In: fitted_model.summary()
Out:
```

OLS Regression Results			
Dep. Variable:	y	R-squared:	0.741
Model:	OLS	Adj. R-squared:	0.734
Method:	Least Squares	F-statistic:	108.1
Date:	Tue, 29 Sep 2015	Prob (F-statistic):	6.95e-135
Time:	21:45:28	Log-Likelihood:	-1498.8
No. Observations:	506	AIC:	3026.
Df Residuals:	492	BIC:	3085.
Df Model:	13		
Covariance Type:	nonrobust		

	coef	std err	t	P>|t|	[95.0% Conf. Int.]
const	36.4911	5.104	7.149	0.000	26.462 46.520
CRIM	-0.1072	0.033	-3.276	0.001	-0.171 -0.043
ZN	0.0464	0.014	3.380	0.001	0.019 0.073
INDUS	0.0209	0.061	0.339	0.735	-0.100 0.142
CHAS	2.6886	0.862	3.120	0.002	0.996 4.381
NOX	-17.7958	3.821	-4.658	0.000	-25.302 -10.289
RM	3.8048	0.418	9.102	0.000	2.983 4.626
AGE	0.0008	0.013	0.057	0.955	-0.025 0.027
DIS	-1.4758	0.199	-7.398	0.000	-1.868 -1.084
RAD	0.3057	0.066	4.608	0.000	0.175 0.436
TAX	-0.0123	0.004	-3.278	0.001	-0.020 -0.005
PTRATIO	-0.9535	0.131	-7.287	0.000	-1.211 -0.696
B	0.0094	0.003	3.500	0.001	0.004 0.015
LSTAT	-0.5255	0.051	-10.366	0.000	-0.625 -0.426

Omnibus:	178.029	Durbin-Watson:	1.078
Prob(Omnibus):	0.000	Jarque-Bera (JB):	782.015
Skew:	1.521	Prob(JB):	1.54e-170
Kurtosis:	8.276	Cond. No.	1.51e+04

Basically, the enunciations of the various statistical measures, as presented in the previous chapter, are still valid. We will just devote a few words to remarking on a couple of extra features we couldn't mention before because they are related to the presence of multiple predictors.

First, the adjusted R-squared is something to take note of now. When working with multiple variables, the standard R-squared can get inflated because of the many coefficients inserted into the model. If you are using too many predictors, its measure will diverge perceptibly from the plain R-squared. The adjusted R-squared considers the complexity of the model and reports a much more realistic R-squared measure.

 Just make a ratio between the plain and the adjusted R-squared measure. Check if their difference exceeds 20%. If it does, it means that we have introduced some redundant variables inside our model specification. Naturally, the larger the ratio difference, the more serious the problem.

This is not the case in our example because the difference is quite slight, approximately between 0.741 and 0.734, which translated into a ratio turns out to be *0.741/0.734 = 1.01*, that is just 1% over the standard R-squared.

Then, working with so many variables at a time, coefficients should also be checked for important warnings. The risk involved is having coefficients picking up noisy and non-valuable information. Usually such coefficients will not be far from zero and will be noticeable because of their large standard errors. Statistical t-tests are the right tool to spot them.

> Be aware that variables with a low p-value are good candidates for being removed from the model because there will probably be little proof that their estimated coefficient is different from zero.

In our example, being largely not significant (p-value major of 0.05), the AGE and INDUS variables are represented in the model by coefficients whose usefulness could be seriously challenged.

Finally, the condition number test (Cond. No.) is another previously mentioned statistic that now acquires a fresh importance under the light of a system of predictors. It signals numeric unstable results when trying an optimization based on matrix inversion. The cause of such instability is due to multicollinearity, a problem we are going to expand on in the following paragraphs.

> When a condition number is over the score of 30, there's a clear signal that unstable results are rendering the result less reliable. Predictions may be affected by errors and the coefficients may drastically change when rerunning the same regression analysis with a subset or a different set of observations.

In our case, the condition number is well over 30, and that's a serious warning signal.

Using formulas as an alternative

To obtain the same results using the statsmodels.formula.api and thereby explicating a formula to be interpreted by the Patsy package (http://patsy.readthedocs.org/en/latest/), we use:

```
linear_regression = smf.ols(formula = 'target ~ CRIM + ZN +INDUS + CHAS +
NOX + RM + AGE + DIS + RAD + TAX + PTRATIO + B + LSTAT', data=dataset)

fitted_model = linear_regression.fit()
```

In this case, you have to explicate all the variables to enter into model building by naming them on the right side of the formula. After fitting the model, you can use all the previously seen Statsmodels methods for reporting the coefficients and results.

The correlation matrix

When trying to model the response using a single predictor, we used Pearson's correlation (Pearson was the name of its inventor) to estimate a coefficient of linear association between the predictor and the target. Having more variables in the analysis now, we are still quite interested in how each predictor relates to the response; however, we have to distinguish whether the relation between the variance of the predictor and that of the target is due to unique or shared variance.

The measurement of the association due to unique variance is called **partial correlation** and it expresses what can be guessed of the response thanks to the information uniquely present in a variable. It represents the exclusive contribution of a variable in predicting the response, its unique impact as a direct cause to the target (if you can view it as being a cause though, because, as seen, correlation is not causation).

The shared variance is instead the amount of information that is simultaneously present in a variable and in other variables in the dataset at hand. Shared variance can have many causes; maybe one variable causes or it just interferes with the other (as we described in the previous chapter in the *Correlation is not causation* section). Shared variance, otherwise called **collinearity** (between two variables) or multicollinearity (among three or more variables), has an important effect, worrisome for the classical statistical approach, less menacing for the data science one.

For the statistical approach, it has to be said that high or near perfect multicollinearity not only often renders coefficient estimations impossible (matrix inversion is not working), but also, when it is feasible, it will be affected by imprecision in coefficient estimation, leading to large standard errors of the coefficients. However, the predictions won't be affected in any way and that leads us to the data science points of view.

Having multicollinear variables, in fact, renders it difficult to select the correct variables for the analysis (since the variance is shared, it is difficult to figure out which variable should be its causal source), leading to sub-optimal solutions that could be resolved only by augmenting the number of observations involved in the analysis.

To determine the manner and number of predictors affecting each other, the right tool is a correlation matrix, which, though a bit difficult to read when the number of the features is high, is still the most direct way to ascertain the presence of shared variance:

```
X = dataset.ix[:,:-1]
correlation_matrix = X.corr()
print (correlation_matrix)
```

This will give the following output:

```
              CRIM        ZN     INDUS      CHAS       NOX        RM       AGE  \
CRIM      1.000000 -0.199458  0.404471 -0.055295  0.417521 -0.219940  0.350784
ZN       -0.199458  1.000000 -0.533828 -0.042697 -0.516604  0.311991 -0.569537
INDUS     0.404471 -0.533828  1.000000  0.062938  0.763651 -0.391676  0.644779
CHAS     -0.055295 -0.042697  0.062938  1.000000  0.091203  0.091251  0.086518
NOX       0.417521 -0.516604  0.763651  0.091203  1.000000 -0.302188  0.731470
RM       -0.219940  0.311991 -0.391676  0.091251 -0.302188  1.000000 -0.240265
AGE       0.350784 -0.569537  0.644779  0.086518  0.731470 -0.240265  1.000000
DIS      -0.377904  0.664408 -0.708027 -0.099176 -0.769230  0.205246 -0.747881
RAD       0.622029 -0.311948  0.595129 -0.007368  0.611441 -0.209847  0.456022
TAX       0.579564 -0.314563  0.720760 -0.035587  0.668023 -0.292048  0.506456
PTRATIO   0.288250 -0.391679  0.383248 -0.121515  0.188933 -0.355501  0.261515
B        -0.377365  0.175520 -0.356977  0.048788 -0.380051  0.128069 -0.273534
LSTAT     0.452220 -0.412995  0.603800 -0.053929  0.590879 -0.613808  0.602339

              DIS       RAD       TAX   PTRATIO         B     LSTAT
CRIM     -0.377904  0.622029  0.579564  0.288250 -0.377365  0.452220
ZN        0.664408 -0.311948 -0.314563 -0.391679  0.175520 -0.412995
INDUS    -0.708027  0.595129  0.720760  0.383248 -0.356977  0.603800
CHAS     -0.099176 -0.007368 -0.035587 -0.121515  0.048788 -0.053929
NOX      -0.769230  0.611441  0.668023  0.188933 -0.380051  0.590879
RM        0.205246 -0.209847 -0.292048 -0.355501  0.128069 -0.613808
AGE      -0.747881  0.456022  0.506456  0.261515 -0.273534  0.602339
DIS       1.000000 -0.494588 -0.534432 -0.232471  0.291512 -0.496996
RAD      -0.494588  1.000000  0.910228  0.464741 -0.444413  0.488676
TAX      -0.534432  0.910228  1.000000  0.460853 -0.441808  0.543993
PTRATIO  -0.232471  0.464741  0.460853  1.000000 -0.177383  0.374044
B         0.291512 -0.444413 -0.441808 -0.177383  1.000000 -0.366087
LSTAT    -0.496996  0.488676  0.543993  0.374044 -0.366087  1.000000
```

At first glance, some high correlations appear to be present in the order of the absolute value of 0.70 (highlighted by hand in the matrix) between TAX, NOX, INDUS, and DIS. That's fairly explainable since DIS is the distance from employment centers, NOX is a pollution indicator, INDUS is the quota of non-residential or commercial buildings in the area, and TAX is the property tax rate. The right combination of these variables can well hint at what the productive areas are.

A faster, but less numerical representation is to build a heat map of the correlations:

In:

```
def visualize_correlation_matrix(data, hurdle = 0.0):
    R = np.corrcoef(data, rowvar=0)
    R[np.where(np.abs(R)<hurdle)] = 0.0
    heatmap = plt.pcolor(R, cmap=mpl.cm.coolwarm, alpha=0.8)
    heatmap.axes.set_frame_on(False)
    heatmap.axes.set_yticks(np.arange(R.shape[0]) + 0.5, minor=False)
    heatmap.axes.set_xticks(np.arange(R.shape[1]) + 0.5, minor=False)
```

```
heatmap.axes.set_xticklabels(variables, minor=False)
plt.xticks(rotation=90)
heatmap.axes.set_yticklabels(variables, minor=False)
plt.tick_params(axis='both', which='both', bottom='off', \
top='off', left = 'off', right = 'off')
plt.colorbar()
plt.show()
```

```
visualize_correlation_matrix(X, hurdle=0.5)
```

This will give the following output:

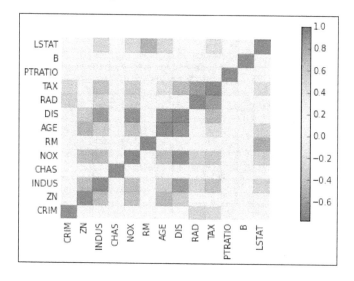

Having a cut at 0.5 correlation (which translates into a 25% shared variance), the heat map immediately reveals how **PTRATIO** and **B** are not so related to other predictors. As a reminder of the meaning of variables, **B** is an indicator quantifying the proportion of colored people in the area and **PTRATIO** is the pupil-teacher ratio in the schools of the area. Another intuition provided by the map is that a cluster of variables, namely **TAX, INDUS, NOX,** and **RAD,** is confirmed to be in strong linear association.

An even more automatic way to detect such associations (and figure out numerical problems in a matrix inversion) is to use eigenvectors. Explained in layman's terms, eigenvectors are a very smart way to recombine the variance among the variables, creating new features accumulating all the shared variance. Such recombination can be achieved using the NumPy `linalg.eig` function, resulting in a vector of eigenvalues (representing the amount of recombined variance for each new variable) and eigenvectors (a matrix telling us how the new variables relate to the old ones):

```
In: corr = np.corrcoef(X, rowvar=0)
    eigenvalues, eigenvectors = np.linalg.eig(corr)
```

After extracting the eigenvalues, we print them in descending order and look for any element whose value is near to zero or small compared to the others. Near zero values can represent a real problem for normal equations and other optimization methods based on matrix inversion. Small values represent a high but not critical source of multicollinearity. If you spot any of these low values, keep a note of their index in the list (Python indexes start from zero).

```
In: print (eigenvalues)
Out: [ 6.12265476  1.43206335  1.24116299  0.85779892  0.83456618
0.65965056  0.53901749  0.39654415  0.06351553  0.27743495  0.16916744
0.18616388  0.22025981]
```

Using their index position in the list of eigenvalues, you can recall their specific vector from eigenvectors, which contains all the variable loadings — that is, the level of association with the original variables. In our example, we investigate the eigenvector at index 8. Inside the eigenvector, we notice values at index positions 2, 8, and 9, which are indeed outstanding in terms of absolute value:

```
In: print (eigenvectors[:,8])
Out: [-0.04552843  0.08089873  0.25126664 -0.03590431 -0.04389033
-0.04580522  0.03870705  0.01828389  0.63337285 -0.72024335 -0.02350903
0.00485021 -0.02477196]
```

We now print the variables' names to know which ones contribute so much by their values to build the eigenvector:

```
In: print (variables[2], variables[8], variables[9])
Out: INDUS RAD TAX
```

Having found the multicollinearity culprits, what remedy could we use for such variables? Removal of some of them is usually the best solution and that will be carried out in an automated way when exploring how variable selection works in *Chapter 6, Achieving Generalization*.

Revisiting gradient descent

In continuity with the previous chapter, we carry on our explanation and experimentation with gradient descent. As we have already defined both the mathematical formulation and their translation into Python code, using matrix notation, we don't need to worry if now we have to deal with more than one variable at a time. Having used the matrix notation allows us to easily extend our previous introduction and example to multiple predictors with just minor changes to the algorithm.

In particular, we have to take note that, by introducing more parameters to be estimated during the optimization procedure, we are actually introducing more dimensions to our line of fit (turning it into a hyperplane, a multidimensional surface) and such dimensions have certain communalities and differences to be taken into account.

Feature scaling

Working with different features requires more attention when estimating the coefficients because of their similarities which can cause a variance increase of the estimates, as we initially discussed. Multicollinearity between variables also has other drawbacks because it can also make matrix inversion (the matrix operation at the core of the normal equation coefficient estimation) very difficult, if not impossible, to achieve; such a problem is due to a mathematical limitation of the algorithm. Gradient descent, instead, is not affected at all by reciprocal correlation, allowing us to estimate reliable coefficients even in the presence of perfect collinearity.

Anyway, though being quite resistant to problems that affect other approaches, its simplicity also makes it vulnerable to other common problems, such as the different scale present in each feature. In fact, some features in your data may be represented by measurements in units, some in decimals, and others in thousands, depending on what aspect of reality each feature represents. In our real estate example, one feature could be the number of rooms, another one could be the percentage of certain pollutants in the air, and finally, the average value of a house in the neighborhood. When it is the case that the features have a different scale, though the algorithm will be processing each of them separately, optimization will be dominated by the variables with the more extensive scale. Working in a space of dissimilar dimensions will require more iterations before convergence to a solution (and sometimes there might be no convergence at all).

The remedy is very easy; it is just necessary to put all the features on the same scale. Such an operation is called **feature scaling**. Feature scaling can be achieved through standardization or normalization. Normalization rescales all the values in the interval between zero and one (usually, but different ranges are also possible), whereas standardization operates by removing the mean and dividing by standard deviation to obtain a unit variance. In our case, standardization is preferable, both because it easily permits retuning the obtained standardized coefficients into their original scale and also because, by centering all the features at the zero mean, it makes the error surface more tractable by many machine learning algorithms, in a much more effective way than just rescaling the maximum and minimum of a variable.

An important reminder when applying feature scaling is that changing the scale of the features implies that you will have to use rescaled features also for predictions, unless you can recalculate the coefficients as if the variables had never been rescaled.

Let's try the algorithm, first using standardization based on the Scikit-learn `preprocessing` module:

```
In: from sklearn.preprocessing import StandardScaler
    observations = len(dataset)
    variables = dataset.columns
    standardization = StandardScaler()
    Xst = standardization.fit_transform(X)
    original_means = standardization.mean_
    originanal_stds = standardization.std_
    Xst = np.column_stack((Xst,np.ones(observations)))
    y   = dataset['target'].values
```

In the preceding code, we just standardized the variables using the `StandardScaler` class from Scikit-learn. This class can fit a data matrix, record its column means and standard deviations, and operate a transformation on itself, as well as on any other similar matrix, standardizing the column data. With this method, after fitting we keep a track of means and standard deviations that have been used because they will come in handy later when we have to recalculate the coefficients using the original scale:

```
In: import random

    def random_w( p ):
        return np.array([np.random.normal() for j in range(p)])
    def hypothesis(X,w):
        return np.dot(X,w)

    def loss(X,w,y):
        return hypothesis(X,w) - y

    def squared_loss(X,w,y):
        return loss(X,w,y)**2

    def gradient(X,w,y):
        gradients = list()
        n = float(len( y ))
        for j in range(len(w)):
            gradients.append(np.sum(loss(X,w,y) * X[:,j]) / n)
```

```
        return gradients


    def update(X,w,y, alpha=0.01):
        return [t - alpha*g for t, g in zip(w, gradient(X,w,y))]


    def optimize(X,y, alpha=0.01, eta = 10**-12, iterations = 1000):
        w = random_w(X.shape[1])
        path = list()
        for k in range(iterations):
            SSL = np.sum(squared_loss(X,w,y))
            new_w = update(X,w,y, alpha=alpha)
            new_SSL = np.sum(squared_loss(X,new_w,y))
            w = new_w
            if k>=5 and (new_SSL - SSL <= eta and \
            new_SSL - SSL >= -eta):
                path.append(new_SSL)
                return w, path
            if k % (iterations / 20) == 0:
                path.append(new_SSL)
        return w, path


    alpha = 0.02
    w, path = optimize(Xst, y, alpha, eta = 10**-12, \
    iterations = 20000)
    print ("These are our final standardized coefficients: " + ', \
    '.join(map(lambda x: "%0.4f" % x, w)))
```

```
Out: These are our final standardized coefficients: -0.9204, 1.0810,
0.1430, 0.6822, -2.0601, 2.6706, 0.0211, -3.1044, 2.6588, -2.0759,
-2.0622, 0.8566, -3.7487, 22.5328
```

The code we are using is not at all different from the code we used in the previous chapter with the exception of its input, which is now made up of multiple standardized variables. In this case, the algorithm reaches a convergence in fewer iterations and uses a smaller alpha than before because in our previous example our single variable actually was unstandardized. Observing the output, we now need a way to rescale the coefficients to their variables' characteristics and we will be able to report the gradient descent solution in unstandardized form.

Another point to mention is our choice of alpha. After some tests, the value of `0.02` has been chosen for its good performance on this very specific problem. Alpha is the learning rate and during optimization it can be fixed or changeable, accordingly to a line search method, modifying its value in order to minimize as far as possible the cost function at each single step of the optimization process. In our example, we opted for a fixed learning rate and we had to look for its best value by trying a few optimization values and deciding on which minimized the cost in the minor number of iterations.

Unstandardizing coefficients

Given a vector of standardized coefficients from a linear regression and its bias, we can recall the formulation of the linear regression, which is:

$$y = \beta_0 + \sum \beta_i x_i$$

The previous formula, transforming the predictors using their mean and standard deviation, is actually equivalent (after a few calculations) to such an expression:

$$y = \left(\hat{\beta}_0 - \sum \frac{\hat{\beta}_i * \bar{x}_i}{\delta_i} \right) + \sum \left(\frac{\hat{\beta}_i}{\delta_i} * x_i \right)$$

In our formula, $\bar{x}$ represents the original mean and δ the original variance of the variables.

By comparing the different parts of the two formulas (the first parenthesis and the second summation), we can calculate the bias and coefficient equivalents when transforming a standardized coefficient into an unstandardized one. Without replicating all the mathematical formulas, we can quickly implement them into Python code and immediately provide an application showing how such calculations can transform gradient descent coefficients:

```
In: unstandardized_betas = w[:-1] / originanal_stds
    unstandardized_bias  = w[-1] -np.sum((original_means /
    originanal_stds) * w[:-1])
    print ('%8s: %8.4f' % ('bias', unstandardized_bias))
    for beta,varname in zip(unstandardized_betas, variables):
            print ('%8s: %8.4f' % (varname, beta))
```

Out:

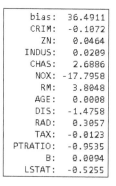

```
    bias:  36.4911
    CRIM:  -0.1072
      ZN:   0.0464
   INDUS:   0.0209
    CHAS:   2.6886
     NOX: -17.7958
      RM:   3.8048
     AGE:   0.0008
     DIS:  -1.4758
     RAD:   0.3057
     TAX:  -0.0123
 PTRATIO:  -0.9535
       B:   0.0094
   LSTAT:  -0.5255
```

As an output from the previous code snippet, you will get a list of coefficients identical to our previous estimations with both Scikit-learn and Statsmodels.

Estimating feature importance

After having confirmed the values of the coefficients of the linear model we have built, and after having explored the basic statistics necessary to understand if our model is working correctly, we can start auditing our work by first understanding how a prediction is made up. We can obtain this by accounting for each variable's role in the constitution of the predicted values. A first check to be done on the coefficients is surely on the directionality they express, which is simply dictated by their sign. Based on our expertise on the subject (so it is advisable to be knowledgeable about the domain we are working on), we can check whether all the coefficients correspond to our expectations in terms of directionality. Some features may decrease the response as we expect, thereby correctly confirming that they have a coefficient with a negative sign, whereas others may increase it, so a positive coefficient should be correct. When coefficients do not correspond to our expectations, we have **reversals**. Reversals are not uncommon and they can actually reveal that things work in a different way than we expected. However, if there is much multicollinearity between our predictors, reversals could be just due to the higher uncertainty of estimates: some estimates may be so uncertain that the optimization processes have allocated them a wrong sign. Consequently, when a linear regression doesn't confirm our expectations, it is better not to jump to any quick conclusion; instead, closely inspect all the statistical measures pointing toward multicollinearity.

A second check is done on the impact of the variable on the model — that is, how much of the predicted result is dominated by variations in feature. Usually, if the impact is low, reversals and other difficulties caused by the variable (it could be from an unreliable source, for instance, or very noisy — that is, measured imprecisely) are less disruptive for the predictions or can even be ignored.

Introducing the idea of impact also presents the possibility of making our model economic in terms of the number of modeled coefficients. Up to now, we have just concentrated on the idea that it is desirable to fit data in the best way possible and we didn't check if our predictive formula generalizes well to new data. Starting to rank the predictors could help us make new simpler models (by just selecting only the most important features in the model) and simpler models are less prone to errors when in the production phase.

In fact, if our objective is not simply to fit our present data maximally with a formula, but to also fit future data well, it is necessary to apply the principle of Occam's razor. This suggests that, given more correct answers, simpler models are always preferable to more complex ones. The core idea is not to make an explanation, that is a linear model, more complex than it should be, because complexity may hide overfitting.

Inspecting standardized coefficients

Extending our interpretation of the linear model from one single variable to a host of them, we can still read each single coefficient as the unit change inducted on the response variable by each predictor (keeping the other predictors constant).

Intuitively, larger coefficients seem to impact more on the result of the linear combination; however, as we noticed while revisiting gradient descent, different variables may have different scales and their coefficients may incorporate this. Being smaller or larger in terms of coefficient may just be because of the variable's relative scale in comparison to the other features involved in the analysis.

By standardizing variables, we place them under a similar scale where a unit is the standard deviation of the variable itself. Variables extending from high to low values (with a larger range) tend to have a greater standard deviation and you should expect them to be reduced. By doing so, most variables with a normal-like distribution should be reduced in the range $-3 < x < +3$, thus allowing a comparison on their contribution to the prediction. Highly skewed distributions won't be standardized in the range $-3 < x < +3$. The transformation will be beneficial anyway because their range is going to be largely reduced and after that it will even make sense to compare different distributions because then they will all represent the same unit measure—that is, the unit variance. After standardization, larger coefficients can be interpreted as major contributions to establishing the result (a weighted summation, so the result will resemble larger weights more closely). Using standardized coefficients, we can therefore confidently rank our variables and spot those contributing less.

Let's proceed to an example using our Boston dataset. This time we will be using the `LinearRegression` method from Scikit-learn because we do not need to do a linear model for its statistical properties, but just a working model using a fast and scalable algorithm:

```
In: linear_regression = linear_model.LinearRegression(normalize=False,
fit_intercept=True)
```

In such an initialization, apart from the `fit_intercept` parameter that explicates the insertion of a bias into the design of model, the `normalize` option indicates whether we intend to rescale all the variables in the range between zero and one. Such a transformation is different from statistical standardization and we will omit it for the moment by setting it in a `False` state:

```
In: from sklearn.preprocessing import StandardScaler
    from sklearn.pipeline import make_pipeline
    standardization = StandardScaler()
    Stand_coef_linear_reg = make_pipeline(standardization,\
    linear_regression)
```

Besides the `StandardScaler` seen before, we also import from Scikit-learn the convenient `make_pipeline` wrapper, which allows us to establish a sequence of operations to be done automatically on our data before feeding it to the linear regression analysis. Now, the `Stand_coef_linear_reg` pipeline will execute a statistical standardization on data before regressing it, thus outputting standardized coefficients:

```
In: linear_regression.fit(X,y)
for coef, var in sorted(zip(map(abs,linear_regression.coef_), \
            dataset.columns[:-1]), reverse=True):
        print ("%6.3f %s" % (coef,var))
```

Out:

```
17.796 NOX
 3.805 RM
 2.689 CHAS
 1.476 DIS
 0.953 PTRATIO
 0.525 LSTAT
 0.306 RAD
 0.107 CRIM
 0.046 ZN
 0.021 INDUS
 0.012 TAX
 0.009 B
 0.001 AGE
```

As a first step, we output the coefficients of the regression on unstandardized data. As seen before, the output seems dominated by the huge coefficient of the NOX variable, which overlooks (with its absolute value of about 17.8) minor coefficients of 3.8 and less. However, we may question whether it could be so after also standardizing the variables:

```
In: Stand_coef_linear_reg.fit(X,y)
for coef, var in \
sorted(zip(map(abs,Stand_coef_linear_reg.steps[1][1].coef_), \
dataset.columns[:-1]), reverse=True):
            print ("%6.3f %s" % (coef,var))
```

Out:

```
3.749 LSTAT
3.104 DIS
2.671 RM
2.659 RAD
2.076 TAX
2.062 PTRATIO
2.060 NOX
1.081 ZN
0.920 CRIM
0.857 B
0.682 CHAS
0.143 INDUS
0.021 AGE
```

Having all the predictors on a similar scale now, we can easily provide a more realistic interpretation of each coefficient. Clearly, it appears that a unit change has more impact when it involves the variables LSTAT, DIS, RM, RAD, and TAX. LSTAT is the percentage of lower status population, and this aspect explains its relevancy.

Using standardized scales has certainly pointed us at the most important variables but it is still not a complete overview of the predictive power of each variable because:

- Standardized coefficients represent how well the model works out its predictions because large coefficients heavily impact the resulting response: though having a large coefficient is certainly a hint of how important a variable is, it tells us just a part of the role that the variable plays in reducing the error of the estimates and in making our predictions more accurate

- Standardized coefficients can be ranked but their unit, though similar in scale, is somehow abstract (the standard deviation of each variable) and relative to the data at hand (so we shouldn't compare the standardized coefficients of different datasets because their standard deviations could be different)

One solution could be to integrate the importance estimate based on standardized coefficients, instead using some measure related to the error measure.

Comparing models by R-squared

From a general point of view, we can evaluate a model by comparing how better it does in respect of a simple mean, and that's the coefficient of determination, R-squared.

R-squared can estimate how good a model is; therefore, by comparing the R-squared of our model against alternative models where the variables have been removed, we can get an idea of how predictive each removed variable is. All we have to do is compute the difference between the coefficients of determination of the initial model against the model without that variable. If the difference is large, the variable is very important in the determination of a better R-squared and of a better model.

In our case, we have to first record what the R-squared is when we build the model with all the variables present. We can name such a value our baseline of comparison:

```
In: from sklearn.metrics import r2_score
    linear_regression = linear_model.LinearRegression(normalize=False,\
    fit_intercept=True)
def r2_est(X,y):
    return r2_score(y,linear_regression.fit(X,y).predict(X))


print ('Baseline R2: %0.3f' %  r2_est(X,y))


Out:Baseline R2: 0.741
```

After that, all we have to do is to remove one variable at a time from the set of predictors, to estimate again the regression model recording its coefficient of determination, and subtract it from the baseline value we got from the complete regression model:

```
In: r2_impact = list()
    for j in range(X.shape[1]):
        selection = [i for i in range(X.shape[1]) if i!=j]
        r2_impact.append(((r2_est(X,y) - \
        r2_est(X.values [:,selection],y)) ,dataset.columns[j]))
    for imp, varname in sorted(r2_impact, reverse=True):
        print ('%6.3f %s' %  (imp, varname))


Out:
```

```
0.057 LSTAT
0.044 RM
0.029 DIS
0.028 PTRATIO
0.011 NOX
0.011 RAD
0.006 B
0.006 ZN
0.006 TAX
0.006 CRIM
0.005 CHAS
0.000 INDUS
0.000 AGE
```

After we get all the differences, each one representing the contribution of each variable to the R-squared, we just have to rank them and we will then have an idea of which variables contribute more in reducing the error of the linear model; this is a different point of view from knowing which variable contributed the most to the response value. Such a contribution is called the partial R-squared.

Apart from suggesting we use both measures (standardized coefficients and partial Rsquared) to separate relevant variables from irrelevant ones, by using the partial Rsquared you can actually directly compare the importance of the variables because using ratios does make sense here (so you can tell that a variable is twice as important as another because it reduces the error twice as much).

Another noticeable point is that partial R-squareds are not really a decomposition of the initial R-squared measure. In fact, only if the predictors are uncorrelated by summing all the partial scores will you get the precise coefficient of determination of the full model. This is due to collinearity between variables. Therefore, when you remove a variable from the model, you certainly do not remove all its informative variance since correlated variables, containing similar information to the removed variable, are kept in the model. It may happen that, if you have two highly correlated variables, removing each in turn won't change the R-squared by much because, as one is removed, the other one will provide the missing information (thus, the double-check with the standardized coefficient is not redundant at all).

There are more sophisticated methods to estimate the variable importance, but these two methods should provide you with enough insight. Knowing what variables impact your results more strongly can provide you with the means to:

1. Try to explain the results to management in a reasonable and understandable way.
2. Prioritize your work, in terms of data cleaning, preparation, and transformation, by concentrating first on the features most relevant to the success of your project.

3. Conserve resources, in particular memory, as less data is used when building and using the regression model.

If you would like to use importance to exclude irrelevant variables using one of the measures we presented, the safest way would be to recalculate the ranking every time you decide to exclude a variable from the set. Otherwise, using a single ranking may risk hiding the true importance of highly correlated variables (and that's true for both the methodologies, though standardized coefficients are a bit more revealing).

Such an approach is certainly time-consuming, but it is necessary when you notice that your model, though presenting a good fit on your present data, cannot generalize well to new observations.

We are going to discuss such circumstances in more depth in *Chapter 6, Achieving Generalization*, when we will illustrate the best ways to reduce your predictor set, maintaining (simplifying your solution) and even improving your predictive performances (generalizing more effectively).

Interaction models

Having explained how to build a regression model with multiple variables and having touched on the theme of its utilization and interpretation, we start from this paragraph to explore how to improve it. As a first step, we will work on its fit with present data. In the following chapters, devoted to model selection and validation, we will concentrate on how to make it really generalizable—that is, capable of correctly predicting on new, previously unseen data.

As we previously reasoned, the beta coefficients in a linear regression represent the link between a unit change in the predictors and the response variations. The assumptions at the core of such a model are of a constant and unidirectional relationship between each predictor and the target. It is the linear relationship assumption, having the characteristics of a line where direction and fluctuation are determined by the angular coefficient (hence the name linear regression, hinting at the operation of regressing, tracing back to the linear form from some data evidence). Although a good approximation, a linear relationship is a simplification often not true in real data. In fact, most relationships are non-linear, showing bends and curves and alternating different fluctuations in increase and decrease.

The good news is that we do not have to limit ourselves to the originally provided features, but we can modify them in order to *straighten* their relationship with the target variable. In fact, the more similarity between the predictor and the response, the better the fit and the fewer prediction errors in the training set.

Consequently, we can say that:

- We can improve our linear regression by transforming predictor variables in various ways

- We can measure such improvement using the partial R-squared, since every transformation should impact on the quantity of residual errors and ultimately on the coefficient of determination

Discovering interactions

One of the first sources of non-linearity is due to possible interactions between predictors. Two predictors interact when the effect of one of them on the response variable varies in respect of the values of the other predictors.

In mathematical formulation, interaction terms (the interacting variables) have to be multiplied by themselves for our linear model to catch the supplementary information of their relation as expressed in this example of a model with two interacting predictors:

$$y = \beta_0 + \beta_1 x_1 + \beta_2 x_2 + \beta_{12} x_1 x_2$$

An easy-to-remember example of an interaction in a regression model is the role of engine noise in the evaluation of a car. If you are going to model the preference for car models, you will immediately notice that the engine noise can either decrease or increase consumer preference for the car, depending on the price of the car (or its category, which is a proxy of monetary value). In fact, if the car is inexpensive being silent is clearly a must-have, but if the car is expensive (such as a Ferrari or another sports car) the noise is an outstanding benefit (clearly when in it, you want to have everyone notice the cool car you are driving).

It may sound a little bit tricky to deal with interaction, but actually it isn't; after all, you are just transforming a variable role in a linear regression based on another one. Finding interaction terms can be achieved in two different ways, the first one being domain knowledge — that is, knowing directly the problem you are modeling and incorporating your expertise in it. When you do not have such an expertise, an automatic search over the possible combinations will suffice if it is well tested using a revealing measure such as R-squared.

The best way to illustrate the automatic search approach is to show an example in Python using the `PolynomialFeatures` from Scikit-learn, a function that allows both interactions and polynomial expansions (we are going to talk about them in the next paragraph):

```
In: from sklearn.preprocessing import PolynomialFeatures

    from sklearn.metrics import r2_score

    linear_regression = linear_model.LinearRegression(normalize=False,\
    fit_intercept=True)

    create_interactions = PolynomialFeatures(degree=2, \
    interaction_only=True, include_bias=False)
```

By the `degree` parameter we define how many variables to put into the interaction, it being possible to have three or even more variables interact with each other. Interactions in statistics are called two-way effects, three-way effects, and so on, depending on the number of variables involved (whereas the original variables are instead called the main effects).

```
In: def r2_est(X,y):

            return r2_score(y,linear_regression.fit(X,y).predict(X))

baseline = r2_est(X,y)

print ('Baseline R2: %0.3f' % baseline)


Out: Baseline R2: 0.741


in: Xi = create_interactions.fit_transform(X)

  main_effects = create_interactions.n_input_features_
```

After recalling the baseline R-squared value, the code creates a new input data matrix using the `fit_transform` method, enriching the original data with the interaction effects of all the variables. At this point, we create a series of new linear regression models, each one containing all the main effects plus a single interaction. We measure the improvement, calculate the difference with the baseline, and then report only interactions over a certain threshold. We can decide on a threshold just above zero or a threshold we determine based on a statistical test. In our example we decided on an arbitrary threshold, aiming at reporting all R-squared increment above `0.01`:

```
In: for k,effect in \
    enumerate(create_interactions.powers_[(main_effects):]):

      termA, termB = variables[effect==1]

      increment = r2_est(Xi[:,list(range(0,main_effects)) \
      +[main_effects+k]],y) - baseline

      if increment > 0.01:

        print ('Adding interaction %8s *%8s R2: %5.3f' % \
          (termA, termB, increment))
```

Out:

```
Adding interaction    CRIM *    CHAS R2: 0.011
Adding interaction    CRIM *      RM R2: 0.021
Adding interaction      ZN *      RM R2: 0.013
Adding interaction   INDUS *      RM R2: 0.038
Adding interaction   INDUS *     DIS R2: 0.013
Adding interaction     NOX *      RM R2: 0.027
Adding interaction      RM *     AGE R2: 0.024
Adding interaction      RM *     DIS R2: 0.018
Adding interaction      RM *     RAD R2: 0.049
Adding interaction      RM *     TAX R2: 0.054
Adding interaction      RM * PTRATIO R2: 0.041
Adding interaction      RM *       B R2: 0.020
Adding interaction      RM *   LSTAT R2: 0.064
```

Relevant interaction effects are clearly made up by the variable 'RM' (one of the most important ones, as seen before) and the strongest improvement is given by its interaction with another key feature, LSTAT. An important take away would be that we add it to our original data matrix, as a simple multiplication between the two:

```
In: Xi = X
   Xi['interaction'] = X['RM']*X['LSTAT']
   print ('R2 of a model with RM*LSTAT interaction: %0.3f' % \
   r2_est(Xi,y))
```

Out: R2 of a model with RM*LSTAT interaction: 0.805

Polynomial regression

As an extension of interactions, polynomial expansion systematically provides an automatic means of creating both interactions and non-linear power transformations of the original variables. Power transformations are the bends that the line can take in fitting the response. The higher the degree of power, the more bends are available to fit the curve.

For instance, if you have a simple linear regression of the form:

$$y = \beta_0 + \beta_1 x$$

By a second degree transformation, called **quadratic**, you will get a new form:

$$y = \beta_0 + \beta_1 x + \beta_3 x^2$$

By a third degree transformation, called **cubic**, your equation will turn into:

$$y = \beta_0 + \beta_1 x + \beta_3 x^2 + \beta_4 x^3$$

If your regression is a multiple one, the expansion will create additional terms (interactions) increasing the number of new features derived from the expansion. For instance, a multiple regression made up of two predictors (x_1 and x_2), expanded using the quadratic transformation, will become:

$$y = \beta_0 + \beta_1 x_1 + \beta_2 x_2 + \beta_3 x_1 x_2 + \beta_4 x_1^2 + \beta_5 x_2^2$$

Before proceeding, we have to note two aspects of the expansion procedure:

- Polynomial expansion rapidly increases the number of predictors
- Higher-degree polynomials translate into high powers of the predictors, posing problems for numeric stability, thus requiring suitable numeric formats or standardizing numeric values that are too large

Testing linear versus cubic transformation

By setting the `interaction_only` parameter off in the `PolynomialFeatures` function seen before, we can get the full polynomial transformation of our input matrix, not just simply the interactions as before:

In:
```
from sklearn.preprocessing import PolynomialFeatures
from sklearn.pipeline import make_pipeline
from sklearn.preprocessing import StandardScaler

linear_regression = linear_model.LinearRegression(normalize=False, \
fit_intercept=True)
create_cubic = PolynomialFeatures(degree=3, interaction_only=False, \
include_bias=False)
create_quadratic = PolynomialFeatures(degree=2, interaction_only=False, \
include_bias=False)
```

```
linear_predictor = make_pipeline(linear_regression)
quadratic_predictor = make_pipeline(create_quadratic, \
linear_regression)
cubic_predictor = make_pipeline(create_cubic, linear_regression)
```

By sending both `PolynomialFeatures` and `LinearRegression` into a pipeline we can create a function automatically by a single command, expanding out data and regressing it. As an experiment, we try to model the `'LSTAT'` variable alone for best clarity, remembering that we could have expanded all the variables at once:

```
predictor = 'LSTAT'
x = dataset['LSTAT'].values.reshape((observations,1))
xt = np.arange(0,50,0.1).reshape((50/0.1,1))
x_range = [dataset[predictor].min(),dataset[predictor].max()]
y_range = [dataset['target'].min(),dataset['target'].max()]

scatter = dataset.plot(kind='scatter', x=predictor, y='target', \
xlim=x_range, ylim=y_range)
regr_line = scatter.plot(xt, linear_predictor.fit(x,y).predict(xt), \
'-', color='red', linewidth=2)
```

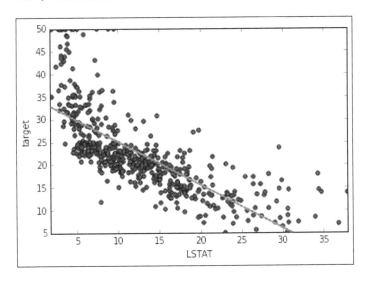

Our first fit is the linear one (a simple linear regression) and from the scatterplot we can notice that the line is not representing well the cloud of points relating to `'LSTAT'` with the response; most likely we need a curve. Instead of testing a second degree transformation that will turn into a parabola, we immediately try a cubic transformation: using two bends, we should obtain a better fit:

```
scatter = dataset.plot(kind='scatter', x=predictor, y='target', \
xlim=x_range, ylim=y_range)

regr_line = scatter.plot(xt, cubic_predictor.fit(x,y).predict(xt), \
'-', color='red', linewidth=2)
```

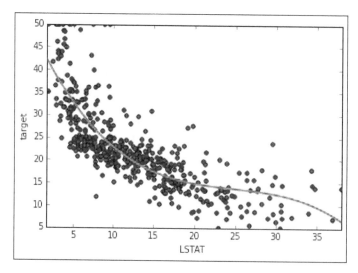

Our graphic check confirms that now we have a more credible representation of how `'LSTAT'` and the response relate. We question whether we cannot do better using even higher-degree transformations.

Going for higher-degree solutions

To test a higher degree of polynomial transformations, we prepare a script that creates the expansion and reports its R-squared measure. We then try to plot the function with the highest degree in the series and have a look at how it fits the data points:

```
In: for d in [1,2,3,5,15]:

    create_poly = PolynomialFeatures(degree=d,\
    interaction_only=False, include_bias=False)

    poly = make_pipeline(create_poly, StandardScaler(),\
    linear_regression)

    model = poly.fit(x,y)

    print ("R2 degree - %2i polynomial :%0.3f" \
        %(d,r2_score(y,model.predict(x))))
```

Out:

```
R2 degree -  1 polynomial :0.544
R2 degree -  2 polynomial :0.641
R2 degree -  3 polynomial :0.658
R2 degree -  5 polynomial :0.682
R2 degree - 15 polynomial :0.695
```

Noticeably, there is a huge difference in the coefficient of determination between the linear model and the quadratic expansion (second-degree polynomial). The measure jumps from 0.544 to 0.641, a difference that increases up to 0.682 when reaching the fifth degree. Preceding to even higher degrees, the increment is not so astonishing, though it keeps on growing, reaching 0.695 when the degree is the fifteenth. As the latter is the best result in terms of coefficient of determination, having a look at the plot on the data cloud will reveal a not so smooth fit, as we can see with lower degrees of polynomial expansion:

```
In: scatter = dataset.plot(kind='scatter', x=predictor,\
        y='target', xlim=x_range, ylim=y_range)

  regr_line = scatter.plot(xt, model.predict(xt), '-',\
  color='red', linewidth=2)
```

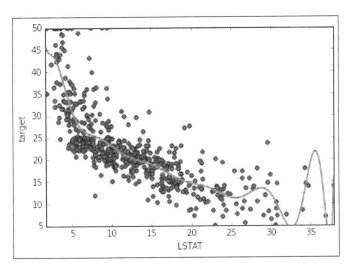

Observing closely the resulting curve, you will surely notice how, by such a high degree, the curve tends strictly to follow the distribution of points, going erratic when the density diminishes at the fringes of the range of the predictors' values.

Introducing underfitting and overfitting

Polynomial regression offers us the right occasion for starting to talk about model complexity. We have not explicitly tested it, but you may already have got the feeling that, by increasing the degree of the polynomial expansion, you are going to always reap better fits. We say more: the more variables you have in your model, the better, until you will have such a large number of betas, likely equal or almost equal to the number of your observations, that your predictions will be perfect.

Decaying performances due to over-parameterization (an excess of parameters to be learned by the model) is a problem of linear regression and of many other machine learning algorithms. The more parameters you add, the better the fit because the model will cease to intercept the rules and regularities of your data but will start, in such an embarrassment of riches, to populate the many available coefficients with all the erratic and erroneous information present in the data. In such a situation, the model won't learn general rules but it will just be memorizing the dataset itself in another form.

This is called **overfitting**: fitting the data at hand so well that the result is far from being an extraction of the form of the data to draw predictions from; the result is just a mere memorization. On the other side, another problem is **underfitting** — that is, when you are using too few parameters for your prediction. The most straightforward example is fitting a non-linear relation using a simple linear regression; clearly, it won't match the curve bends and some of its predictions will be misleading.

There are appropriate tools for verifying if you are underfitting or, more likely, overfitting and they will be discussed in *Chapter 6, Achieving Generalization*, (the chapter explaining data science); in the meantime, don't overfit too much with high-degree polynomials!

Summary

In this chapter, we have carried on introducing linear regression, extending our example from a simple to a multiple one. We have revisited the previous outputs from the Statsmodels linear functions (the classical statistical approach) and gradient descent (the data science engine).

We started experimenting with models by removing selected predictors and evaluating the impact of such a move from the point of view of the R-squared measure. Meanwhile we also discovered reciprocal correlations between predictors and how to render more linear relations between each predictor and the target variable by intercepting the interactions and by means of polynomial expansion of the features.

In the next chapter, we will progress again and extend the regression model to make it viable for classification tasks, turning it into a probabilistic predictor. The conceptual jump into the world of probability will allow us to complete the range of possible problems where linear models can be successfully applied.

Logistic Regression

In this chapter, another supervised method is introduced: classification. We will introduce the simplest classifier, the Logistic Regressor, which shares the same foundations as the Linear Regressor, but it targets classification problems.

In the following chapter, you'll find:

- A formal and mathematical definition of the classification problem, for both binary and multiclass problems
- How to evaluate classifier performances — that is, their metrics
- The math behind Logistic Regression
- A revisited formula for SGD, specifically built for Logistic Regression
- The multiclass case, with Multiclass Logistic Regression

Defining a classification problem

Although the name Logistic Regression suggests a regression operation, the goal of Logistic Regression is classification. In a very rigorous world such as statistics, why is this technique ambiguously named? Simple, the name is not wrong at all, and it makes perfect sense: it just requires a bit of an introduction and investigation. After that you'll fully understand why it's named Logistic Regression, and you'll no longer think that it's a wrong name.

First, let's introduce what a classification problem is, what a classifier is, how it operates, and what its output is.

In the previous chapter, we presented regression as the operation of estimating a continuous value in a target variable; mathematically speaking, the predicted variable is a real number in the range $(-\infty, +\infty)$. Classification, instead, predicts a class, that is, an index in a finite set of classes. The simplest case is named binary classification, and the output is typically a Boolean value (`true`/`false`). If the class is `true` the sample is typically called a *positive sample*; otherwise it's a *negative sample*.

To state some examples, here are some questions that refer to a binary classification problem:

- Is this email spam?
- Is my house worth at least $200,000?
- Is the banner/email clicked/opened by the user?
- Is the current document about finance?
- Is there a person in the image? Is it a man or a woman?

 Putting a threshold on the output of a regression problem, to determine whether the value is greater or lower than a fixed threshold, is actually a binary classification problem.

When the output can have multiple values (that is, the predicted label is a categorical variable), the classification is named a multiclass one. Usually, the possible labels are named levels or classes, and the list of them should be finite and known in advance (or else it will be an unsupervised problem, not a supervised one).

Examples of multiclass classification problems are:

- Which kind of flower is this?
- What's the primary topic of this webpage?
- Which kind of network attack am I experiencing?
- Which digit/letter is drawn in the image?

Formalization of the problem: binary classification

Let's start now with the simplest type of classification: the **binary classification**. Don't worry; in a few pages things are going to be more complex when we focus on the multiclass classification.

Formally, the generic observation is an *n*-dimensional feature vector (x_i) paired with its label: the generic *i*-th can be written as:

$$(x_i, y_i) : x_i \in \mathbb{R}^n, y_i \in \{0,1\}$$

The model underneath the classifier is a function and is called a **classification function**, which can be either linear or non linear. The form of the function is the following:

$$f : \mathbb{R}^n \to \{0,1\}$$

During the prediction task, the classification function is applied to a new feature vector, and the output of the classifier represents the class to which the input sample is classified, that is, the predicted label. A perfect classifier predicts, for every possible input, the correct class y.

The feature vector x should comprise numbers. If you're dealing with categorical features (such as gender, membership, and words), you should be able to take that variable to one or more numeric variables (usually binary). We'll see more about this point later on in the book, in *Chapter 5, Data Preparation*, which is devoted to data preparation of variables into the most suitable form for regression.

To have a visual understanding of what's going on, let's consider now a binary classification problem, where every feature has two dimensions (a 2-D problem). Let's first define the input dataset; here the `make_classifier` method of the Scikit-learn library comes in very handy. It creates a dummy dataset for classification, providing the number of classes, the dimensionality of the problem, and the number of observations as parameters. Additionally, you should specify that each feature is informative (and there are no redundancies) and each class is composed of a single cluster of points:

```
In:
%matplotlib inline

import matplotlib.pyplot as plt
from sklearn.datasets import make_classification

X, y = make_classification(n_samples=100, n_features=2,
                           n_informative=2, n_redundant=0,
                           n_clusters_per_class=1,
                           class_sep = 2.0, random_state=101)
```

```
plt.scatter(X[:, 0], X[:, 1], marker='o', c=y,
            linewidth=0, edgecolor=None)
plt.xlabel('Feature 1')
plt.ylabel('Feature 2')
plt.show()
```

Out:

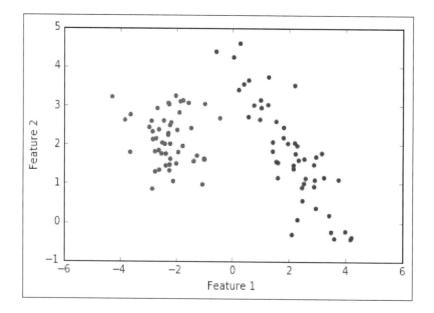

Assessing the classifier's performance

To understand if a classifier is a good one, or equivalently, to identify the classifier with the best performance in the classification task, we need to define some metrics. There is no single metric since the classification goal can be different—for example, the correctness or completeness of a defined label, minimization of the number of misclassifications, correct ordering in respect of the likelihood of having a certain label, and quite a few others. All the measures can be derived from the classification matrix after having applied a cost matrix: the outcome highlights which errors are more expensive and which are not so expensive in terms of results.

Metrics exposed here can be used for both binary and multiclass classification. Although it is not a measure of performance, let's start from the confusion matrix, the simplest metric that gives us a visual impact of the correct classifications and the misclassification errors for each class. On the rows there are the true labels, on the column the predicted one. Let's also create a dummy label set and a predicted set for the following experiments. In our example the original labels are six 0 and four 1; the classifier misclassified entries are two 0 and one 1:

```
In:
y_orig = [0,0,0,0,0,0,1,1,1,1]
y_pred = [0,0,0,0,1,1,1,1,1,0]
```

Let's now create the confusion matrix for this experiment:

```
In:
from sklearn.metrics import confusion_matrix
confusion_matrix(y_orig, y_pred)
Out:
array([[4, 2],
       [1, 3]])
```

From this matrix we can extract some evidence:

- The number of samples is 10 (the sum of the whole matrix).
- The number of samples labeled 0 in the original is 6; 1s are 4 (the sum for the lines). These numbers are named support.
- The number of samples labeled 0 in the predicted dataset is 5; 1s are 5 (the sum as columns).
- Correct classifications are 7 (the sum of the diagonal).
- Misclassifications are 3 (the sum of all numbers not on the diagonal).

A perfect classification example would have had all the numbers on the diagonal, and 0 elsewhere.

This matrix can also be represented graphically, using a heatmap. This is a very impactful representation, especially when dealing with multiclass problems:

```
In:
plt.matshow(confusion_matrix(y_orig, y_pred))
plt.title('Confusion matrix')
plt.colorbar()
plt.ylabel('True label')
```

```
plt.xlabel('Predicted label')
plt.show()
```

Out:

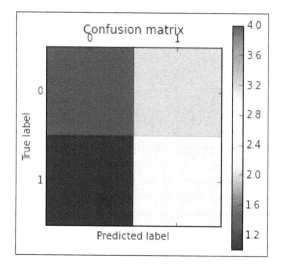

The first measure we're going to explore to evaluate the classifier's performance is accuracy. Accuracy is the percentage of correct classifications, over the total number of samples. You can derive this error measure directly from the confusion matrix by dividing the sum over the diagonal by the sum of the elements in the matrix. The best possible accuracy is `1.0` and the worst one is `0.0`. In the preceding example, accuracy amounts to *7/10 = 0.7.*

Using Python, this becomes:

In:

```
from sklearn.metrics import accuracy_score
accuracy_score(y_orig, y_pred)
```

Out:

```
0.69999999999999996
```

Another very popular measure is precision. It considers only one label and counts the percentage of correct classifications on that label. While considering our label "1", the precision is the number in the bottom right of the confusion matrix, divided by the sum of the elements in the second column — that is, *3/5=0.6.* Values are bounded between 0 and 1, where 1 is the best possible result and 0 the worst.

Note that this function in Scikit-learn expects a binary input, where only the class under examination is marked as `true` (this is sometime named a *class indicator*). To extract a precision score for each label, you should then make each class a binary vector:

```
In:
from sklearn.metrics import precision_score
precision_score(y_orig, y_pred)
Out:
0.59999999999999998
```

Paired with precision you'll frequently find another error measure, recall. If precision is about the quality of what you got (that is, the quality of the results marked with the label 1), recall is about the quality of what you could have gotten – that is, how many instances of 1 you've been able to extract properly. Also, here, this measure is class-based, and to compute the recall score for class 1 you should divide the bottom right number in the confusion matrix by the sum of the second line, that is, *3/4=0.75*. Recall is bounded 0 and 1; the best score is 1 and means that all the instances of "1" in the original dataset have been correctly classified as "1"; a score equal to 0 means that no "1"s have been classified properly:

```
In:
from sklearn.metrics import recall_score
recall_score(y_orig, y_pred)
Out:
0.75
```

Precision and recall are two metrics that indicate how well the classifier performed on a class. Merge their score, using a harmonic average, and you'll get the comprehensive f1-score, helping you to figure out at a glance the performance on both error measures.

Mathematically:

$$f1 = 2 \cdot \frac{precision \cdot recall}{precision \,|\, recall}$$

In Python this is easier:

```
In:
from sklearn.metrics import f1_score
f1_score(y_orig, y_pred)
Out:
0.66666666666666652
```

In conclusion, if there are so many error scores, which is the best to use? The solution is not very easy, and often it is better to have and evaluate the classifier on all of them. How can we do that? Is it a long function to write? No, Scikit-learn here comes to help us here, providing a method to compute all these scores for each class (this is really handy). Here is how it works:

In:

```
from sklearn.metrics import classification_report
print(classification_report(y_orig, y_pred))
```

Out:

	precision	recall	f1-score	support
0	0.80	0.67	0.73	6
1	0.60	0.75	0.67	4
avg / total	0.72	0.70	0.70	10

Defining a probability-based approach

Let's gradually introduce how logistic regression works. We said that it's a classifier, but its name recalls a regressor. The element we need to join the pieces is the probabilistic interpretation.

In a binary classification problem, the output can be either "0" or "1". What if we check the probability of the label belonging to class "1"? More specifically, a classification problem can be seen as: given the feature vector, find the class (either 0 or 1) that maximizes the conditional probability:

$$P\left(y_i = \text{"1"} \mid x_i\right)$$

Here's the connection: if we compute a probability, the classification problem *looks like* a regression problem. Moreover, in a binary classification problem, we just need to compute the probability of membership of class "1", and therefore it looks like a well-defined regression problem. In the regression problem, classes are no longer "1" or "0" (as strings), but 1.0 and 0.0 (as the probability of belonging to class "1").

Let's now try fitting a multiple linear regressor on a dummy classification problem, using a probabilistic interpretation. We reuse the same dataset we created earlier in this chapter, but first we split the dataset into train and test sets, and we convert the y vector to floating point values:

In:

```
from sklearn.cross_validation import train_test_split
```

```
X_train, X_test, y_train, \
    y_test = train_test_split(X, y.astype(float),\
            test_size=0.33, random_state=101)
```

In:

```
y_test.dtype
```

Out:

```
dtype('float64')
```

In:

```
y_test
```

Out:

```
array([ 0.,   1.,   1.,   0.,   1.,   1.,   0.,   1.,   0.,   0.,   0.,   0.,   1.,
        0.,   1.,   0.,   0.,   1.,   1.,   0.,   0.,   0.,   0.,   0.,   0.,
        0.,   0.,   0.,   1.,   0.,   1.,   0.])
```

Here, with these few methods, we split the datasets into two folds, (train and test) and we converted all the numbers in the *y* array to floating point. In the last cell, we effectively check the operation. Now, if *y = 1.0*, it means that the relative observation is 100% class "1"; *y = 0.0* implies that the observation is 0% class "1". Since it's a binary classification task, it implies that it's also 100% class "0" (note that the percentages here refer to probability).

Let's now proceed with the regression:

In:

```
from sklearn.linear_model import LinearRegression
regr = LinearRegression()
regr.fit(X_train, y_train)
regr.predict(X_test)
```

Out:

```
array([ 0.06688448,  1.01981921,  1.08597427, -0.15225094,  1.05856628,
        0.8156161 ,  0.04837505,  0.7997539 ,  0.18942251, -0.03658995,
       -0.0462575 , -0.09640911,  1.0253004 , -0.17062754,  1.13642842,
        0.14052848, -0.00703683,  0.90903158,  1.26997191,  0.03606483,
       -0.19047191,  0.22476337, -0.05936491, -0.18559975,  0.28378888,
        0.01139188, -0.03559395,  0.22742328,  0.07485246,  1.24545626,
        0.13924533,  1.09388935,  0.35341582])
```

The output—that is, the prediction of the regressor—should be the probability of belonging to class 1. As you can see in the last cell output, that's not a proper probability, since it contains values below 0 and greater than 1. The simplest idea here is clipping results between 0 and 1, and putting a threshold at `0.5`: if the value is >0.5, then the predicted class is "1"; otherwise the predicted class is "0".

This procedure works, but we can do better. We've seen how easy it is to transit from a classification problem to a regression one, and then go back with predicted values to predicted classes. With this process in mind, let's again start the analysis, digging further in its core algorithm while introducing some changes.

In our dummy problem, we applied the linear regression model to estimate the probability of the observation belonging to class "1". The regression model was (as we've seen in the previous chapter):

$$y = X \cdot w$$

Now, we've seen that the output is not a proper probability. To be a probability, we need to do the following:

1. Bound the output between 0.0 and 1.0 (clipping).
2. If the prediction is equal to the threshold (we chose 0.5 previously), the probability should be 0.5 (symmetry).

To have both conditions `true`, the best we could do is to send the output of the regressor through a sigmoid curve, or an S-shaped curve. A sigmoid generically maps values in R (the field of real numbers) to values in the range `[0,1]`, and its value when mapping `0` is `0.5`.

On the basis of such a hypothesis, we can now write (for the first time) the formula underneath the logistic regression algorithm.

$$P\left(y=1 \mid x\right) = \sigma\left(W^T \cdot x\right)$$

Note also that the weight `w[0]` (the bias weight) will take care of the misalignment of the central point of the sigmoid (it's in 0, whereas the threshold is in 0.5).

That's all. That's the logistic regression algorithm. There is just one thing missing: why logistic? What's the σ function?

Well, the answer to both questions is trivial: the standard choice of sigma is the logistic function, also named the inverse-logit function:

$$\sigma(t) = logit^{-1}(t) = \frac{1}{1+e^{-t}}$$

Although there are infinite functions that satisfy the sigmoid constraints, the logistic has been chosen because it's continuous, easily differentiable, and quick to compute. If the results are not satisfactory, always consider that, by introducing a couple of parameters, you can change the steepness and the center of the function.

The sigmoid function is quickly drawn:

```
In:
import numpy as np

def model(x):
    return 1 / (1 + np.exp(-x))

X_vals = np.linspace(-10, 10, 1000)
plt.plot(X_vals, model(X_vals), color='blue', linewidth=3)
plt.ylabel('sigma(t)')
plt.xlabel('t')

plt.show()
Out:
```

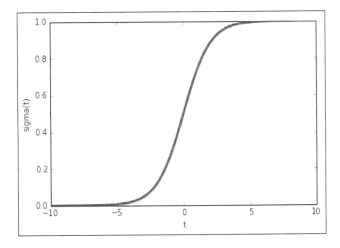

You can immediately see that, for a very low **t**, the function tends to the value **0**; for a very high **t**, the function tends to be **1**, and, in the center, where **t** is **0**, the function is **0.5**. Exactly the sigmoid function we were looking for.

More on the logistic and logit functions

Now, why did we use the inverse of the logit function? Isn't there anything better than that? The answer to this question comes from statistics: we're dealing with probabilities, and the logit function is a great fit. In statistics, the logit function applied to a probability, returns the log-odds:

$$logit(p) = \log\left(\frac{p}{1-p}\right) = \log(p) - \log(1-p)$$

This function transforms numbers from range [0,1] to numbers in $(-\infty, +\infty)$.

Now, let's see if you can intuitively understand the logic behind the selection of the inverse-logit function as the sigmoid function for the logistic regression. Let's first write down the probabilities for both classes, according to this logistic regression equation:

$$P(y = "1"|x) = \frac{1}{1+e^{-t}}$$

$$P(y = "0"|x) = 1 - \frac{1}{1+e^{-t}}$$

Let's now compute the log-odds:

$$\log\left(\frac{P(y = "1"|x)}{P(y = "0"|x)}\right) = W^T \cdot x$$

However, not surprisingly, that's also the **logit** function, applied to the probability of getting a "1":

$$logit(P(y = "1"|x)) = W^T \cdot x$$

The chain of our reasoning is finally closed, and here's why logistic regression is based on, as the definition implies, the logistic function. Actually, logistic regression is a model of the big category of the GLM: the generalized linear model. Each model has a different function, a different formulation, a different operative hypothesis, and not, surprisingly, a different goal.

Let's see some code

First, we start with the dummy dataset we created at the beginning of the chapter. Creating and fitting a logistic regressor classifier is really easy: thanks to Scikit-learn, it just requires a couple of lines of Python code. As for regressors, to train the model you need to call the `fit` method, whereas for predicting the class you just need to call the `predict` method:

In:

```
from sklearn.linear_model import LogisticRegression


clf = LogisticRegression()
clf.fit(X_train, y_train.astype(int))
y_clf = clf.predict(X_test)


print(classification_report(y_test, y_clf))
```

Out:

	precision	recall	f1-score	support
0.0	1.00	0.95	0.98	22
1.0	0.92	1.00	0.96	11
avg / total	0.97	0.97	0.97	33

Note that here we're not making a regression operation; that's why the label vector must comprise integers (or class indexes). The report shown at the bottom shows a very accurate prediction: all the scores are close to 1 for all classes. Since we have 33 samples in the test set, 0.97 means just one case misclassified. That's almost perfect in this dummy example!

Now, let's try to dig under the hood even more. First, we would like to check the decision boundary of the classifier: which part of the bidimensional space has points being classified as "1"; and where are the "0"s? Let's see how you can visually see the decision boundary here:

In:

```
# Example based on:
# Code source: Gaël Varoquaux, Modified for documentation by Jaques
Grobler, License: BSD 3 clause
```

```
h = .02  # step size in the mesh


# Plot the decision boundary. For that, we will assign a color to each
# point in the mesh [x_min, m_max]x[y_min, y_max].
x_min, x_max = X[:, 0].min() - .5, X[:, 0].max() + .5
y_min, y_max = X[:, 1].min() - .5, X[:, 1].max() + .5
xx, yy = np.meshgrid(np.arange(x_min, x_max, h), np.arange(y_min, y_max,
h))
Z = clf.predict(np.c_[xx.ravel(), yy.ravel()])


# Put the result into a color plot
Z = Z.reshape(xx.shape)
plt.pcolormesh(xx, yy, Z, cmap=plt.cm.autumn)


# Plot also the training points
plt.scatter(X[:, 0], X[:, 1], c=y, edgecolors='k', linewidth=0, cmap=plt.
cm.Paired)


plt.xlim(xx.min(), xx.max())
plt.ylim(yy.min(), yy.max())
plt.xticks(())
plt.yticks(())


plt.show()
Out:
```

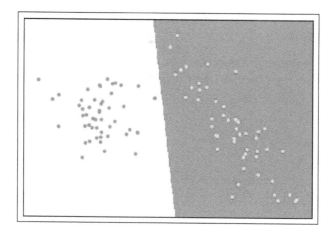

The separation is almost vertical. "1"s are on the left (yellow) side; "0"s on the right (red). From the earlier screenshot, you can immediately perceive the misclassification: it's pretty close to the boundary. Therefore, its probability of belonging to class "1" will be very close to 0.5.

Let's now see the bare probabilities and the weight vector. To compute the probability, you need to use the `predict_proba` method of the classifier. It returns two values for each observation: the first is the probability of being of class "0"; the second the probability for class "1". Since we're interested in class "1", here we just select the second value for all the observations:

```
In:
Z = clf.predict_proba(np.c_[xx.ravel(), yy.ravel()])[:,1]
Z = Z.reshape(xx.shape)
plt.pcolormesh(xx, yy, Z, cmap=plt.cm.autumn)

ax = plt.axes()
ax.arrow(0, 0, clf.coef_[0][0], clf.coef_[0][1], head_width=0.5,
head_length=0.5, fc='k', ec='k')
plt.scatter(0, 0, marker='o', c='k')

plt.xlim(xx.min(), xx.max())
plt.ylim(yy.min(), yy.max())

plt.show()
Out:
```

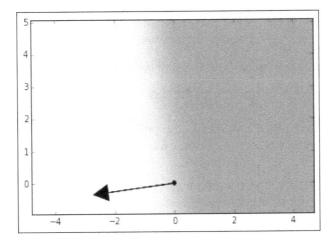

In the screenshot, pure yellow and pure red are where the predicted probability is very close to 1 and 0 respectively. The black dot is the origin *(0,0)* of the Cartesian bidimensional space, and the arrow is the representation of the weight vector of the classifier. As you can see, it's orthogonal to the decision boundary, and it's *pointing* toward the "1" class. The weight vector is actually the model itself: if you need to store it in a file, consider that it's just a couple of floating point numbers and nothing more.

Lastly, I'd want to focus on speed. Let's now see how much time the classifier takes to train and to predict the labels:

```
In:
%timeit clf.fit(X, y)
Out:
1000 loops, best of 3: 291 µs per loop
In:
%timeit clf.predict(X)
Out:
10000 loops, best of 3: 45.5 µs per loop
In:
%timeit clf.predict_proba(X)
Out:
10000 loops, best of 3: 74.4 µs per loop
```

Although timings are computer-specific (here we're training it and predicting using the full 100-point dataset), you can see that Logistic Regression is a very fast technique both during training and when predicting the class and the probability for all classes.

Pros and cons of logistic regression

Logistic regression is a very popular algorithm because of the following:

- It's linear: it's the equivalent of the linear regression for classification.

- It's very simple to understand, and the output can be the most likely class, or the probability of membership.

- It's simple to train: it has very few coefficients (one coefficient for each feature, plus one bias). This makes the model very small to store (you just need to store a vector of weights).

- It's computationally efficient: using some special tricks (see later in the chapter), it can be trained very quickly.

- It has an extension for multiclass classification.

Unfortunately, it's not a perfect classifier and has some drawbacks:

- It's often not very performant, compared to most advanced algorithms, because it tends to underfit (no flexibility: the boundary has to be a line or a hyperplane)
- It's linear: if the problem is non-linear, there is no way to properly fit this classifier onto the dataset

Revisiting gradient descent

In the previous chapter, we introduced the gradient descent technique to speed up processing. As we've seen with Linear Regression, the fitting of the model can be made in two ways: closed form or iterative form. Closed form gives the best possible solution in one step (but it's a very complex and time-demanding step); iterative algorithms, instead, reach the minima step by step with few calculations for each update and can be stopped at any time.

Gradient descent is a very popular choice for fitting the Logistic Regression model; however, it shares its popularity with Newton's methods. Since Logistic Regression is the base of the iterative optimization, and we've already introduced it, we will focus on it in this section. Don't worry, there is no winner or any best algorithm: all of them can reach the very same model eventually, following different paths in the coefficients' space.

First, we should compute the derivate of the loss function. Let's make it a bit longer, and let's start deriving the logistic function:

$$\sigma(t) = \frac{1}{1+e^{-t}}$$

Its first-order derivative is as follows:

$$\sigma'(t) = \frac{\partial}{\partial z}\frac{1}{1+e^{-t}} = \frac{e^{-t}}{\left(1+e^{-t}\right)^2} = \left(\frac{1}{1+e^{-t}}\right)\cdot\left(1-\frac{1}{1+e^{-t}}\right) = \sigma(t)\cdot(1-\sigma(t))$$

This is another reason why logistic regression used the logistic function: its derivate is computationally light. Now, let's assume that the training observations are independent. Computing the likelihood, with respect to the set of weights, is as follows:

$$L(W) = P(Y \mid X; W)$$
$$= \prod_i P(y_i \mid x_i; W)$$
$$= \prod_i \left(\sigma\left(W^T \cdot x_i\right) \right)^{y_i} \cdot \left(1 - \sigma\left(W^T \cdot x_i\right)\right)^{1-y_i}$$

Note that, in the last row, we used a trick based on the fact that y_i can be either 0 or 1. If $y_i=1$, only the first factor of the multiplication is computed; otherwise it's the second factor.

Let's now compute the log-likelihood: it will make things easier:

$$\hat{L}(W) = \log\left(L(W)\right)$$
$$= \sum_i y_i \log\left(\sigma\left(W^T \cdot x_i\right)\right) + (1 - y_i)\log\left(1 - \sigma\left(W^T \cdot x_i\right)\right)$$

Now, we have two considerations to make. First: the SGD works with one point at a time; therefore, the log-likelihood, step-by-step, is just a function of one point. Hence, we can remove the sum over all the points, and name *(x,y)* the point under observation. Second, we need to maximize the likelihood: to do so, we need to extract its partial derivative with respect to the generic k-th coefficient of W.

The math here becomes a bit complex; therefore we will just write the last result (this is the thinking we will use in our model). Deriving and understanding the equations in the middle is given to the reader as homework:

$$\frac{\partial}{\partial w_k} \hat{L}(W) = \cdots = \left(y - \sigma\left(W^T \cdot x\right)\right) \cdot x_k$$

Since we're trying to maximize the likelihood (and its log version), the right formula for updating the weights is the Stochastic Gradient Ascent:

$$W \leftarrow W + \alpha \nabla \hat{L}(W)$$

That's the generic formula. In our case, the update step for each coefficient composing W is as follows:

$$w_k \leftarrow w_k + \alpha \cdot \left(y - \frac{1}{1 + e^{-W^T \cdot x}} \right) \cdot x_k$$

Here, *(x,y)* is the (stochastic) random observation chosen for the update step, and the learning step.

To see a real example of what the SGD produces, check the last section of this chapter.

Multiclass Logistic Regression

The extension to Logistic Regression, for classifying more than two classes, is Multiclass Logistic Regression. Its foundation is actually a generic approach: it doesn't just work for Logistic Regressors, it also works with other binary classifiers. The base algorithm is named **One-vs-rest**, or **One-vs-all**, and it's simple to grasp and apply.

Let's describe it with an example: we have to classify three kinds of flowers and, given some features, the possible outputs are three classes: f1, f2, and f3. That's not what we've seen so far; in fact, this is not a binary classification problem. Instead, it seems very easy to break down this problem into three simpler problems:

- **Problem #1**: Positive examples (that is, the ones that get the label "1") are f1; negative examples are all the others
- **Problem #2**: Positive examples are f2; negative examples are f1 and f3
- **Problem #3**: Positive examples are f3; negative examples are f1 and f2

For all three problems, we can use a binary classifier, as Logistic Regressor, and, unsurprisingly, the first classifier will output $P(y = f1 \mid x)$; the second and the third will output respectively $P(y = f2 \mid x)$ and $P(y = f3 \mid x)$.

To make the final prediction, we just need to select the classifier that emitted the highest probability. Having trained three classifiers, the feature space is not divided in two subplanes, but according to the decision boundary of the three classifiers.

The approach of One-vs-all is very convenient, in fact:

- The number of classifiers to fit is exactly the same as the number of classes. Therefore, the model will be composed by N (where N is the number of classes) weight vectors.
- Moreover, this operation is embarrassingly parallel and the training of the N classifiers can be made simultaneously, using multiple threads (up to N threads).
- If the classes are balanced, the training time for each classifier is similar, and the predicting time is the same (even for unbalanced classes).

For a better understanding, let's make a multiclass classification example, creating a dummy three-class dataset, splitting it as training and test sets, training a Multiclass Logistic Regressor, applying it on the training set, and finally visualizing the boundaries:

In:

```
%reset -f
```

In:

```
%matplotlib inline

import matplotlib.pyplot as plt
from sklearn.datasets import make_classification

X, y = make_classification(n_samples=200, n_features=2,
                           n_classes=3, n_informative=2,
                           n_redundant=0, n_clusters_per_class=1,
                           class_sep = 2.0, random_state=101)

plt.scatter(X[:, 0], X[:, 1], marker='o', c=y, linewidth=0,
edgecolor=None)
plt.show()
```

Out:

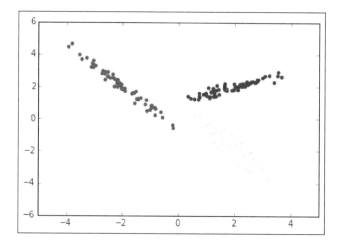

In:

```
from sklearn.cross_validation import train_test_split
```

```
X_train, X_test, y_train, y_test = train_test_split(X, y.astype(float),
                              test_size=0.33, random_state=101)
```

In:

```
from sklearn.linear_model import LogisticRegression


clf = LogisticRegression()
clf.fit(X_train, y_train.astype(int))
y_clf = clf.predict(X_test)
```

In:

```
from sklearn.metrics import classification_report
print(classification_report(y_test, y_clf))
```

Out:

	precision	recall	f1-score	support
0.0	1.00	1.00	1.00	24
1.0	1.00	1.00	1.00	22
2.0	1.00	1.00	1.00	20
avg / total	1.00	1.00	1.00	66

In:

```
import numpy as np


h = .02   # step size in the mesh


x_min, x_max = X[:, 0].min() - .5, X[:, 0].max() + .5
y_min, y_max = X[:, 1].min() - .5, X[:, 1].max() + .5
xx, yy = np.meshgrid(np.arange(x_min, x_max, h), np.arange(y_min, y_max,
h))
Z = clf.predict(np.c_[xx.ravel(), yy.ravel()])


# Put the result into a color plot
Z = Z.reshape(xx.shape)
plt.pcolormesh(xx, yy, Z, cmap=plt.cm.autumn)


# Plot also the training points
plt.scatter(X[:, 0], X[:, 1], c=y, edgecolors='k', cmap=plt.cm.Paired)
```

```
plt.xlim(xx.min(), xx.max())
plt.ylim(yy.min(), yy.max())
plt.xticks(())
plt.yticks(())


plt.show()
```
Out:

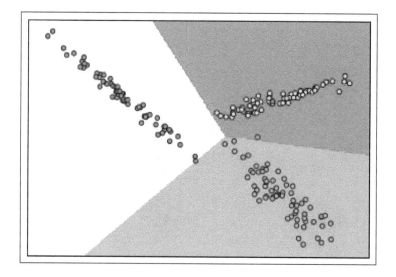

On this dummy dataset, the classifier has achieved a perfect classification (precision, recall, and f1-score are all 1.0). In the last picture, you can see that the decision boundaries define three areas, and create a non-linear division.

Finally, let's observe the first feature vector, its original label, and its predicted label (both reporting class "0"):

```
In:
print(X_test[0])
print(y_test[0])
print(y_clf[0])
Out:
[ 0.73255032  1.19639333]
0.0
0
```

To get its probabilities to belong to each of the three classes, you can simply apply the `predict_proba` method (exactly as in the binary case), and the classifier will output the three probabilities. Of course, their sum is 1.0, and the highest value is, naturally, one for class "0".

```
In:
clf.predict_proba(X_test[0])
Out:
array([[ 0.72797056,  0.06275109,  0.20927835]])
```

An example

We now look at a practical example, containing what we've seen so far in this chapter.

Our dataset is an artificially created one, composed of 10,000 observations and 10 features, all of them informative (that is, no redundant ones) and labels "0" and "1" (binary classification). Having all the informative features is not an unrealistic hypothesis in machine learning, since usually the feature selection or feature reduction operation selects non-related features.

```
In:
X, y = make_classification(n_samples=10000, n_features=10,
                           n_informative=10, n_redundant=0,
                           random_state=101)
```

Now, we'll show you how to use different libraries, and different modules, to perform the classification task, using logistic regression. We won't focus here on how to measure the performance, but on how the coefficients can compose the model (what we've named in the previous chapters).

As a first step, we will use Statsmodel. After having loaded the right modules, we need to add an additional feature to the input set in order to have the bias weight `w[0]`. After that, training the model is really simple: we just need to instantiate a `logit` object and use its `fit` method. Statsmodel will train the model and will show whether it was able to train a model (*Optimization terminated successfully*) or it failed:

```
In:
import statsmodels.api as sm
import statsmodels.formula.api as smf
In:
Xc = sm.add_constant(X)
logistic_regression = sm.Logit(y,Xc)
```

```
fitted_model = logistic_regression.fit()
```

Out:

```
Optimization terminated successfully.
        Current function value: 0.438685
        Iterations 7
```

To get a detailed insight into the model, use the method summary:

In:

```
fitted_model.summary()
```

Out:

Logit Regression Results

Dep. Variable:	y	No. Observations:	10000
Model:	Logit	Df Residuals:	9989
Method:	MLE	Df Model:	10
Date:	Fri, 01 Jan 2016	Pseudo R-squ.:	0.3671
Time:	11:48:59	Log-Likelihood:	-4386.8
converged:	True	LL-Null:	-6931.5
		LLR p-value:	0.000

	coef	std err	z	P>|z|	[95.0% Conf. Int.]
const	0.4299	0.039	11.023	0.000	0.353 0.506
x1	0.0671	0.015	4.410	0.000	0.037 0.097
x2	-0.7828	0.019	-41.947	0.000	-0.819 -0.746
x3	0.1221	0.016	7.815	0.000	0.091 0.153
x4	0.2841	0.016	18.150	0.000	0.253 0.315
x5	0.1469	0.014	10.283	0.000	0.119 0.175
x6	-0.3414	0.019	-17.636	0.000	-0.379 -0.303
x7	0.0503	0.014	3.481	0.000	0.022 0.079
x8	-0.1393	0.014	-9.642	0.000	-0.168 -0.111
x9	0.1127	0.014	7.931	0.000	0.085 0.141
x10	-0.4792	0.018	-27.340	0.000	-0.514 -0.445

Two tables are returned: the first one is about the dataset and model performances; the second is about the weights of the model. Statsmodel provides a lot of information on the model; some of it has been shown in *Chapter 2, Approaching Simple Linear Regression*, about a trained regressor. Here, instead, we have a brief description of the information shown for the classifier:

- **Converged**: This tells whether the classification model has reached convergence while being trained. Use the model only if this parameter is `true`.

- **Log-Likelihood**: This is the logarithm of the likelihood. It's what we previously named.

- **LL-Null**: This is the Log-Likelihood when only the intercept is used as a predictor.

- **LLR p-value**: This is the chi-squared probability of getting a log-likelihood ratio statistically greater than LLR. Basically, it shows how the model is better than guessing with a constant value. LLR is the log-likelihood ratio, that is, the logarithm of the likelihood of the null model (intercept only), divided by the likelihood of the alternate model (full model).

- **Pseudo R-squared**: This can be seen as the proportion of the total variability unexplained by the model. It's computed as *1-Log-likelihood/LL-Null*.

As for the coefficient table, there is one line for each coefficient: `const` is the weight associated to the intercept term (that is, the bias weight); `x1`, `x2`, ... `x10` are the weights associated to the 10 features composing the model. For each of them there are a few values:

- **Coef**: This is the weight in the model associated to that feature.

- **Std err**: This is the standard error of the coefficient, that is its (predicted) standard deviation (across all observations) divided by the square root of the sample size.

- **Z**: This is the ratio between the standard error and the coefficient (it's the stat t-value).

- **P>|z|**: This is the probability of obtaining a t-value greater than z, while sampling from the same population.

- **[95.0% Conf. Int.]**: This is the interval where, with 95% confidence, the real value of the coefficient is. It is computed as *coefficient +/- 1.96 * std err*.

An alternate method to obtain the same result (often used when the model contains a small number of features) is to write down the formula involved in the regression. This is possible thanks to the Statsmodel formula API, which makes the fitting operation similar to what you would use in R. We first need to name the features, then we write down the formula (using the names we set), and lastly we fit the model. With this method, the intercept term is automatically added to the model. Its output, then, is the same as the preceding output:

```
In:
import pandas as pd


Xd = pd.DataFrame(X)
Xd.columns = ['VAR'+str(i+1) for i in range(10)]
Xd['response'] = y


logistic_regression = smf.logit(formula =
    'response ~ VAR1+ VAR2 + VAR3 + VAR4 + \
    VAR5 + VAR6 + VAR7 + VAR8 + VAR9 + VAR10', data=Xd)


fitted_model = logistic_regression.fit()
fitted_model.summary()
Out:
[same output as above]
```

Let's change our approach, and let's now fully implement the stochastic gradient descent formula. Each piece of the formula has a function, and the `main` function is optimization. With respect to the linear regression, here the big difference is the `loss` function, which is the logistic (that is, the sigmoid):

```
In:
from sklearn.preprocessing import StandardScaler
import numpy as np
observations = len(X)
variables = ['VAR'+str(i+1) for i in range(10)]
In:
import random


def random_w( p ):
```

```python
    return np.array([np.random.normal() for j in range(p)])


def sigmoid(X,w):
    return 1./(1.+np.exp(-np.dot(X,w)))


def hypothesis(X,w):
    return np.dot(X,w)


def loss(X,w,y):
    return hypothesis(X,w) - y


def logit_loss(X,w,y):
    return sigmoid(X,w) - y


def squared_loss(X,w,y):
    return loss(X,w,y)**2


def gradient(X,w,y,loss_type=squared_loss):
    gradients = list()
    n = float(len( y ))
    for j in range(len(w)):
        gradients.append(np.sum(loss_type(X,w,y) * X[:,j]) / n)
    return gradients


def update(X,w,y, alpha=0.01, loss_type=squared_loss):
    return [t - alpha*g for t, g in zip(w, gradient(X,w,y,loss_type))]


def optimize(X,y, alpha=0.01, eta = 10**-12, loss_type=squared_loss,
iterations = 1000):
    standardization = StandardScaler()
    Xst = standardization.fit_transform(X)
    original_means, originanal_stds = standardization.mean_,
standardization.std_
    Xst = np.column_stack((Xst,np.ones(observations)))
    w = random_w(Xst.shape[1])
    path = list()
```

```
    for k in range(iterations):
        SSL = np.sum(squared_loss(Xst,w,y))
        new_w = update(Xst,w,y, alpha=alpha, loss_type=logit_loss)
        new_SSL = np.sum(squared_loss(Xst,new_w,y))
        w = new_w
        if k>=5 and (new_SSL - SSL <= eta and new_SSL - SSL >= -eta):
            path.append(new_SSL)
            break
        if k % (iterations / 20) == 0:
            path.append(new_SSL)
    unstandardized_betas = w[:-1] / originanal_stds
    unstandardized_bias = w[-1]-np.sum((original_means /
originanal_stds) * w[:-1])
return np.insert(unstandardized_betas, 0, unstandardized_bias),
path,k


alpha = 0.5
w, path, iterations = optimize(X, y, alpha, eta = 10**-5, loss_
type=logit_loss, iterations = 100000)
print ("These are our final standardized coefficients: %s" % w)
print ("Reached after %i iterations" % (iterations+1))
Out:
These are our final standardized coefficients: [ 0.42991407   0.0670771
-0.78279578   0.12208733   0.28410285   0.14689341
 -0.34143436   0.05031078 -0.1393206     0.11267402 -0.47916908]
Reached after 868 iterations
```

The coefficients produced with the stochastic gradient descent approach are the same as the ones Statsmodels derived previously. The code implementation, as seen before, is not best optimized; though reasonably efficient at working out the solution, it's just an instructive way to understand how SGD works under the hood in the logistic regression task. Try to play around, checking the relation between the number of iterations, alpha, eta, and the final outcome: you'll understand how these parameters are connected, as well as how to select the best settings.

Finally, we switch to the Scikit-learn library, and its implementation of Logistic Regression. Scikit-learn has two implementations: one based on the *classic* solution of the logistic regression optimization, and the other one based on a quick SGD implementation. We'll explore them both.

First, we start with the classic Logistic Regression implementation. The training is really simple, and just requires a couple of parameters. We will set its parameters to the extreme, so the solution is not regularized (C is very high) and the stopping criterion on tolerance is very low. We do that in this example to get the same weights in the model; in a real experiment, these parameters will guide hyperparameter optimization. For more information about regularization, please refer to *Chapter 6, Achieving Generalization*:

```
In:
from sklearn.linear_model import LogisticRegression

clf = LogisticRegression(C=1E4, tol=1E-25, random_state=101)
clf.fit(X,y)
Out:
LogisticRegression(C=10000.0, class_weight=None, dual=False,
        fit_intercept=True, intercept_scaling=1, max_iter=100,
        multi_class='ovr', penalty='l2', random_state=101,
        solver='liblinear', tol=1e-25, verbose=0)
In:
coeffs = [clf.intercept_[0]]
coeffs.extend(clf.coef_[0])
coeffs
Out:
```

```
[0.42991394845314063,
 0.067077096874709585,
 -0.7827957661488677,
 0.12208730826867409,
 0.28410283693190336,
 0.14689340914475549,
 -0.34143434245188609,
 0.050310756492560317,
 -0.1393205915231476,
 0.11267402173781312,
 -0.47916904027905627]
```

As the last model, we try the Scikit-learn implementation of the SGD. Getting the same weights is really tricky, since the model is really complex, and the parameters should be optimized for performance, not for obtaining the same result as for the closed form approach. So, use this example to understand the coefficients in the model, but not for training a real-world model:

```
In:
from sklearn.linear_model import SGDClassifier
```

```
clf = SGDClassifier(loss='log', alpha=1E-4, n_iter=1E2, random_state=101)
clf.fit(X,y)
```

Out:

```
SGDClassifier(alpha=0.0001, average=False, class_weight=None,
      epsilon=0.1, eta0=0.0, fit_intercept=True, l1_ratio=0.15,
      learning_rate='optimal', loss='log', n_iter=100.0,
      n_jobs=1, penalty='l2', power_t=0.5, random_state=101,
      shuffle=True, verbose=0, warm_start=False)
```

In:

```
coeffs = [clf.intercept_[0]]
coeffs.extend(clf.coef_[0])
coeffs
```

Out:

```
[0.42571117875899561,
 0.092754663986175351,
 -0.78381378869544127,
 0.093708745822509473,
 0.1675646650527122,
 0.10596527209458738,
 -0.41091578158018643,
 0.062219832489940362,
 -0.19435965629236054,
 0.2353120824478212,
 -0.48793778455042086]
```

Summary

We've seen in this chapter how to build a binary classifier based on Linear Regression and the logistic function. It's fast, small, and very effective, and can be trained using an incremental technique based on SGD. Moreover, with very little effort (the One-vs-Rest approach), the Binary Logistic Regressor can become multiclass.

In the next chapter, we will focus on how to prepare data: to obtain the maximum from the supervised algorithm, the input dataset must be carefully cleaned and normalized. In fact, real world datasets can have missing data, errors, and outliers, and variables can be categorical and with different ranges of values. Fortunately, some popular algorithms deal with these problems, transforming the dataset in the best way possible for the machine learning algorithm.

5
Data Preparation

After providing solid foundations for an understanding of the two basic linear models for regression and classification, we devote this chapter to a discussion about the data feeding the model. In the next pages, we will describe what can routinely be done to prepare the data in the best way and how to deal with more challenging situations, such as when data is missing or outliers are present.

Real-world experiments produce real data, which, in contrast to synthetic or simulated data, is often very varied. Real data is also quite messy, and frequently it proves wrong in ways that are obvious and some that are, initially, quite subtle. As a data practitioner, you will almost never find your data already prepared in the right form to be immediately analyzed for your purposes.

Writing a compendium of bad data and its remedies is outside the scope of this book, but our intention is to provide you with the basics to help you manage the majority of common data problems and correctly feed your algorithm. After all, the commonly known acronym **garbage in, garbage out** (**GIGO**) is a truth that we have to face and accept.

Throughout this chapter, we will therefore discover a variety of topics, Python classes, and functions that will allow you to:

- Properly scale numeric features and have an easier time not just comparing and interpreting coefficients but also when dealing with unusual or missing values or with very sparse matrices (very common in textual data processing)
- Turn qualitative features into numeric values that can be accepted by a regression model and correctly transformed into predictions
- Transform numeric features in the smartest possible way to convert non-linear relationships in your data into linear ones

- Determine what to do when important data is missing to estimate a replacement or even just let the regression manage the best solution by itself

- Repair any unusual or strange value in your data and make your regression model always work properly

Numeric feature scaling

In *Chapter 3, Multiple Regression in Action,* inside the feature scaling section, we discussed how changing your original variables to a similar scale could help better interpret the resulting regression coefficients. Moreover, scaling is essential when using gradient descent-based algorithms because it facilitates quicker converging to a solution. For gradient descent, we will introduce other techniques that can only work using scaled features. However, apart for the technical requirements of certain algorithms, now our intention is to draw your attention to how feature scaling can be helpful when working with data that can sometimes be missing or faulty.

Missing or wrong data can happen not just during training but also during the production phase. Now, if a missing value is encountered, you have two design options to create a model sufficiently robust to cope with such a problem:

- Actively deal with the missing values (there is a paragraph in this chapter devoted to this)

- Passively deal with it and:
    - Your system throws an error and everything goes down (and remains down till the problem is solved)
    - Your system ignores the missing data and computes the values that are not missing

It is certainly worrying that your prediction system can get struck and could stop, but ignoring it and summing the present values could produce highly biased results. If your regression equation has been designed to work with all its variables, then it cannot work properly when some data is missing. Anyway, let's again recall the linear regression formula:

$$y = \beta_0 + \beta X$$

As you may guess, the bias coefficient is actually there to stay; it will always appear, whatever the situation with your predictors is. Consequently, even in an extreme case, such as when all the X are missing, if you standardize your variables thus they have zero mean.

Let's see this in practice and discover how properly rescaling your predictors can help to fix missing values, allow advanced optimization techniques such as gradient descent, regularization, and stochastic learning (more about the latter two in later chapters), and easily detect outlying and anomalous values.

First, let's upload our basic packages and functions for the analysis:

```
In: import numpy as np
    import pandas as pd
    import matplotlib.pyplot as plt
    from sklearn.datasets import load_boston
    from sklearn import linear_model
    %matplotlib inline
    #To set float output to 5 decimals and to suppress printing of \
    small floating point values using scientific notation
    np.set_printoptions(precision=5, suppress=True)
```

Please notice that the Boston dataset is also reloaded. We refer to *y* as the target variable and to *X* as the predictors' array.

```
In:     boston = load_boston()
    dataset = pd.DataFrame(boston.data, \
    columns=boston.feature_names)
    dataset['target'] = boston.target
    observations = len(dataset)
    variables = dataset.columns[:-1]
    X = dataset.ix[:,:-1]
    y = dataset['target'].values
```

Since we would also like to have a test on the logistic regression, we now transform the target variable into a binary response by putting all values above the score of 25 at level "1".

```
In: yq = np.array(y>25, dtype=int)
```

After this operation, our qualitative response variable is named yq.

Mean centering

For all rescaling operations, we suggest the functions to be found in the preprocessing module of the Scikit-learn package. In particular, we will be using StandardScaler and MinMaxScaler. Like all classes in Scikit-learn, they both have a fit method that will record and store the parameters that allow correct scaling. They also feature a transform method that could be immediately applied on the same data (the fit_transform method will also do the trick) or on any other data, for example data used for validation, testing, or even, later on, production.

The StandardScaler class will rescale your variables by removing the mean, an action also called centering. In fact, in your training set the rescaled variables will all have zero mean and the features will be forced to the unit variance. After fitting, the class will contain the mean_ and std_ vectors, granting you access to the means and standard deviations that made the scaling possible. Therefore, in any following set for testing purpose or predictions in production, you will be able to apply the exact same transformations, thus maintaining the data consistency necessary for the algorithm to work exactly.

The MinMaxScaler class will rescale your variables setting a new minimum and maximum value in the range pointed out by you. After fitting, min_ and scale_ will report the minimum values (subtracted from the original variables) and the scale used for dividing your variables to have the intended maximum values, respectively.

> If you reuse one of the two classes, after being trained, on other new data, the new variables might have different maximum and minimum values, causing the resulting transformed variables to be off-scale (above maximum or below minimum, or with an anomalous value). When this happens, it is important to check if the new data has anomalous values and question whether we used the correct data for the training phase when we defined the transformations and the coefficients.

Let's now upload both the scaling classes and get a remainder of the coefficients and intercept value when fitting a linear regression on the Boston dataset:

```
In: from sklearn.preprocessing import StandardScaler
    from sklearn.preprocessing import MinMaxScaler
    linear_regression = linear_model.LinearRegression(normalize=False,\
    fit_intercept=True)
    linear_regression.fit(X,y)
    print ("coefficients: %s\nintercept: %0.3f" % \
    (linear_regression.coef_,linear_regression.intercept_))
```

`Out:`

```
coefficients: [ -0.10717    0.0464    0.02086    2.68856 -17.79576    3.80475    0.00075
  -1.47576    0.30566   -0.01233   -0.95346    0.00939  -0.52547]
intercept: 36.491
```

 If you get your results from your Jupyter Notebook in scientific notation, it could be helpful to first use `import numpy as np` and then `np.set_printoptions(precision=5, suppress=True)`.

In particular, let's notice the intercept. Given the linear regression formula, we can expect that to be the regression output when all predictors are zero. Let's also have a look at the minimum values to check if they are negative, zero, or positive.

`In: dataset.min()`

`Out:`

```
CRIM             0.00632
ZN               0.00000
INDUS            0.46000
CHAS             0.00000
NOX              0.38500
RM               3.56100
AGE              2.90000
DIS              1.12960
RAD              1.00000
TAX            187.00000
PTRATIO         12.60000
B                0.32000
LSTAT            1.73000
target           5.00000
dtype: float64
```

Given the range in our variables, there could never be a situation when all the predictors are zero, implying that the intercept, though still functional and essential for the proper working of our model, is not representing any really expected value.

Now, as a first scaling operation, let's just center the variables, that is, remove the mean, and see if this action changes something in our linear regression.

```
In: centering = StandardScaler(with_mean=True, with_std=False)
    linear_regression.fit(centering.fit_transform(X),y)
    print ("coefficients: %s\nintercept: %s" % \
    (linear_regression.coef_,linear_regression.intercept_))
```

Out:

```
coefficients: [ -0.10717    0.0464     0.02086    2.68856 -17.79576    3.80475    0.00075
  -1.47576    0.30566   -0.01233   -0.95346    0.00939   -0.52547]
intercept: 22.533
```

Though the coefficients have remained the same, now the intercept is **22.533**, a value that has a particular meaning in our Boston Housing prices problem:

```
In: print ('mean: %0.3f' % np.mean(y))
```

Out:mean: 22.533

Having the intercept valued as the average target value means that when one or more values are missing we expect them to automatically get a zero value if we centered the variable, and our regression will naturally tend to output the average value of the target variable.

Standardization

At this point, we can also try scaling everything to unit variance and check the results:

```
In: standardization = StandardScaler(with_mean=True, with_std=True)
    linear_regression.fit(standardization.fit_transform(X),y)
    print ("coefficients: %s\nintercept: %0.3f" % \
    (linear_regression.coef_,linear_regression.intercept_))
```

Out:

```
coefficients: [-0.92041   1.08098   0.14297   0.6822    -2.06009   2.67064   0.02112 -3.10445
  2.65879  -2.0759   -2.06216   0.85664  -3.74868]
intercept: 22.533
```

As expected, now the coefficients are different, and each one now represents the unit change in the target after a modification in the predictors' equivalent to a standard deviation. However, the scales are not fully comparable if the distributions of our predictors are not normal (standardization implies a normal bell-shaped distribution), yet we can now compare the impact of each predictor and allow both the automatic handling of missing values and the correct functioning of advanced algorithms.

Normalization

Normalization rescales as standardization, by acting on ranges of the predictors, but it has different properties. In fact, when using normalization the zero value is the minimum value in the range of values of each predictor. That means that zero doesn't represent the mean anymore. Moreover, rescaling between the maximum and the minimum can become misleading if there are anomalous values at either one of the extremities (most of your values will get squeezed around a certain region in [0,1], usually in the center of the range).

```
In: scaling  = MinMaxScaler(feature_range=(0, 1))
  linear_regression.fit(scaling.fit_transform(X),y)
  print ("coefficients: %s\nintercept: %0.3f" % \
  (linear_regression.coef_,linear_regression.intercept_))
```

Out:

```
coefficients: [ -9.53495   4.63952   0.56907   2.68856  -8.64874  19.857      0.07293
 -16.22877   7.03007  -6.46058  -8.96256   3.72488 -19.04291]
intercept: 26.613
```

Applying the `MinMaxScaler` in a range of 0 and 1 drastically changes both the coefficients and the intercept, but this could be acceptable under certain circumstances. In fact, when working with big data derived from textual data or logs, we sometimes realize that the matrices we are working on are not especially populated with values, zero often being the most frequent value to be encountered. To speed up the calculations and allow huge matrices to be kept in memory, matrices are stored in a sparse format.

Sparse matrices do not occupy all the memory necessary for their size, they just store coordinates and non-zero values. In such situations, standardizing the variables would change zero to the mean and a large number of previously zero cells would have to be defined, causing the matrix to occupy much more memory. Scaling between zero and one allows taking values in a comparable order and keeping all previously zero entries, thus not modifying the matrix dimensions in memory.

The logistic regression case

A special discussion has to be devoted to logistic regression. As we illustrated in the previous chapter, in logistic regression we model the odds ratio of the probability of response. We can use the standardized coefficients as a trick to face missing data, as seen with linear regression, but things then turn out to be a bit different from when we try to guess a target numeric value in linear regression analysis.

Let's explore an example that could clarify the matter. We will be using the Boston dataset to demonstrate the logistic regression case and we will use the yq vector, previously defined, as a response variable. For the logistic regression, we won't be using the Scikit-learn implementation this time but rather the Statsmodels package, so we can easily show some insights about the coefficients in the model:

```
In: import statsmodels.api as sm
    Xq = sm.add_constant(standardization.fit_transform(X))
    logit = sm.Logit(yq, Xq)
    result = logit.fit()
    print (result.summary())
```

Out:

```
Optimization terminated successfully.
         Current function value: 0.206632
         Iterations 9
                          Logit Regression Results
==============================================================================
Dep. Variable:                      y   No. Observations:                  506
Model:                          Logit   Df Residuals:                      492
Method:                           MLE   Df Model:                           13
Date:                Tue, 20 Oct 2015   Pseudo R-squ.:                   0.6289
Time:                        16:33:29   Log-Likelihood:                 -104.56
converged:                       True   LL-Null:                        -281.76
                                        LLR p-value:                  9.147e-68
==============================================================================
                 coef    std err          z      P>|z|      [95.0% Conf. Int.]
------------------------------------------------------------------------------
const         -3.0541      0.356     -8.572      0.000      -3.752     -2.356
x1            -0.0949      0.389     -0.244      0.807      -0.857      0.667
x2             0.2543      0.252      1.008      0.314      -0.240      0.749
x3            -0.7570      0.403     -1.880      0.060      -1.546      0.032
x4             0.2452      0.205      1.195      0.232      -0.157      0.648
x5            -0.7924      0.519     -1.527      0.127      -1.810      0.225
x6             1.3244      0.318      4.168      0.000       0.702      1.947
x7             0.0982      0.313      0.314      0.754      -0.515      0.712
x8            -1.2390      0.345     -3.591      0.000      -1.915     -0.563
x9             2.7664      0.719      3.849      0.000       1.358      4.175
x10           -1.8228      0.680     -2.682      0.007      -3.155     -0.491
x11           -0.7635      0.264     -2.888      0.004      -1.282     -0.245
x12           -0.2062      0.349     -0.591      0.554      -0.890      0.477
x13           -2.6208      0.521     -5.031      0.000      -3.642     -1.600
==============================================================================
```

Using the standardized predictors, as in a linear regression, we can interpret the coefficients in terms of the same scale and consider the intercept as the response when all predictors have an average value. Contrary to linear regression, in logistic regression a unit change in predictors changes the odds ratio of the response of a quantity equivalent to the exponentiation of the coefficients themselves:

```
In: print ('odd ratios of coefficients: %s' % np.exp(result.params))
```

```
Out: odd ratios of coefficients: [  0.04717   0.90948   1.2896    0.46908
1.2779    0.45277   3.75996   1.10314   0.28966  15.9012    0.16158
0.46602   0.81363   0.07275]
```

We recall how odds ratios are calculated: given a certain probability p of an event, an odds ratio is the ratio between p and its complement to 1, odds *ratio = p / (1−p)*. When the odds ratio is equivalent to 1, our probability is exactly 0.5. When the probability is above 0.5 the odds ratio is above 1; when, on the contrary, our probability is less than 0.5 then the odds ratio is below 1. By applying the natural logarithm (as logistic regression does), the values are distributed around the zero value (50% probability). Clearly working with probabilities is more intuitive therefore, a simple transformation, the sigmoid transformation, will convert the coefficients to more understandable probabilities:

```
In: def sigmoid(p):

  return 1 / (1 + np.exp(-p))


  print ('intercept: %0.3f' % result.params[0])
  print ('probability of value above 25 when all predictors are \
  average: %0.3f' %        sigmoid(result.params[0]))
```

```
Out: intercept: -3.054
    probability of value above 25 when all predictors
    are average: 0.045
```

Transforming the intercept into a probability using the sigmoid function, we obtain `0.045`, which is the probability of a house value above `25` when all predictors bear the mean value. Please notice that such a probability is different from the average probability in the sample:

```
In: print ('average likelihood of positive response: %0.3f' %
      (sum(yq) /float(len(yq))))
```

```
Out: average likelihood of positive response: 0.245
```

In fact, that's the baseline probability of having a house value above 25, taking account of any possible value of the predictors. What we extracted from logistic regression is instead a particular probability, not a general one. You can actually get a comparable likelihood when you model a logistic regression with only an intercept (the so-called null model), thus allowing the predictors to vary freely:

```
In: C = np.ones(len(X))
    logit = sm.Logit(yq, C)
    result = logit.fit()
    print (result.summary())
    print ('\nprobability of value above 25 using just a constant: %0.3f' %
sigmoid(result.params[0]))
```

Out:

```
Optimization terminated successfully.
         Current function value: 0.556842
         Iterations 5
                      Logit Regression Results
=================================================================
Dep. Variable:                    y   No. Observations:            506
Model:                        Logit   Df Residuals:                505
Method:                         MLE   Df Model:                      0
Date:              Tue, 20 Oct 2015   Pseudo R-squ.:             0.000
Time:                      16:33:29   Log-Likelihood:          -281.76
converged:                     True   LL-Null:                 -281.76
                                      LLR p-value:                 nan
=================================================================
                 coef    std err          z      P>|z|      [95.0% Conf. Int.]
-----------------------------------------------------------------
const          -1.1251      0.103    -10.886      0.000     -1.328    -0.923
=================================================================

probability of value above 25 using just a constant: 0.245
```

Qualitative feature encoding

Beyond numeric features, which have been the main topic of this section so far, a great part of your data will also comprise qualitative variables. Databases especially tend to record data readable and understandable by human beings; consequently, they are quite crowded by qualitative data, which can appear in data fields in the form of text or just single labels explicating information, such as telling you the class of an observation or some of its characteristics.

For a better understanding of qualitative variables, a working example could be a weather dataset. Such a dataset describes conditions under which you would want to play tennis because of weather information such as outlook, temperature, humidity, and wind, which are all kinds of information that can be rendered by numeric measurements. However, you will easily find such data online and recorded in datasets with their qualitative translations such as sunny or overcast, rather than numeric satellite/weather-station measurements. We will work on this kind of data to demonstrate how it is still possible to transform it in such a way that it can be included effectively into a linear model:

```
In: outlook     = ['sunny', 'overcast', 'rainy']
    temperature = ['hot', 'mild', 'cool']
    humidity    = ['high', 'normal']
    windy       = ['TRUE', 'FALSE']


    weather_dataset = list()


    for o in outlook:
      for t in temperature:
        for h in humidity:
          for w in windy:
            weather_dataset.append([o,t,h,w])


    play = [0, 0, 1, 1, 1, 0, 1, 1, 0, 0, 0, 1, 1, 1, 1, 1, 1, 1, 1, 1, 0,
0, 1, 1, 0, 0, 0, 1, 0, 1, 0, 1, 0, 0, 0, 1]
```

A linear regressor can analyze qualitative data only after having been properly transformed into a numeric value. A common type of qualitative data comprises nominal variables, which are expressed by a limited set of textual labels. For instance, a nominal variable could be the color of a product or the outlook of the weather (as in our weather example). The textual values that a variable can assume are called levels; in our example, outlook has three levels: sunny, overcast and rainy, all of them represented as strings.

If we think that any of these can be present or not (each label excludes the other), we can easily transform each nominal variable with n levels into n distinct variables, each one telling us if a certain characteristic is present or not. If we use the value of 1 for denoting the presence of the level and 0 for its absence (like binary coding, such as in computers), we will have a working transformation of qualitative information into a numeric one (technically it is a Boolean, but for practical purposes we model it as a 0 – 1 numeric integer). Such transformed variables are called indicator or binary variables in machine learning terminology, whereas in statistics they are described as **dichotomies** (a more technical term) or dummies variables. They act in a regression formula as modifiers of the intercept when the level is present.

When the levels of a variable are ordered, there's another possible transformation. For instance, they can be qualitative labels such as good, average, acceptable, and bad. In such an occurrence, the labels can also be converted into growing or decreasing numbers following the ordering of the meaning of the labels. Therefore, in our example, good could be 3, average 2, acceptable 1, and bad 0. Such encoding directly translates a qualitative variable into a numeric one, but it works only with labels that can be ordered (that is, where you can define *greater than* and *lower than* relations). The transformation implies, since a single coefficient will be calculated in the regression model for all the levels, that the difference in the outcome passing from good to average is the same as passing from acceptable to bad. In reality, this is often not true due to non-linearity. In such a case, binary encoding is still the best solution.

Dummy coding with Pandas

The fastest way to transform a set of qualitative variables into binary ones is using a Pandas function, get_dummies:

```
In: import pandas as pd
    df = pd.DataFrame(weather_dataset, columns=['outlook', \
    'temperature', 'humidity', 'windy'])
```

After transforming all your data into a Pandas DataFrame, it is quite easy to call single variables and single cases to be transformed into binary variables:

```
In: print (pd.get_dummies(df.humidity).ix[:5,:])
Out:     high   normal
    0      1       0
    1      1       0
    2      0       1
    3      0       1
    4      1       0
    5      1       0
```

Pandas can really transform all your variables in a breeze; all you need is to point out the DataFrame you want to entirely transform or specify just the variables to be converted:

```
In: dummy_encoding = pd.get_dummies(df)
```

After the transformation, a regression model can immediately analyze the resulting new DataFrame:

```
In: import statsmodels.api as sm
    X = sm.add_constant(dummy_encoding)
    logit = sm.Logit(play, X)
    result = logit.fit()
    print (result.summary())
```

Out:

```
Optimization terminated successfully.
         Current function value: 0.292346
         Iterations 32
                         Logit Regression Results
==============================================================================
Dep. Variable:                      y   No. Observations:                   36
Model:                          Logit   Df Residuals:                       29
Method:                           MLE   Df Model:                            6
Date:                Tue, 20 Oct 2015   Pseudo R-squ.:                  0.5744
Time:                        16:33:30   Log-Likelihood:                -10.524
converged:                       True   LL-Null:                       -24.731
                                        LLR p-value:                 7.856e-05
==============================================================================
                     coef    std err          z      P>|z|      [95.0% Conf. Int.]
------------------------------------------------------------------------------
const              0.2393   1.76e+07   1.36e-08      1.000    -3.44e+07   3.44e+07
outlook_overcast   2.9833   6.69e+07   4.46e-08      1.000    -1.31e+08   1.31e+08
outlook_rainy     -2.1746   6.69e+07  -3.25e-08      1.000    -1.31e+08   1.31e+08
outlook_sunny     -0.5695   6.69e+07  -8.51e-09      1.000    -1.31e+08   1.31e+08
temperature_cool  -2.1996      6e+07  -3.66e-08      1.000    -1.18e+08   1.18e+08
temperature_hot    0.3045      6e+07   5.07e-09      1.000    -1.18e+08   1.18e+08
temperature_mild   2.1344      6e+07   3.55e-08      1.000    -1.18e+08   1.18e+08
humidity_high     -2.0459   2.24e+07  -9.15e-08      1.000    -4.38e+07   4.38e+07
humidity_normal    2.2851   2.24e+07   1.02e-07      1.000    -4.38e+07   4.38e+07
windy_FALSE        1.3162   4.47e+07   2.94e-08      1.000    -8.77e+07   8.77e+07
windy_TRUE        -1.0770   4.47e+07  -2.41e-08      1.000    -8.77e+07   8.77e+07
==============================================================================
```

Some regression methods do not really like you to have all the binary variables expressing a qualitative variable (but this is not so in our case). Certain optimization methods do not love perfect collinearity, such as in the case of a complete binarization (in fact, if you know all the other dichotomies, then the remaining ones can be perfectly guessed by summing the others—it has value 1 when the sum of the others is zero). In such a case, you just need to drop a level of your choice from each set of binary variables. By doing so, the omitted coefficient will be incorporated into the intercept and the regression model will just work as before, though with a different set of variables and coefficients:

```
In: X.drop(['outlook_sunny', 'temperature_mild', 'humidity_normal',
'windy_FALSE'], inplace=True, axis=1)

  logit = sm.Logit(play, X)

  result = logit.fit()

  print (result.summary())
```

Out:

```
Optimization terminated successfully.
         Current function value: 0.292346
         Iterations 8
                     Logit Regression Results
=================================================================
Dep. Variable:                   y   No. Observations:            36
Model:                       Logit   Df Residuals:                29
Method:                        MLE   Df Model:                     6
Date:             Tue, 20 Oct 2015   Pseudo R-squ.:           0.5744
Time:                     16:33:30   Log-Likelihood:         -10.524
converged:                    True   LL-Null:                -24.731
                                     LLR p-value:          7.856e-05
=================================================================
                    coef    std err        z      P>|z|    [95.0% Conf. Int.]
-----------------------------------------------------------------
const             5.4055      2.196    2.462      0.014     1.102    9.709
outlook_overcast  3.5528      1.721    2.064      0.039     0.179    6.927
outlook_rainy    -1.6051      1.357   -1.183      0.237    -4.265    1.055
temperature_cool -4.3340      1.867   -2.322      0.020    -7.993   -0.675
temperature_hot  -1.8299      1.478   -1.238      0.216    -4.727    1.067
humidity_high    -4.3310      1.645   -2.633      0.008    -7.555   -1.107
windy_TRUE       -2.3932      1.325   -1.807      0.071    -4.989    0.203
=================================================================
```

get_dummies presents only one drawback: it constructs the binary variables directly, reading the levels from the dataset you are converting. Consequently, if you first build a set of binary variables from a sample and then another one from another sample of your same data, it can produce different transformed datasets because of rare levels not appearing in one of the samples.

DictVectorizer and one-hot encoding

The Scikit-learn package offers a way, though a bit less direct, to consistently transform your qualitative variables into numeric ones.

The DictVectorizer class can read datasets made of a list of dictionaries, properly transform the string label data into a set of binaries, and leave the numeric data untouched. If instead you already have qualitative variables coded as numeric types in your dataset, all you need is to transform them to string values before having them processed by DictVectorizer.

All you have to do is first create a dictionary representation of your dataset, as in the following example:

```
In: from sklearn.feature_extraction import DictVectorizer
    vectorizer = DictVectorizer(sparse = False)
    dict_representation = [{varname:var for var, varname in \
    zip(row,['outlook', 'temperature', 'humidity', 'windy'])}
    for row in weather_dataset]
    print (dict_representation[0])
    print (vectorizer.fit_transform(dict_representation))


Out: {'windy': 'TRUE', 'humidity': 'high', 'temperature': 'hot',
'outlook': 'sunny'}
  [[ 1.   0.   0.   0.   1.   0.   1.   0.   0.   1.]
   [ 1.   0.   0.   0.   1.   0.   1.   0.   1.   0.]
   [ 0.   1.   0.   0.   1.   0.   1.   0.   0.   1.]
...
```

A dictionary representation is in the form of a list of dictionaries whose keys are the variables' names and whose values are their numeric or label value. To obtain such a representation, you will need to duplicate your dataset, and that could represent a big limitation if you are working with little memory available.

On the other hand, the class keeps memory of the transformations and thus everything can be exactly replicated on any other data sample using the transform method, overcoming the limitation we've seen with the Pandas get_dummies method.

You can also easily visualize the transformations by calling the `features_names_` method.

```
In: print (vectorizer.feature_names_)
```

```
Out: ['humidity=high', 'humidity=normal', 'outlook=overcast', \
      'outlook=rainy', 'outlook=sunny', 'temperature=cool', \
      'temperature=hot', 'temperature=mild', 'windy=FALSE', \
      'windy=TRUE']
```

If the limit number of binarizations does not justify the entire conversion of the dataset into a dictionary representation, by using the `LabelEncoder` and `LabelBinarizer` class, available in the `preprocessing` package in Scikit-learn, you can encode and transform a single variable at a time.

`LabelEncoder` turns the labels into numbers and `LabelBinarizer` transforms the numbers into dichotomies. The consistency of all such operations across different samples is guaranteed by the `fit` and `transforms` methods that are characteristic of all the classes present in Scikit-learn, where `fit` picks and records the parameters from data and the `transform` method applies it to new data afterwards.

Let's test a transformation on the outlook variable. We first convert the text labels into numbers:

```
In: from sklearn.preprocessing import LabelEncoder, LabelBinarizer
label_encoder = LabelEncoder()
print (label_encoder.fit_transform(df.outlook))
```

```
Out: [2 2 2 2 2 2 2 2 2 2 2 0 0 0 0 0 0 0 0 0 0 0 1 1 1 1 1 1 1 1 1
 1 1]
```

The assigned numbers are given by the position of the label in the list that you get using an `inverse_transform` method:

```
In: label_encoder.inverse_transform([0,1,2])
```

```
Out: array(['overcast', 'rainy', 'sunny'], dtype=object)
```

Or by just requiring the recorded classes, glancing at the `classes_` internal variable:

```
In: print (label_encoder.classes_)
```

```
Out: ['overcast' 'rainy' 'sunny']
```

Once numerically encoded, `LabelBinarizer` can transform everything into indicator variables, allowing you to decide what values should be placed in the dichotomy.

In fact, if you worry about missing values, you can encode the negative value as -1, leaving the missing case at 0 (in that case, the missing value will be passively taken in charge by the intercept as seen before).

```
In: label_binarizer = LabelBinarizer(neg_label=0, pos_label=1, \
    sparse_output=False)
    print (label_binarizer.fit_transform( \
    label_encoder.fit_transform(df.outlook)))
```

```
Out: [[0 0 1]
     [0 0 1]
     [0 0 1]
...
```

Another great advantage of this method is that it allows sparse representations, thus saving memory when working with large datasets.

Feature hasher

One-hot encoding is a powerful transformation that allows any kind of data to be represented just using a binary variable. Using the same approach, you can even transform text into variables that can be analyzed by a linear regression model.

The idea is to transform any occurrence of a certain word in the text into a specific binary variable, so the model will assign a binary value connected to the presence of a word in the text. For instance, if you want to analyze the Latin motto *Nomina sunt consequentia rerum* (that means "names follow things"), you can force all the text to lowercase and enumerate all the distinct words present in the text by tokenizing them. By doing so, you intend to separate them (in our case, the tokenization is quite simple, we just split by spaces) in a way that it is often referred to as a **bag of words (BoW)** representation:

```
In: your_text = 'Nomina sunt consequentia rerum'
mapping_words_in_text = {word:position for position, word in
enumerate(set(your_text.lower().split(' ')))}
print (mapping_words_in_text)
```

```
Out: {'rerum': 0, 'sunt': 1, 'consequentia': 2, 'nomina': 3}
```

The preceding code just transforms all your textual data into a dictionary containing the lowercase words and their positional index in a vector of binary variables.

The length of this vector is the length of the dictionary, and each binary flag has unit value when the corresponding word is present in the analyzed text. Therefore, the vector for all our phrase is [1,1,1,1] and the vector for a phrase just containing the word 'rerum' should be [1,0,0,0] because the positional index of the word is 0.

Figuratively, you can imagine our vector as a line of lamps; each time, you turn on only those whose corresponding word is present in the text you are analyzing.

Transforming a word into an indicator is just a starting point. You can also count how many times a word appears in a text and normalize that count by considering the length of the text you are transforming. In fact, in longer text, certain words have a higher chance of appearing multiple times than in shorter ones. By normalizing the word count, for instance, in such a way that the sum of word counts cannot be over a certain number, it will appear like reducing all texts to the same length. These are just some of the possible transformations that are part of **natural language processing** (**NLP**), and they are viable for a linear regression model.

The Scikit-learn package offers a specialized class for automatically transforming text into vectors of binary variables; this is the CountVectorizer class. It allows the transformation of a list or array of textual data into a sparse matrix. Setting the binary parameter to True, when transforming the data with just binary encoding, represents the sparse matrix as a set of unit values in correspondence to the texts where a word is present. As a simple example, we can encode this series of texts:

```
In: corpus = ['The quick fox jumped over the lazy dog', 'I sought a dog
wondering around with a bird', 'My dog is named Fido']
```

The only common word in the corpus (the term for a collection of documents subject to a linguistic analysis, so it is common to have a bilingual corpus or even a more heterogeneous one) is 'dog'. This should be reflected in our matrix; in fact, just a single column always has the unit value:

```
In: from sklearn.feature_extraction.text import CountVectorizer
textual_one_hot_encoder = CountVectorizer(binary=True)
textual_one_hot_encoder.fit(corpus)
vectorized_text = textual_one_hot_encoder.transform(corpus)
print(vectorized_text.todense())

Out: [[0 0 1 0 1 0 1 1 0 0 1 1 0 1 0 0]
```

```
[1 1 1 0 0 0 0 0 0 0 0 0 1 0 1 1]
[0 0 1 1 0 1 0 0 1 1 0 0 0 0 0 0]]
```

To visualize the resulting matrix as an output, which would otherwise just be made up of the coordinates where the unit values are in the matrix, we need to make the resulting sparse matrix dense using the `.todense()` method.

> Being a toy dataset, such transformation won't imply much in our example. Beware of doing the same when your corpus is large because that could cause an out-of-memory error on your system.

We notice that the third column has three units, so we imagine that it could represent the word `'dog'`. We can verify that by requiring a list representing the dictionary and the positional arrangement of words using the `.get_feature_names()` method:

```
In: print (textual_one_hot_encoder.get_feature_names())
```

```
Out: ['around', 'bird', 'dog', 'fido', 'fox', 'is', 'jumped', 'lazy',
'my', 'named', 'over', 'quick', 'sought', 'the', 'with', 'wondering']
```

Leveraging the ability to quickly build dictionaries of words, you can transform and use it even for the prediction of text.

The only trouble you can incur using such a representation is when you encounter a word never seen before. Let's see what happens:

```
In: print (textual_one_hot_encoder.transform(['John went home today']).
todense())
```

```
Out: [[0 0 0 0 0 0 0 0 0 0 0 0 0 0 0 0]]
```

Such behavior should actually have been expected. Since no word of the phrase has been encountered before, it doesn't have any space to fit in the vectorized text.

A quick and working solution would be to define a very large sparse vector (which until filled with data won't occupy much space, no matter the dimensions) and to use the specific characteristics of hash functions to deterministically assign a position to every word in the vector, without having the need to observe the word itself before the assignment. This is also called the **hashing trick** and can be applied using the Scikit-learn `HashingVectorizers`.

```
In: from sklearn.feature_extraction.text import HashingVectorizer
    hashing_trick = HashingVectorizer(n_features=11, binary=True, \
    norm=None, non_negative=True)
```

```
M = hashing_trick.transform(corpus)
print (M.todense())
```

```
Out: [[ 1.   0.   0.   1.   1.   0.   0.   1.   0.   0.   0.]
      [ 0.   0.   0.   1.   0.   1.   0.   1.   1.   0.   0.]
      [ 0.   0.   0.   1.   0.   0.   0.   1.   1.   0.   0.]]
```

The `HashingVectorizer` class has quite a few options for you to explore, especially for text treatment, such as allowing more sophisticated tokenizing (even custom ones), the removal of common words, stripping accents, and the parsing of different encodings.

In a replica of what we have done before with `CountVectorizer`, we fixed an output vector of 11 elements. By doing so, we can notice and discuss two relevant characteristics of the preceding output.

First, clearly the position of the words is different (it depends on the hash function), and we cannot get back a dictionary of what word is in what position (but we can be confident that the hashing function has done its job properly). Now, we have no fear of vectorizing any previously unseen new text:

```
In: print (hashing_trick.transform(['John is the owner of that dog']).
todense())
```

```
Out: [[1.   1.   1.   0.   0.   0.   0.   0.   0.   0.   0.]]
```

The second thing is that, by observing well the distributions of unit values in the matrix, you have values concentrating on certain positions, whereas others are left empty. This is due to *the collision problem* with hash functions when bounded in a limited number of positions (actually we set the `n_features` parameter to 11 for ease of understanding, though in a real analysis it is good practice to set it to higher figures).

 To avoid any unwanted collision, a good `n_features` value is between 2**21 and 2**24, depending on the expected variety of text (the more variety, the larger the vector should be).

Numeric feature transformation

Numeric features can be transformed, regardless of the target variable. This is often a prerequisite for better performance of certain classifiers, particularly distance-based. We usually avoid (besides specific cases such as when modeling a percentage or distributions with long queues) transforming the target, since we will make any pre-existent linear relationship between the target and other features non-linear.

We will keep on working on the Boston Housing dataset:

```
In: import numpy as np
  boston = load_boston()
  labels = boston.feature_names
  X = boston.data
  y = boston.target
  print (boston.feature_names)


Out: ['CRIM' 'ZN' 'INDUS' 'CHAS' 'NOX' 'RM' 'AGE' 'DIS' \
      'RAD' 'TAX' 'PTRATIO' 'B' 'LSTAT']
```

As before, we fit the model using `LinearRegression` from Scikit-learn, this time measuring its R-squared value using the `r2_score` function from the `metrics` module:

```
In: linear_regression = \
  linear_model.LinearRegression(fit_intercept=True)
  linear_regression.fit(X, y)


  from sklearn.metrics import r2_score
  print ("R-squared: %0.3f" % r2_score(y, \
  linear_regression.predict(X)))


Out: R-squared: 0.741
```

Observing residuals

Residuals are what's left from the original response when the predicted value is removed. It is numeric information telling us what the linear model wasn't able to grasp and predict by its set of coefficients and intercepts.

Obtaining residuals when working with Scikit-learn requires just one operation:

```
In: residuals = y - linear_regression.predict(X)
  print ("Head of residual %s" % residuals[:5])
  print ("Mean of residuals: %0.3f" % np.mean(residuals))
  print ("Standard deviation of residuals: %0.3f" \
  % np.std(residuals))


Out: Head of residual [-6.00821 -3.42986  4.12977  4.79186  8.25712]
    Mean of residuals: 0.000
    Standard deviation of residuals: 4.680
```

The residuals of a linear regression always have mean zero and their standard deviation depends on the size of the error produced. Residuals can provide insight on an unusual observation and non-linearity because, after telling us about what's left, they can direct us to specific troublesome data points or puzzling patterns in data.

For the specific problem of detecting non-linearity, we are going to use a plot based on residuals called the **partial residual plot**. In this plot, we compare the regression residuals summed with the values derived from the modeled coefficient of a variable against the original values of the variable itself:

```
In: var = 7 # the variable in position 7 is DIS
    partial_residual = residuals + X[:,var] * \
    linear_regression.coef_[var]
    plt.plot(X[:,var], partial_residual, 'wo')
    plt.xlabel(boston.feature_names[var])
    plt.ylabel('partial residuals')
    plt.show()
Out:
```

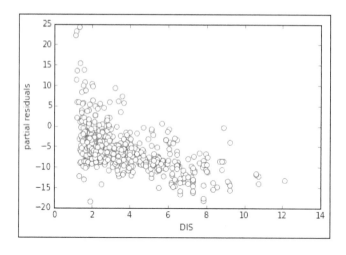

After having calculated the residual of the regression, we decide to inspect one variable at a time. After picking up our selected variable, we create a partial residual by summing the residuals of the regression with the multiplication of the variable values multiplied by its coefficient. In such a way, we *extract* the variable from the regression line and we put it in the residuals. Now, as partial residuals, we have both the errors and the coefficient-weighted variable. If we plot it against the variable itself, we can notice whether there is any non-linear pattern. If there is one, we know that we should try some modification.

In our case, there is some sign that the points bend after the value 2 of our variable, a clear non-linearity sign such as any bend or pattern different from an elongated, straight cloud of points. Square, inverse, logarithmic transformations can often solve such problems without adding new terms, such as when using the polynomial expansion:

```
In: X_t = X.copy()
    X_t[:,var] = 1./np.sqrt(X_t[:,var])
    linear_regression.fit(X_t, y)
    partial_residual = residuals + X_t[:,var] * \
    linear_regression.coef_[var]
    plt.plot(X_t[:,var], partial_residual, 'wo')
    plt.xlabel(boston.feature_names[var])
    plt.ylabel('partial residuals')
    plt.show()
    print ("R-squared: %0.3f" % r2_score(y, \
    linear_regression.predict(X_t)))
```

```
Out: R-squared: 0.769
```

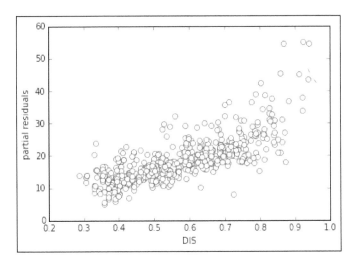

Just notice how an inverse square transformation rendered the partial residual plot straighter, something that is reflected in a higher R-squared value, indicating an increased capacity of the model to capture the data distribution.

As a rule, the following transformations should always be tried (singularly or in combination) to find a fix for a non-linearity:

Function names	Functions
Logarithmic	`np.log(x)`
Exponential	`np.exp(x)`
Squared	`x**2`
Cubed	`x**3`
Square root	`np.sqrt(x)`
Cube root	`x**(1./3.)`
Inverse	`1. / x`

Some of the transformations suggested in the preceding table won't work properly after normalization or otherwise in the presence of zero and negative values: logarithmic transformation needs positive values above zero, square root won't work with negative values, and inverse transformation won't operate with zero values. Sometimes adding a constant may help (like in the case of `np.log(x+1)`). Generally, just try the possible transformations, according to your data values.

Summarizations by binning

When it is not easy to figure out the exact transformation, a quick solution could be to transform the continuous numeric variable into a series of binary variables, thus allowing the estimation of a coefficient for each single part of the numeric range of the variable.

Though fast and convenient, this solution will increase the size of your dataset (unless you use a sparse representation of the matrix) and it will risk too much overfitting on your data.

First, you divide your values into equally spaced bins and you notice the edges of the bins using the `histogram` function from Numpy. After that, using the `digitize` function, you convert the value in their bin number, based on the bin boundaries provided before. Finally, you can transform all the bin numbers into binary variables using the previously present `LabelBinarizer` from Scikit-learn.

At this point, all you have to do is replace the previous variable with this new set of binary indicators and refit the model for checking the improvement:

```
In: import numpy as np
    from sklearn.preprocessing import LabelBinarizer
    LB = LabelBinarizer()
    X_t = X.copy()
    edges = np.histogram(X_t[:,var], bins=20)[1]
    binning = np.digitize(X_t[:,var], edges)
    X_t = np.column_stack((np.delete(X_t, var, \
    axis=1),LB.fit_transform(binning)))
    linear_regression.fit(X_t, y)
    print ("R-squared: %0.3f" % r2_score(y, \
    linear_regression.predict(X_t)))
```

```
Out: R-squared: 0.768
```

Missing data

Missing data appears often in real-life data, sometimes randomly in random occurrences, more often because of some bias in its recording and treatment. All linear models work on complete numeric matrices and cannot deal directly with such problems; consequently, it is up to you to take care of feeding suitable data for the algorithm to process.

Even if your initial dataset does not present any missing data, it is still possible to encounter missing values in the production phase. In such a case, the best strategy is surely that of dealing with them passively, as presented at the beginning of the chapter, by standardizing all the numeric variables.

 As for as indicator variables, in order to passively intercept missing values, a possible strategy is instead to encode the presence of the label as 1 and its absence as -1, leaving the zero value for missing values.

When missing values are present from the beginning of the project, it is certainly better to deal with them explicitly, trying to figure out if there is any systematic pattern behind missing values. In Python arrays, upon which both the Pandas and Scikit-learn packages are built, missing values are marked by a special value, **Not a Number (NaN)**, which is repeatable using the value available from the NumPy constant nan.

Creating a toy array with a missing value is easy:

```
In: import Numpy as np
    example = np.array([1,2,np.nan,4,5])
    print (example)
```

```
Out: [ 1.   2.   nan   4.   5.]
```

Also discovering where missing values are in a vector (the result is a vector of Booleans):

```
In: print (np.isnan(example))
```

```
Out: [False False  True False False]
```

Replacing all missing elements can be done easily by slicing or by the function nan_to_num, which turns every nan to zero:

```
In: print (np.nan_to_num(example))
```

```
Out: [ 1.   2.   0.   4.   5.]
```

Using slicing, you could decide to use something more sophisticated than a constant, such as the mean of valid elements in the vector:

```
In: missing = np.isnan(example)
    replacing_value = np.mean(example[~missing])
    example[missing] = replacing_value
    print (example)
```

```
Out: [ 1.   2.   3.   4.   5.]
```

Missing data imputation

Consistency of treatment between samples of data is essential when working with predictive models. If you replace the missing values with a certain constant or a particular mean, that should be consistent during both the training and the production phase. The Scikit-learn package offers the Imputer class in the preprocessing module which can learn a solution by the fit method and then consistently apply it by the transform one.

Let's start demonstrating it after putting some missing values in the Boston dataset:

```
In: from random import sample, seed
    import numpy as np
    seed(19)
    Xm = X.copy()
    missing = sample(range(len(y)), len(y)//4)
    Xm[missing,5] = np.nan
    print ("Header of Xm[:,5] : %s" % Xm[:10,5])
```

```
Out: Header of Xm[:,5] : [ 6.575    nan  7.185    nan  7.147  6.43
     6.012  6.172    nan  6.004]
```

 It is quite unlikely that you will get the same result due to the random nature of the sampling process. Please notice that the exercise sets a seed so you can count on the same results on your PC.

Now about a quarter of observations in the variable should be missing. Let's use `Imputer` to replace them using a mean:

```
In: from sklearn.preprocessing import Imputer
    impute = Imputer(missing_values = 'NaN', strategy='mean', axis=1)
    print ("Header of imputed Xm[:,5] : %s" % \
    impute.fit_transform(Xm[:,5])[0][:10])
```

```
Out: Header of imputed Xm[:,5] : [ 6.575    6.25446  7.185    6.25446
     7.147    6.43     6.012    6.172  6.25446  6.004 ]
```

Imputer allows you to define any value as missing (sometimes in a re-elaborated dataset missing values could be encoded with negative values or other extreme values) and to choose alternative strategies rather than the mean. Other alternatives are **median** and **mode**. The median is useful if you suspect that outlying values are influencing and biasing the average (in house prices, some very expensive and exclusive houses or areas could be the reason). Mode, the most frequent value, is instead the optimal choice if you are working with discrete values (for instance a sequence of integer values with a limited range).

Keeping track of missing values

If you suspect that there is some bias in the missing value pattern, by imputing them you will lose any trace of it. Before imputing, a good practice is to create a binary variable recording where all missing values were and to add it as a feature to the dataset. As seen before, it is quite easy using NumPy to create such a new feature, transforming the Boolean vector created by `isnan` into a vector of integers:

```
In: missing_indicator = np.isnan(Xm[:,5]).astype(int)
  print ("Header of missing indicator : %s" \
  % missing_indicator[:10])
```

```
Out: Header of missing indicator : [0 1 1 0 0 0 0 0 1 1]
```

The linear regression model will create a coefficient for this indicator of missing values and, if any pattern exists, its informative value will be captured by a coefficient.

Outliers

After properly transforming all the quantitative and qualitative variables and fixing any missing data, what's left is just to detect any possible outlier and to deal with it by removing it from the data or by imputing it as if it were a missing case.

An outlier, sometimes also referred to as an anomaly, is an observation that is very different from all the others you have observed so far. It can be viewed as an unusual case that stands out, and it could pop up due to a mistake (an erroneous value completely out of scale) or simply a value that occurred (rarely, but it occurred). Though understanding the origin of an outlier could help to fix the problem in the most appropriate way (an error could be legitimately removed; a rare case could be kept or capped or even imputed as a missing case), what is of utmost concern is the effect of one or more outliers on your regression analysis results. Any anomalous data in a regression analysis means a distortion of the regression's coefficients and a limit on the ability of the model to correctly predict usual cases.

Despite the importance of controlling outliers, unfortunately practitioners often overlook this activity because, in contrast to the other preparations illustrated throughout the chapter, omitting to detect outliers won't stop the analysis you are working on and you will get your regression coefficients and results (both probably quite inexact). However, having an analysis run smoothly to the end doesn't mean that everything is fine with the analysis itself. An outlier can distort an analysis in two ways depending on whether the anomalous value is on the target variable or on the predictors.

In order to detect outliers, there are a few approaches, some based on the observation of variables taken singularly (the single-variable, or univariate, approach), and some based on reworking all the variables together into a synthetic measure (the multivariate approach).

The best single variable approach is based on the observation of standardized variables and on the plotting of box plots:

- Using standardized variables, everything scoring further than the absolute value of three standard deviations from the mean is suspect, though such a rule of thumb doesn't generalize well if the distribution is not normal

- Using boxplots, the **interquartile range** (shortened to **IQR**; it is the difference between the values at the 75th and the 25th percentile) is used to detect suspect outliers beyond the 75th and 25th percentiles. If there are examples whose values are outside the IQR, they can be considered suspicious, especially if their value is beyond 1.5 times the IQR's boundary value. If they exceed 3 times the IQR's limit, they are almost certainly outliers.

 The Scikit-learn package offers a couple of classes for automatically detecting outliers using sophisticated approaches: `EllipticEnvelope` and `OneClassSVM`. Though a treatise of both these complex algorithms is out of scope here, if outliers or unusual data is the main problem with your data, we suggest having a look at this web page for some quick recipes you can adopt in your scripts: `http://scikit-learn.org/stable/modules/outlier_detection.html`. Otherwise, you could always read our previous book *Python Data Science Essentials*, *Alberto Boschetti* and *Luca Massaron*, *Packt Publishing*.

Outliers on the response

The first step in looking for outliers is to check the response variable. In observing plots of the variable distribution and of the residuals of the regression, it is important to check if there are values that, because of a too high or too low value, are out of the main distribution.

Usually, unless accompanied by outlying predictors, outliers in the response have little impact on the estimated coefficients; however, from a statistical point of view, since they affect the amount of the root-squared error, they reduce the explained variance (the squared r) and inflate the standard errors of the estimate. Both such effects represent a problem when your approach is a statistical one, whereas they are of little concern for data science purposes.

To figure out which responses are outliers, we should first monitor the target distribution. We start by recalling the Boston dataset:

```
In: boston = load_boston()
    dataset = pd.DataFrame(boston.data, columns=boston.feature_names)
    labels = boston.feature_names
    X = dataset
    y = boston.target
```

A `boxplot` function can hint at any outlying values in the target variable:

```
In: plt.boxplot(y,labels=('y'))
plt.show()
```

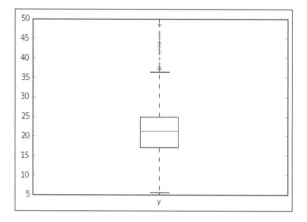

The box display and its whiskers tell us that quite a few values are out of the IQR, so they are suspect ones. We also notice a certain concentration at the value 50; in fact the values are capped at 50.

At this point, we can try to build our regression model and inspect the resulting residuals. We will standardize them using the Root Mean Squared error. An easy approach to implement though it is not the most precise, it is still enough good to reveal any significant problem:

```
In: scatter = plt.plot(linear_regression.predict(X), \
    standardized_residuals, 'wo')
    plt.plot([-10,50],[0,0], "r-")
    plt.plot([-10,50],[3,3], "r--")
    plt.plot([-10,50],[-3,-3], "r--")
    plt.xlabel('fitted values')
    plt.ylabel('standardized residuals')
    plt.show()
```

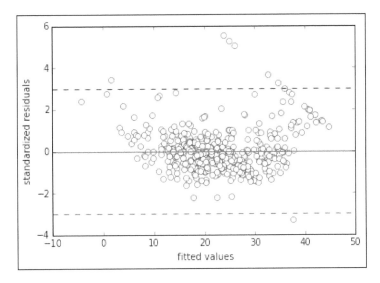

Making a scatterplot of the values fitted by the regression against the standardized residuals, we notice there are a few outlying cases over three standard deviations from the zero mean. The capped values especially, clearly visible in the graph as a line of points, seem problematic.

Outliers among the predictors

As we inspected the target variable, it is now time to have a look also at the predictors. If unusual observations were outliers in the target variable, similar cases in the predictors are instead named influential or high leverage observations because they can really make an impact on more than the **sum of squared errors** (**SSE**), this time influencing coefficients and the intercept—in a word, the entire regression solution (that's why they are so important to catch).

After standardizing, we start having a look at the distributions using boxplots:

```
In: standardization = StandardScaler(with_mean=True, with_std=True)
    Xs = standardization.fit_transform(X)
    boxplot = plt.boxplot(Xs[:,0:7],labels=labels[0:7])
```

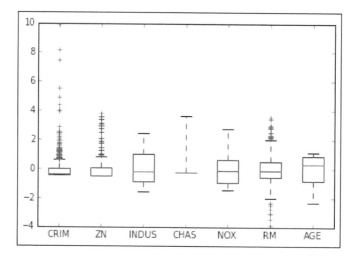

```
In: boxplot = plt.boxplot(Xs[:,7:13],labels=labels[7:13])
```

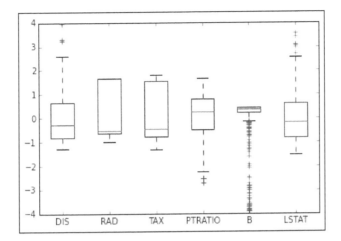

After observing all the boxplots, we can conclude that there are variables with restricted variance, such as **B**, **ZN**, and **CRIM**, which are characterized by a long tail of values. There are also some suspect cases from **DIS** and **LSTAT**. We can delimit all these cases by looking for the values above the represented thresholds, variable after variable, but it would be helpful to catch all of them at once.

Principal Component Analysis (PCA) is a technique that can reduce complex datasets into fewer dimensions, the summation of the original variables of the dataset. Without delving too much into the technicalities of the algorithm, you just need to know that the new dimensions produced by the algorithm have decreasing explicatory power; consequently, plotting the top ones against each other is just like plotting all the dataset's information. By glancing at such synthetic representations, you can spot groups and isolated points that, if very far from the center of the graph, are also quite influential on the regression model.

```
In: from sklearn.decomposition import PCA
    pca = PCA()
    pca.fit(Xs)
    C = pca.transform(Xs)
    print (pca.explained_variance_ratio_)
```

```
Out: [ 0.47097  0.11016  0.09547  0.06598  0.0642   0.05074 \
      0.04146  0.0305   0.02134  0.01694  0.01432  0.01301  0.00489]
```

```
In: import numpy as np
    import matplotlib.pyplot as plt
    explained_variance = pca.explained_variance_ratio_
    plt.title('Portion of explained variance by component')
    range_ = [r+1 for r in range(len(explained_variance))]
    plt.bar(range_,explained_variance, color="b", alpha=0.4, \
    align="center")
    plt.plot(range_,explained_variance,'ro-')
    for pos, pct in enumerate(explained_variance):
       plt.annotate(str(round(pct,2)), (pos+1,pct+0.007))
    plt.xticks(range_)
    plt.show()
```

Out:

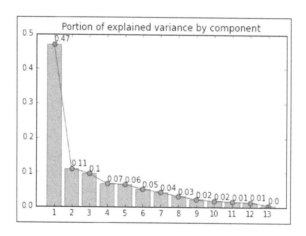

The first dimension created by PCA can explain 47% of the dataset's information, the second and the third 11% and 9.5%, respectively (the `explained_variance_ratio_` method can provide you with such information). Now all we have to do is to plot the first dimension against the second and the third and look for lonely points away from the center because those are our high leverage cases to be investigated:

```
In: scatter = plt.scatter(C[:,0],C[:,1], facecolors='none', \
    edgecolors='black')
    plt.xlabel('Dimension 1')
    plt.ylabel('Dimension 2')
```

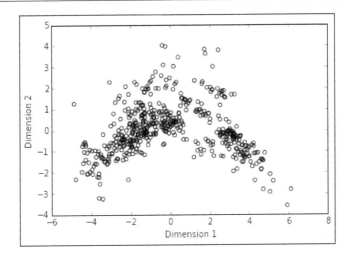

```
In: scatter = plt.scatter(C[:,0],C[:,2], facecolors='none', \
edgecolors='black')
    plt.xlabel('Dimension 1')
    plt.ylabel('Dimension 3')
```

Out:

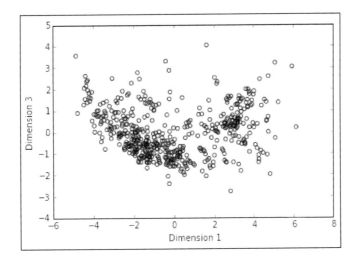

Removing or replacing outliers

After being able to detect outliers and influential observations, we just need to discuss what we can do with them. You might believe it's OK just to delete them but, on the contrary, removing or replacing an outlier is something to consider carefully.

In fact, outlying observations may be justified by three reasons (their remedies change accordingly):

- They are outliers because they are rare occurrences, so they appear unusual with regard to other observations. If this is the case, removing the data points could not be the correct solution because the points are part of the distribution you want to model and they stand out just because of chance. The best solution would be to increase the sample number. If augmenting your sample size is not possible, then remove them or try to resample in order to avoid having them drawn.

- Some errors have happened in the data processing and the outlying observations are from another distribution (some data has been mixed, maybe from different times or another geographical context). In this case, prompt removal is called for.

- The value is a mistake due to faulty input or processing. In such an occurrence, the value has to be considered as missing and you should perform an imputation of the now missing value to get a reasonable value.

As a rule, just keep in mind that removing data points is necessary only when the points are different from the data you want to use for prediction and when, by removing them, you get direct confirmation that they had a lot of influence on the coefficients or on the intercept of the regression model. In all other cases, avoid any kind of selection in order to improve the model since it is a form of data snooping (more on the topic of how data snooping can negatively affect your models in the next chapter).

Summary

In this chapter, we have dealt with many different problems that you may encounter when preparing your data to be analyzed by a linear model.

We started by discussing rescaling variables and understanding how new variables' scales not only permit a better insight into the data, but also help us deal with unexpectedly missing data.

Then, we learned how to encode qualitative variables and deal with the extreme variety of possible levels with unpredictable variables and textual information just by using the hashing trick. We then returned to quantitative variables and learned how to transform in a linear shape and obtain better regression models.

Finally, we dealt with some possible data pathologies, missing and outlying values, showing a few quick fixes that, in spite of their simplicity, are extremely effective and performant.

At this point, before proceeding to more sophisticated linear models, we just need to illustrate the data science principles that can help you obtain really good working predictive engines and not just mere mathematical curve fitting exercises. And that's precisely the topic of the next chapter.

6

Achieving Generalization

We have to confess that, until this point, we've delayed the crucial moment of truth when our linear model has to be put to the test and verified as effectively predicting its target. Up to now, we have just considered whether we were doing a good modeling job by naively looking at a series of good-fit measures, all just telling us if the linear model could be apt at predicting based solely on the information in our training data.

Unless you love sink-or-swim situations, in much the same procedure you'd employ with new software before going into production, you need to apply the correct tests to your model and to be able to anticipate its live performance.

Moreover, no matter your level of skill and experience with such types of models, you can easily be misled into thinking you're building a good model just on the basis of the same data you used to define it. We will therefore introduce you to the fundamental distinction between in-sample and out-of-sample statistics and demonstrate how they risk diverging when you use too many predictors, too few predictors, or simply just the wrong ones.

Here we are then, ready at last to check whether we have done a good job or have to rethink everything from scratch. In this pivotal chapter of the book, before proceeding to more complex techniques, we will introduce you to key data science recipes to thoroughly test your model, fine-tune it optimally, make it economical, and pit it against real, fresh data without any concerns.

In this chapter, you'll get to know how to:

- Test your models, using the most appropriate cost measure, on a validation/test set or using cross-validation
- Select the best features on the basis of statistical tests and experiments
- Make your model more economical by tweaking the cost function
- Use stability selection, an almost automated method for variable selection

Checking on out-of-sample data

Until this point in the book, we have striven to make the regression model fit data, even by modifying the data itself (inputting missing data, removing outliers, transforming for non-linearity, or creating new features). By keeping an eye on measures such as R-squared, we have tried our best to reduce prediction errors, though we have no idea to what extent this was successful.

The problem we face now is that we shouldn't expect a well fit model to automatically perform well on any new data during production.

While defining and explaining the problem, we recall what we said about underfitting. Since we are working with a linear model, we are actually expecting to apply our work to data that has a linear relationship with the response variable. Having a linear relationship means that, with respect to the level of the response variable, our predictors always tend to constantly increase (or decrease) at the same rate. Graphically, on a scatterplot, this is refigured by a straight and very elongated cloud of points that could be crossed by a straight regression line with little or minimal prediction error.

When the relationship is instead non-linear, the rate of change and direction are mutable (alternatively increasing or decreasing). In such a situation, in order to have the linear model work better, we will have to try to make the relationship straight by opportune transformations. Otherwise we will have to try guessing the response by a not-always-successful approximation of a non-linear shape to a linear one.

If for instance the relationship is quadratic (so the functional shape is that of a parabola), using a line will pose the problem of a systematic underestimation or overestimation of the predicted values at certain ranges in the predictor's values. This systematic error is called bias and it is typical of simple models such as linear regression. A prediction model with a high bias will systematically tend to generate erroneous predictions in certain situations. Since inaccuracy of predictions is an undesirable characteristic for a tool that should be able to provide effective forecasts, we have to strive to achieve a better fit to the response by adding new variables and transforming the present ones by polynomial expansion or other transformations. Such efforts constitute the so-called **feature creation phase**.

By doing so, we may find ourselves in a different but no less problematic situation. In fact, when we render our model more and more complex, it will not just better fit the response by catching more and more parts of the unknown function that ties it to the predictors, but also, by adding more and more terms, we are enabling our model to receive that part of the information that is exclusively specific to the data at hand (we call this noise), making it more and more unable to work properly with different data.

You could think about it as a *power of memorization* so that, the more complex the learning algorithm, the more space there will be to fit not-so-useful information from the data we are using for learning. This memorization brings very inconvenient consequences. Though our model appears to have a good fit on our data, as soon as it is applied to a different set, it reveals its inability to predict correctly. In such a situation, contrary to before when the errors were systematic (systematic under- or over-estimation), errors will appear to be erratic, depending on the dataset. This is called variance of the estimates and it could prove more of a problem to you because it can leave you unaware of its existence until you test it against real data. It tends to strike in more complex algorithms and, in its simplest form, linear regression tends to present a higher bias on the estimates than variance. Anyway, adding too many terms and interactions or resorting to polynomial expansion does expose linear models to overfitting.

Testing by sample split

Since we expect the ability to generalize to new data from a model and since we are seldom interested in just fitting or simply memorizing the present data, we need to take some cautionary steps as we build our model. To fight against this problem, the practice of learning from data has defined over the years a series of procedures, based on the scientific method of validating and testing, that we are going to illustrate and practice ourselves.

First, if we want our model to generalize well on new data, we have to test it in such a situation. This means that, if getting new data is not an easy task or a feasible one, we should reserve some data for our tests from the beginning. We can achieve that by randomly splitting our data into two parts, a training set and a test set, using 70–80 percent of the data for the training part and the residual 20–30 percent for testing purposes.

Scikit-learn's `cross_validation` module offers a series of methods that can help us in dealing with all these operations. Let's try it by operating on our usual Boston Housing dataset:

```
In: import pandas as pd
from sklearn.datasets import load_boston
boston = load_boston()
dataset = pd.DataFrame(boston.data,
columns=boston.feature_names)
dataset['target'] = boston.target
observations = len(dataset)
variables = dataset.columns[:-1]
X = dataset.ix[:,:-1]
y = dataset['target'].values
```

After having loaded it, let's first split it into train and test parts:

```
In: from sklearn.cross_validation import train_test_split
X_train, X_test, y_train, y_test = train_test_split(X, y,
test_size=0.30, random_state=101)
print ("Train dataset sample size: %i" % len(X_train))
print ("Test dataset sample size: %i" % len(X_test))

Out:    Train dataset sample size: 354
Test dataset sample size: 152
```

`train_test_split` will separate the data according to the specified quota for testing indicated in the `test_size` parameter. The split will be a random one, and you can deterministically control the results (for replication purposes) using a specific numeric seed in the `random_state` parameter (our choice for the seed is `101`).

Sometimes, reserving an out-of-sample (comprising what is not in-sample—that is, used as a sample for learning from training activity data) is not enough, because we may have to tune some parameters or make specific choices and we want to test the alternatives without having to use the test data. The solution is to reserve another part of our data for validation purposes, which implies checking what parameters could be optimal for our model. We can achieve that using `train_test_split` in two steps:

```
In: X_train, X_out_sample, y_train, y_out_sample = \
train_test_split(X, y, test_size=0.40, random_state=101)
X_validation, X_test, y_validation, y_test = \
train_test_split(X_out_sample, y_out_sample, test_size=0.50,
random_state=101)
print ("Train dataset sample size: %i" % len(X_train))
print ("Validation dataset sample size: %i" % len(X_validation))
print ("Test dataset sample size: %i" % len(X_test))
Out:    Train dataset sample size: 303
Validation dataset sample size: 101
Test dataset sample size: 102
```

Cross-validation

Though helpful in measuring the true error of an hypothesis, dividing your data into train and test (and sometimes also into validation) sets presents some risks that you have to take into account:

- Since it involves sub-sampling (you casually draw out a part of your initial sample), you may incur the risk of drawing sets that are too favorable or unfavorable for training and testing

- By leaving aside a portion of your sample, you reduce the number of examples to learn from, whereas linear models need as many as possible in order to reduce the variance of the estimates, disambiguate collinear variables, and properly model non-linearity

Though we always suggest drawing a small test sample (say 10% of the data) as a final check of the validity of your work, the best way to avoid the aforementioned problems, and easily manage different comparisons of models and parameters, is to apply cross-validation, which requires you to split your data for both training and testing but it does so repetitively until every observation has played the role of training and testing.

In other words, you decide how many mutually exclusive parts to split your data into, then you repeatedly keep on training your model using all the folds but a different one every time; this plays the role of a test set.

 The number of parts you split your data into is usually set to 3, 5, 10, or 20 and you decide on a large number of splits (each one called a **fold**) when you have little training data.

When you have completed the validation, using every single split available as the test set, you first take the average of the results, which tells you with a good degree of accuracy the overall performance of your model when faced with new data (new but not too dissimilar from the one you have at hand). Then you also notice the standard deviation of the cross-validated performances. This is important because, if there's a high deviation (over half of the average performance value), it can indicate that the model has a high variance of the estimates and that it needs more data to work well.

In the following example, you can look at how `KFold` and `StratifiedKFold` (from the Scikit-learn's `cross_validation` module) work.

They are both iterators: you draw the indices for training and testing for each round of cross validation, with the sole difference that `KFold` just applies a random draw. Instead, `StratifiedKFold` takes account of the distribution of a target variable that you want distributed in your training and test samples as if it were on the original set.

As parameters to both classes, you should provide:

- The count of observations to `KFold` and the target vector to `StratifiedKFold`
- The number of folds (10 is usually the standard choice, but you can decrease the number of folds if you have many observations, or you can increase it if your dataset is small)

You should also decide:

- Whether to shuffle the data or take it as it is (shuffling is always recommended)

- Whether to apply a random seed and make the results replicable

```
In: from sklearn.cross_validation import cross_val_score, \
KFold, StratifiedKFold
from sklearn.metrics import make_scorer
from sklearn.preprocessing import PolynomialFeatures
from sklearn.linear_model import LinearRegression
import numpy as np
def RMSE(y_true, y_pred):
    return np.sum((y_true -y_pred)**2)
lm = LinearRegression()
cv_iterator = KFold(n=len(X), n_folds=10, shuffle=True,\
random_state=101)
edges = np.histogram(y, bins=5)[1]
binning = np.digitize(y, edges)
stratified_cv_iterator = StratifiedKFold(binning, n_folds=10,\
shuffle=True, random_state=101)

second_order=PolynomialFeatures(degree=2, interaction_only=False)
third_order=PolynomialFeatures(degree=3, interaction_only=True)

over_param_X = second_order.fit_transform(X)
extra_over_param_X = third_order.fit_transform(X)
cv_score = cross_val_score(lm, over_param_X, y, cv=cv_iterator,\
scoring='mean_squared_error', n_jobs=1)
```

 The n_jobs parameter will set the number of threads involved in the computation of the results by leveraging parallel computations. When it is set to -1 it will automatically use all the available threads, speeding up the calculations to the maximum on your computer. Anyway, depending on the system you are working on, sometimes setting the parameter to something different than 1 will cause problems, slowing down the results. In our examples, as a precautionary measure, it is always set to 1, but you can change its value if you need to cut short the computational time.

At first, we try to get the cross-validation score of an over-parameterized model (a second-degree polynomial expansion of the original features of the Boston dataset). Please notice that the results are negative (though they are squared errors) because of the internals of the automatic function for computing the cross-validation of a model, cross_val_score, from Scikit-learn. This function requires the model, the features, and the target variable as input. It also accepts a cross validation iterator of your choice for the parameter cv, a string for scoring indicating the name of the scoring function to be used (more on this can be found at: http://scikit-learn. org/stable/modules/model_evaluation.html); and finally the number of threads working in parallel on your PC by specifying n_jobs (1 indicates that only one thread is working whereas –1 indicates all the available threads in the system are used):

```
In: print (cv_score)

Out: [-10.79792467 -19.21944292  -8.39077691 -14.79808458
-10.90565129  -7.08445784 -12.8788423   -16.80309722 -32.40034131
-13.66625192]
```

The mean squared error is negative because of the internals of the function, which can only maximize, whereas our cost metric has to be minimized; this is why it has become negative

After removing the sign, we can take both the average and the standard deviation. Here, we can also notice that the standard deviation is high, and maybe we should then try to control the distribution of the target variable, since in the real estate business there are outlying observations due to very rich residential areas:

```
In: print ('Cv score: mean %0.3f std %0.3f' %
(np.mean(np.abs(cv_score)), np.std(cv_score)))
Out: Cv score: mean 14.694 std 6.855
```

To apply such a control, we stratify the target variable; that is, we divide it into bins and we expect the bin distribution to be kept during the cross-validation process:

```
In:cv_score = cross_val_score(lm, over_param_X, y,\
cv=stratified_cv_iterator, scoring='mean_squared_error', \
n_jobs=1)
print ('Cv score: mean %0.3f std %0.3f' % \
        (np.mean(np.abs(cv_score)), np.std(cv_score)))
Out: Cv score: mean 13.584 std 5.226
```

In the end, controlling for the response distribution really lowers the standard deviation of the estimated error (and our expected average). A successful stratification attempt in cross-validation suggests that we should train on a correctly distributed training sample, otherwise we may achieve an outcome model not always working properly due to bad sampling.

> As a final remark on the topic of cross-validation, we suggest using it mostly for evaluating parameters, and always relying on a small drawn out test set for performance validation. In fact, it is a bit tricky, but if you cross-validate too many times (for example changing the seed) looking for the best performance, you will end up with the best result, which is another form of overfitting called snooping (this also happens if you do the same with the test set). Instead, when you use cross-validation to choose between parameters, you just decide on the best among the options, not on the absolute cross-validation value.

Bootstrapping

Sometimes, if the training data is really small, even dividing into folds can penalize how the model is trained. The statistical technique of bootstrapping allows repeating the training and testing validation sequence (allowing precise estimations of both the mean and standard deviation of expected results) for a large number of times by trying to replicate the underlying distribution of the data.

Bootstrapping is based on sampling with repetition, which implies allowing an observation to be drawn multiple times. Usually bootstraps draw the number of observations equivalent to the original size of the dataset. Also, there's always a part of the observations that it is left untouched, equivalent to a third of the available observations, which can be used for validating:

```
In: import random
def Bootstrap(n, n_iter=3, random_state=None):
        """
        Random sampling with replacement cross-validation generator.
        For each iter a sample bootstrap of the indexes [0, n) is
        generated and the function returns the obtained sample
        and a list of all the excluded indexes.
        """
        if random_state:
            random.seed(random_state)
        for j in range(n_iter):
            bs = [random.randint(0, n-1) for i in range(n)]
            out_bs = list({i for i in range(n)} - set(bs))
```

```
         yield bs, out_bs

boot = Bootstrap(n=10, n_iter=5, random_state=101)
for train_idx, validation_idx in boot:
print (train_idx, validation_idx)
```

The output will be shown as the following:

```
[9, 3, 8, 5, 7, 0, 8, 3, 9, 3] [1, 2, 4, 6]
[4, 7, 3, 5, 7, 1, 4, 3, 2, 1] [0, 8, 9, 6]
[7, 8, 5, 3, 7, 5, 3, 6, 6, 3] [0, 1, 2, 9, 4]
[1, 6, 7, 4, 3, 1, 9, 5, 4, 6] [0, 8, 2]
[6, 3, 6, 1, 6, 6, 0, 7, 3, 8] [9, 2, 4, 5]
```

As illustrated by the preceding example (unfortunately, this method is not part of Scikit-learn, having being recently deprecated), in a set of 10 observations, on average four observations are left available for testing purposes. However, in a bootstrapping process, it is not just the left out cases that provide insight. A model is in fact fitted to the training dataset, and we can also inspect how the coefficients are determined in the bootstrap replications, thus allowing us to figure out how stable each coefficient is:

```
In: import numpy as np
boot = Bootstrap(n=len(X), n_iter=10, random_state=101)
lm = LinearRegression()
bootstrapped_coef = np.zeros((10,13))
for k, (train_idx, validation_idx) in enumerate(boot):
        lm.fit(X.ix[train_idx,:],y[train_idx])
        bootstrapped_coef[k,:] = lm.coef_
```

For instance, the tenth coefficient index (PTRATIO) is quite stable in both sign and value:

```
In: print(bootstrapped_coef[:,10])

Output: [-1.04150741 -0.93651754 -1.09205904 -1.10422447 -0.9982515
-0.79789273 -0.89421685 -0.92320895 -1.0276369  -0.79189224]
```

Whereas the sixth coefficient (AGE) has great variability, often even changing sign:

```
In: print(bootstrapped_coef[:,6])

Out: [-0.01930727  0.00053026 -0.00026774  0.00607945  0.02225979
-0.00089469  0.01922754  0.02164681  0.01243348 -0.02693115]
```

In conclusion, bootstrap is a form of replication that can be run as many times as you decide, and this allows you to create multiple models and evaluate their results in a similar way to a cross-validation procedure.

Greedy selection of features

By following our experiments throughout the book, you may have noticed that adding new variables is always a great success in a linear regression model. That's especially true for training errors and it happens not just when we insert the right variables but also when we place the wrong ones. Puzzlingly, when we add redundant or non-useful variables, there is always a more or less positive impact on the fit of the model.

The reason is easily explained; since regression models are high-bias models, they find it beneficial to augment their complexity by increasing the number of coefficients they use. Thus, some of the new coefficients can be used to fit the noise and other details present in data. It is precisely the memorization/overfitting effect we discussed before. When you have as many coefficients as observations, your model can become saturated (that's the technical term used in statistics) and you could have a perfect prediction because basically you have a coefficient to learn every single response in the training set.

Let's make this concept more concrete with a quick example using a training set (in-sample observations) and a test set (out-sample observations). Let's start by finding out how many cases and features we have and what the baseline performance is (for both in-sample and out-sample):

```
In: from sklearn.metrics import mean_squared_error
from sklearn.linear_model import LinearRegression
from sklearn.cross_validation import train_test_split
X_train, X_test, y_train, y_test = train_test_split(X, y,
test_size=0.30, random_state=3)
lm = LinearRegression()
lm.fit(X_train,y_train)
print ('Train (cases, features) = %s' % str(X_train.shape))
print ('Test  (cases, features) = %s' % str(X_test.shape))
print ('In-sample  mean squared error %0.3f' % mean_squared_error(
        y_train,lm.predict(X_train)))
print ('Out-sample mean squared error %0.3f' % mean_squared_error(
        y_test,lm.predict(X_test)))

Out:   Train (cases, features) = (354, 13)
Test  (cases, features) = (152, 13)
In-sample  mean squared error 22.420
Out-sample mean squared error 22.440
```

The best approach would be to use a cross validation or bootstrap for such an experiment, not just a plain train/test split, but we want to make it fast, and that's the reason why we decided on such a solution. We assure you that using more sophisticated estimation techniques doesn't change the results of the experiment.

Therefore, we have similar in-sample and out-sample errors. We can start working on improving our model using polynomial expansions:

```
In: from sklearn.preprocessing import PolynomialFeatures
second_order=PolynomialFeatures(degree=2, interaction_only=False)
third_order=PolynomialFeatures(degree=3, interaction_only=True)
```

First, we apply the second-order polynomial expansion:

```
In: lm.fit(second_order.fit_transform(X_train),y_train)
print ('(cases, features) = %s' % str(second_order.fit_transform(
        X_train).shape))
print ('In-sample  mean squared error %0.3f' %
mean_squared_error(y_train,lm.predict(second_order.fit_transform(
        X_train))))
print ('Out-sample mean squared error %0.3f' %
mean_squared_error(y_test,lm.predict(second_order.fit_transform(
        X_test))))
Out:    (cases, features) = (354, 105)
In-sample  mean squared error 5.522
Out-sample mean squared error 12.034
```

It seems that the good in-sample results have little correspondence with the out-sample test. Though the out-sample performance has improved, the lack of comparability in results is a clear sign of overfitting; there are some more useful coefficients in the model but most of them are just there to catch noise in data.

We now go to extremes and we test the third-degree polynomial expansion (using only interactions though):

```
In: lm.fit(third_order.fit_transform(X_train), y_train)
print ('(cases, features) = %s' % str(third_order.fit_transform(
        X_train).shape))
print ('In-sample  mean squared error %0.3f' %
mean_squared_error(y_train,lm.predict(third_order.fit_transform(
        X_train))))
print ('Out-sample mean squared error %0.3f' %
mean_squared_error(y_test,lm.predict(third_order.fit_transform(
        X_test))))
```

```
Out:    (cases, features) = (354, 378)
In-sample  mean squared error 0.438
Out-sample mean squared error 85777.890
```

Now, clearly something very bad has happened to our model. Having more coefficients than observations (p>n), we achieved a perfect fit on our training set. However, on the out-sample validation, it seems that our model achieved the same performance as a random number generator. In the next few paragraphs, we will show you how to take advantage of an increased number of features without incurring any of the problems demonstrated by the previous code snippets.

The Madelon dataset

For the task of selecting the best subset of variables among many noisy and collinear ones, we decided to accompany our usual Boston house dataset with a tricky one, the Madelon dataset (https://archive.ics.uci.edu/ml/datasets/Madelon). It is an artificial dataset (that is generated using an algorithm) presented at the NIPS 2003 (the seventh Annual Conference on Neural Information Processing Systems) during a contest on feature selection.

The dataset is particularly challenging because it has been generated by placing 32 distinct clusters of points (16 from the positive group, 16 from the negative one) on the vertices of a five-dimension hypercube. The resulting 500 features and 2,000 cases have been extracted from various transformations of the five metric dimensions. To make things harder, some random numbers have been added to the features to act as noise and a few responses have been flipped (the flipped ones amount to 1%). All these intricate transformations make dealing with the modeling quite difficult, especially for linear models, since the relationship of most of the features with the response is definitely non-linear. This is really helpful for our exemplification because it clearly demonstrates how a direct inclusion of all the features is detrimental to the accuracy of out-of-sample predictions.

To download and make available on your computer such an interesting and challenging dataset, please carry out the following instructions and allow some time for your computer to download the data from the external website where it is stored:

```
In: try:
import urllib.request as urllib2
  except:
    import urllib2
  import numpy as np
  train_data = 'https://archive.ics.uci.edu/ml/machine-learning-
  databases/madelon/MADELON/madelon_train.data'
  validation_data = 'https://archive.ics.uci.edu/ml/
  machine-learning-databases/madelon/MADELON/madelon_valid.data'
```

```
train_response = 'https://archive.ics.uci.edu/ml/
  machine-learning-databases/madelon/MADELON/madelon_train.labels'
  validation_response = 'https://archive.ics.uci.edu/ml/
  machine-learning-databases/madelon/madelon_valid.labels'
try:
     Xt = np.loadtxt(urllib2.urlopen(train_data))
     yt = np.loadtxt(urllib2.urlopen(train_response))
     Xv = np.loadtxt(urllib2.urlopen(validation_data))
     yv = np.loadtxt(urllib2.urlopen(validation_response))
except:
    # In case downloading the data doesn't works,
# just manually download the files into the working directory
     Xt = np.loadtxt('madelon_train.data')
     yt = np.loadtxt('madelon_train.labels')
     Xv = np.loadtxt('madelon_valid.data')
     yv = np.loadtxt('madelon_valid.labels')
```

After finishing loading both the training and validation sets, we can start exploring some of the information available:

```
In: print ('Training set: %i observations %i feature' %
(Xt.shape))
   print ('Validation set: %i observations %i feature' %
(Xv.shape))
Out:  Training set: 2000 observations 500 feature
     Validation set: 600 observations 500 feature
```

Naturally, we won't touch the validation set (we won't even glance at it or it would be snooping), but we can try to figure out the situation with the training set:

```
In:from scipy.stats import describe
   print (describe(Xt))
```

The output is quite lengthy and it is put in matrix form (therefore it is not reported here), but it really tells us everything about the mean, min, max, variance, skewness, and kurtosis for each feature in the dataset. A fast glance through it doesn't reveal anything special; however, it explicits that all the variables have an approximately normal distribution and that they have a limited range of values. We can proceed with our exploration using a graphical representation of correlations among the variables:

```
import matplotlib.pyplot as plt
import matplotlib as mpl
%matplotlib inline

def visualize_correlation_matrix(data, hurdle = 0.0):
    R = np.corrcoef(data, rowvar=0)
```

```
R[np.where(np.abs(R)<hurdle)] = 0.0
heatmap = plt.pcolor(R, cmap=mpl.cm.coolwarm, alpha=0.8)
heatmap.axes.set_frame_on(False)
plt.xticks(rotation=90)
plt.tick_params(axis='both', which='both', bottom='off',\
            top='off', left = 'off',right = 'off')
plt.colorbar()
plt.show()

visualize_correlation_matrix(Xt[:,100:150], hurdle=0.0)
```

Check the following screenshot:

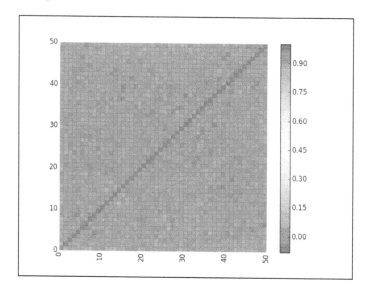

After a glance at a portion of the features and their respective correlation, we can notice that just a couple of them have a significant correlation, whereas the others are mildly related. This gives the impression of noisy relationships between them, thus rendering an effective selection quite complicated.

As a last step, we check how a simple logistic regression model would score in terms of the error measured using the area under the curve metric.

 Area under the curve (AUC) is a measure derived from comparing the rate of correct positive results against the rate of incorrect ones at different classification thresholds. It is a bit tricky to calculate, so we suggest always relying on the `roc_auc_score` function from the `sklearn.metrics` module.

Logistic regression classifies an observation as positive if the threshold is over 0.5 since such a split is always proved to be optimal, but we can freely change that threshold. To increase the precision at a top selection of results we just raise the threshold from 0.5 to 1.0 (raising the threshold increases the accuracy in the selected range). Instead, if we intend to increase the total number of guessed positive cases we just choose a threshold inferior to 0.5 down to almost 0.0 (lowering the threshold increases the coverage of positive cases in the selected range).

The AUC error measure helps us determine whether our predictions are ordered properly, no matter their effective precision in terms of value. Thus, AUC is the ideal error measure to evaluate an algorithm for selection. If you order results properly based on probability, no matter if the guessed probability is correct or not, you can simply pick the correct selection to be used by your project by changing the 0.5 threshold — that is, by taking a certain number of the top results.

In our case, the baseline AUC measure is `0.602`, a quite disappointing value since a random selection should bring us a `0.5` value (`1.0` is the maximum possible):

```
In: from sklearn.cross_validation import cross_val_score
    from sklearn.linear_model import LogisticRegression
    logit = LogisticRegression()
    logit.fit(Xt,yt)

    from sklearn.metrics import roc_auc_score
    print ('Training area under the curve: %0.3f' % \
    roc_auc_score(yt,logit.predict_proba(Xt)[:,1]))
    print ('Validation area under the curve: %0.3f' % \
    roc_auc_score(yv,logit.predict_proba(Xv)[:,1]))

Out:   Training area under the curve: 0.824
    Validation area under the curve: 0.602
```

Univariate selection of features

Given this new tricky dataset, we really have to deal with a large number of either irrelevant or redundant features. Hopefully, after removing them all, our model should increase its performance, and this is indicated by the large difference in AUC score between the in-sample and out-sample values that we got from our last code snippet.

In addition, if interpreting your model is a valuable addition, you really should remove non-useful variables, striving for the simplest possible form of your linear model as dictated by Occam's razor, a commonplace practice in science, favoring simpler solutions against more complex ones when their difference in performance is not marked.

Feature selection can help in both increasing the model out-sample performance and its human readability by retaining only the most predictive set of variables in the model, in some cases just the best ones and in others the set that works the best in unison.

There are quite a few feature selection methods. The simplest approach is the univariate method, which evaluates how good a variable is by estimating its predictive value when taken alone in respect of the response.

This usually involves using statistical tests, and Scikit-learn offers three possible tests:

- The f_regression class, which works out an F-test (a statistical test for comparing different regression solutions) and a p-value (interpretable as the probability value in which we observed a difference by chance) and reveals the best features for a regression

- The f_class, which is an Anova F-test (a statistical test for comparing differences among classes), another statistical and related method that will prove useful for classification problems

- The Chi2 class, which is a chi-squared test (a statistical test on count data), a good choice when your problem is classification and your answer variable is a count or a binary (in every case, a positive number such as units sold or money earned)

All such tests output a score and a statistical test expressed by a p-value. High scores, confirmed by small p-values (under 0.05, indicating a low probability that the score has been obtained by luck), will provide you with confirmation that a certain variable is useful for predicting your target.

In our example, we will use f_class (since we are working on a classification problem now) and we will have the SelectPercentile function help us by selecting a certain percentage of high-scoring features:

```
In: from sklearn.feature_selection import SelectPercentile, f_classif
selector = SelectPercentile(f_classif, percentile=50)
selector.fit(Xt,yt)
variable_filter = selector.get_support()
```

After selecting the upper half, hoping to have cut off the most irrelevant features and to have kept the important ones, we plot our results on an histogram to reveal the distribution of the scores:

```
In: plt.hist(selector.scores_, bins=50, histtype='bar')
plt.grid()
plt.show()
```

Look at the following screenshot:

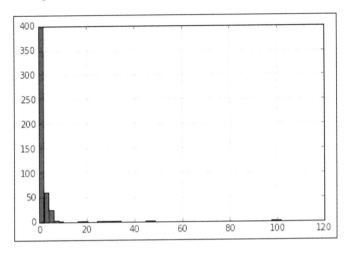

Noticeably, most scores are near zero, with a few high-ranking ones. Now we are going to pick the features we assume to be important by directly selecting a threshold empirically chosen for its convenience:

```
In: variable_filter = selector.scores_ > 10
print ("Number of filtered variables: %i" % \
np.sum(variable_filter))
from sklearn.preprocessing import PolynomialFeatures
interactions = PolynomialFeatures(degree=2,
interaction_only=True)
Xs = interactions.fit_transform(Xt[:,variable_filter])
print ("Number of variables and interactions: %i" % Xs.shape[1])

Out:    Number of filtered variables: 13
Number of variables and interactions: 92
```

Now, we have reduced our dataset to just the core features. At this point, it does make sense to test a polynomial expansion and try to automatically catch any relevant non-linear relationship in our model:

```
In: logit.fit(Xs,yt)
Xvs = interactions.fit_transform(Xv[:,variable_filter])
·print ('Validation area Under the Curve ' + \
        'before recursive \ selection:   %0.3f' % \
        roc_auc_score(yv,logit.predict_proba(Xvs)[:,1]))

Out:    Validation area Under the Curve before
recursive selection: 0.808
```

The resulting validation score (out-sample) is about 0.81, a very promising value given our initial overfitted score of 0.82 on the training set. Of course, we can decide to stop here or try to go on filtering even the polynomial expansion; feature selection is really a never-ending job, though after a certain point you have to realize that only slightly incremental results are possible from further tuning.

Recursive feature selection

The only problem with univariate selection is that it will decide the best features by considering each feature separately from the others, not verifying how they work together in unison. Consequently, redundant variables are not infrequently picked (due to collinearity).

A multivariate approach, such as recursive elimination, can avoid this problem; however, it is more computationally expensive.

Recursive elimination works by starting with the full model and by trying to exclude each variable in turn, evaluating the removal effect by cross-validation estimation. If certain variables have a negligible effect on the model's performance, then the elimination algorithm just prunes them. The process stops when any further removal is proven to hurt the ability of the model to predict correctly.

Here is a demonstration of how RFECV, Scikit-learn's implementation of recursive elimination, works. We will use the Boston dataset enhanced by second-degree polynomial expansion, thus working on a regression problem this time:

```
In: from sklearn.feature_selection import RFECV
from sklearn.cross_validation import KFold
from sklearn.cross_validation import train_test_split
X_train, X_test, y_train, y_test = \
    train_test_split(X, y, test_size=0.30, random_state=1)

lm = LinearRegression()
cv_iterator = KFold(
    n=len(X_train), n_folds=10, shuffle=True, random_state=101)
recursive_selector = RFECV(estimator=lm, step=1, cv=cv_iterator,
scoring='mean_squared_error')
recursive_selector.fit(second_order.fit_transform(X_train),
y_train)
print ('Initial number of features : %i' %
        second_order.fit_transform(X_train).shape[1])
print ('Optimal number of features : %i' %
        recursive_selector.n_features_)

Out:    Initial number of features : 105
Optimal number of features : 52
```

Given an estimator (our model), a cross validation iterator, and an error measure, RFECV will find out after a while that half of the features can be dropped from the model without fear of worsening its performance:

```
In: essential_X_train = recursive_selector.transform(
    second_order.fit_transform(X_train))
essential_X_test  = recursive_selector.transform(
    second_order.fit_transform(X_test))
lm.fit(essential_X_train, y_train)
print ('cases = %i features = %i' % essential_X_test.shape)
print ('In-sample  mean squared error %0.3f' % \
mean_squared_error(y_train,lm.predict(essential_X_train)))
print ('Out-sample mean squared error %0.3f' % \
mean_squared_error(y_test,lm.predict(essential_X_test)))

Out:   cases = 152 features = 52
In-sample  mean squared error 7.834
Out-sample mean squared error 11.523
```

A test-based check will reveal that now the out-sample performance is 11.5. For further confirmation, we can also run a cross-validation and obtain a similar result:

```
In: edges = np.histogram(y, bins=5)[1]
binning = np.digitize(y, edges)
stratified_cv_iterator = StratifiedKFold(binning, n_folds=10,
shuffle=True, random_state=101)
essential_X = recursive_selector.transform(
    second_order.fit_transform(X))
cv_score = cross_val_score(
    lm, essential_X, y, cv=stratified_cv_iterator,
    scoring='mean_squared_error', n_jobs=1)
print ('Cv score: mean %0.3f std %0.3f' % (np.mean(np.abs(cv_score)),
np.std(cv_score)))

Out: Cv score: mean 11.400 std 3.779
```

Regularization optimized by grid-search

Regularization is another way to modify the role of variables in a regression model to prevent overfitting and to achieve simpler functional forms. The interesting aspect of this alternative approach is that it actually doesn't require manipulating your original dataset, making it suitable for systems that learn and predict online from large amounts of features and observations, without human intervention. Regularization works by enriching the learning process using a penalization for too complex models to shrink (or reduce to zero) coefficients relative to variables that are irrelevant for your prediction term or are redundant, as they are highly correlated with others present in the model (the collinearity problem seen before).

Ridge (L2 regularization)

The idea behind ridge regression is simple and straightforward: if the problem is the presence of many variables, which affect the regression model because of their coefficient, all we have to do is reduce their coefficient so their contribution is minimized and they do not influence the result so much.

Such a result is easily achieved by working out a different cost function. Working on the error in respect of the answer, the cost function can be balanced by imposing a penalization value depending on how large the coefficients are.

In the following formula, a reprisal of the formula in the *Chapter 2, Approaching Simple Linear Regression* paragraph *Gradient descent at work*, the weight update is modified by the presence of a negative term, which is the square of the weight reduced by a factor expressed by lambda. Consequently, the larger the coefficient, the more it will be reduced during the update phase of the gradient descent optimization:

$$w_j = w_j - \frac{\alpha}{n} * \left(\sum (Xw - y) * x_j - \lambda * w_j^2 \right)$$

In the preceding formula, each single coefficient j, whose value is represented by w_j, is updated by the gradient descent learning rate α / n, where n is the number of observations. The learning rate is multiplied by the summed deviance of the prediction (the gradient). The novelty is the presence in the gradient of a penalization, calculated as the squared coefficient multiplied by a λ lambda coefficient.

In this way, the error will be propagated to the coefficients only if there is an advantage (a large deviance in predictions), otherwise the coefficients will be reduced in value. The advantage is controlled by the λ lambda value, which has to be found empirically according to the specific model that we are building.

An example will clarify how this new approach works. First, we have to use the `Ridge` class from Scikit-learn, if our problem is a regression, or we use the penalty parameter in the `LogisticRegression` specification (`LogisticRegression(C=1.0, penalty='l2', tol=0.01)`):

```
In: from sklearn.linear_model import Ridge
ridge = Ridge(normalize=True)
ridge.fit(second_order.fit_transform(X), y)
lm.fit(second_order.fit_transform(X), y)
```

The impact of regularization on the model is controlled by the `alpha` parameter in the `Ridge`, and by the `C` parameter in `LogisticRegression`.

The smaller the value of `alpha`, the less the coefficient values are controlled by the regularization, the higher its value with increased regularization, the more the coefficients are shrunk. Its functioning can be easily memorized as a shrinkage parameter: the higher the value, the higher the shrinkage of the complexity of the model. However, the C parameter in `LogisticRegression` is exactly the inverse, with smaller values corresponding to high regularization ($alpha = 1/2C$).

After having completely fitted the model, we can have a look at how the values of coefficients are defined now:

```
In: print ('Average coefficient: Non regularized = %0.3f Ridge = \
%0.3f' % (np.mean(lm.coef_), np.mean(ridge.coef_)))
print ('Min coefficient: Non regularized = %0.3f Ridge = %0.3f' \
% (np.min(lm.coef_), np.min(ridge.coef_)))
print ('Max coefficient: Non regularized = %0.3f Ridge = %0.3f' \
% (np.max(lm.coef_), np.max(ridge.coef_)))

Out:   Average coefficient: Non regularized = 1.376 Ridge = -0.027
Min coefficient: Non regularized = -40.040 Ridge = -2.013
Max coefficient: Non regularized = 142.329 Ridge = 1.181
```

Now, the average coefficient value is almost near zero and the values are placed in a much shorter range than before. In the regularized form, no single coefficient has the weight to influence or, worse, disrupt a prediction.

Grid search for optimal parameters

Until now, we haven't had much to decide about the model itself, no matter whether we decided on a logistic or a linear regression. All that mattered was to properly transform our variables (and actually, we have learned that this is not an easy task either); however, the introduction of the L2 parameter brings forth much more complexity since we also have to heuristically set a value to maximize the performance of the model.

Keeping on working with cross-validation, which ensures we evaluate the performance of our model in a realistic way, a good solution to this problem is to check systematically the result of our model given a range of possible values of our parameter.

The `GridSearchCV` class in the Scikit-learn package can be set using our preferred `cv` iterator and scoring after setting a dictionary explicating what parameters have to be changed in the model (the key) and a range of values to be evaluated (a list of values related to the key), finally assigning it to the `param_grid` parameter of the class:

```
In: from sklearn.grid_search import GridSearchCV
edges = np.histogram(y, bins=5)[1]
```

```
binning = np.digitize(y, edges)
stratified_cv_iterator = StratifiedKFold(
    binning, n_folds=10,shuffle=True, random_state=101)
search = GridSearchCV(
    param_grid={'alpha':np.logspace(-4,2,7)},
    estimator=ridge, scoring ='mean_squared_error',
    n_jobs=1, refit=True, cv=stratified_cv_iterator)
search.fit(second_order.fit_transform(X), y)
print ('Best alpha: %0.5f' % search.best_params_['alpha'])
print ('Best CV mean squared error: %0.3f' % np.abs(
        search.best_score_))


Out:   Best alpha: 0.00100
Best CV mean squared error: 11.883
```

The result of the search, which can take some time when there are many possible model variations to test, can be explored using the attribute grid_scores_:

```
In: search.grid_scores_
Out:
[mean: -12.45899, std: 5.32834, params: {'alpha': 0.0001},
 mean: -11.88307, std: 4.92960, params: {'alpha': 0.001},
 mean: -12.64747, std: 4.66278, params: {'alpha': 0.01},
 mean: -16.83243, std: 5.28501, params: {'alpha': 0.1},
 mean: -22.91860, std: 5.95064, params: {'alpha': 1.0},
 mean: -37.81253, std: 8.63064, params: {'alpha': 10.0},
 mean: -66.65745, std: 10.35740, params: {'alpha': 100.0}]
```

The maximum scoring value (actually using RMSE we should minimize the result, so the grid search works with the negative value of RMSE) is achieved when alpha is 0.001. In addition, the standard deviation of the cross-validation score is minimal in respect of our possible solutions, confirming to us that it is the best solution available at hand.

If you would like to further optimize the results, just explore, using a second grid search, the range of values around the winning solution – that is, in our specific case from 0.0001 to 0.01, you may find a slightly better value in terms of expected results or stability of the solution (expressed by the standard deviation).

Naturally, GridSearchCV can be used effectively when more parameters to be optimized are involved. Please be aware that the more parameters, the more trials have to be made, and the resulting number is a combination—that is, a multiplication—of all the possible values to be tested. Consequently, if you are testing four values of a hypermeter and four of another one, in the end you will need 4×4 trials and, depending on the cross-validation folds, let's say in our case 10, you'll have your CPU compute $4 \times 4 \times 10 = 160$ models. Searches that are more complex may even involve testing thousands of models, and although GridSearchCV can parallelize all its computations, in certain cases it can still be a problem. We are going to address a possible solution in the next paragraph.

We have illustrated how to grid-search using the more general GridSearchCV. There is anyway a specialized function for automatically creating out-of-the-box a cross-validated optimized ridge regression using Scikit-learn: RidgeCV. There are automated classes also for the other regularization variants we are going to illustrate, LassoCV and ElasticNetCV. Actually, these classes, apart from being more synthetic than the approach we described, are much faster in finding the best parameter because they follow an optimization path (so they actually do not exhaustively search along the grid).

Random grid search

Searching for good combinations of hyper-parameters in a grid is a really time-consuming task, especially if there are many parameters; the number of combinations can really explode and thus your CPU can take a long time to compute the results.

Moreover, it is often the case that not all hyper-parameters are important; in such a case, when grid-searching, you are really wasting time checking on a large number of solutions that aren't really distinguishable from one another, while instead omitting to check important values on critical parameters.

The solution is a random grid search, which is not only much speedier than the grid search, but it is also much more efficient, as pointed out in a paper by the scholars James Bergstra and Yoshua Bengio (http://www.jmlr.org/papers/volume13/bergstra12a/bergstra12a.pdf).

Random search works by sampling possible parameters from ranges or distribution that you point out (the NumPy package has quite a lot of distributions that can be used, but for this test we found that logspace function is ideal for systematically exploring the L1/L2 range). Given a certain number of trials, there is a high chance that you can get the right hyper-parameters.

Here, we try using just `10` values sampled from `100` possible ones (so reducing our running time to `1/10` in respect of a grid search):

```
In: from sklearn.grid_search import RandomizedSearchCV
from scipy.stats import expon
np.random.seed(101)
search_func=RandomizedSearchCV(
    estimator=ridge, n_jobs=1, iid=False, refit=True, n_iter=10,
    param_distributions={'alpha':np.logspace(-4,2,100)},
    scoring='mean_squared_error', cv=stratified_cv_iterator)

search_func.fit(second_order.fit_transform(X), y)
print ('Best alpha: %0.5f' % search_func.best_params_['alpha'])
print ('Best CV mean squared error: %0.3f' % np.abs(
        search_func.best_score_))

Out:   Best alpha: 0.00046
Best CV mean squared error: 11.790
```

> As a heuristic, the number of trials of a random search depends on the number of possible combinations that may be tried under a grid search. As a matter of statistical probability, it has been empirically observed that the most efficient number of random trials should be between 30 and 60. More than 60 random trials is unlikely to bring many more performance improvements from tuning hyper parameters than previously assessed.

Lasso (L1 regularization)

Ridge regression is not really a selection method. Penalizing the useless coefficients through keeping them all in the model won't provide much clarity about what variables work the best in your linear regression and won't improve its comprehensibility.

The lasso regularization, a recent addition by Rob Tibshirani, using the absolute value instead of the quadratic one in the regularization penalization, does help to shrink many coefficient values to zero, thus making your vector of resulting coefficients sparse:

$$w_j = w_j - \frac{\alpha}{n} * \left(\sum (Xw - y) * x_j + \lambda * |w_j| \right)$$

Again, we have a formula similar to the previous one for L2 regularization but now the penalization term is made up of λ lambda multiplied by the absolute value of the coefficient.

The procedure is the same as in the ridge regression; you just have to use a different class called `Lasso`. If instead your problem is a classification one, in your logistic regression you just have to specify that the parameter `penalty` is `'l1'`:

```
In: from sklearn.linear_model import Lasso
lasso = Lasso(alpha=1.0, normalize=True, max_iter=10**5)
#The following comment shows an example of L1 logistic regression
#lr_l1 = LogisticRegression(C=1.0, penalty='l1', tol=0.01)
```

Let's check what happens to the previously seen regularization of the linear regression on the Boston dataset when using `Lasso`:

```
In: from sklearn.grid_search import RandomizedSearchCV
from scipy.stats import expon
np.random.seed(101)
search_func=RandomizedSearchCV(
    estimator=lasso, n_jobs=1, iid=False, refit=True, n_iter=15,
    param_distributions={'alpha':np.logspace(-5,2,100)},
    scoring='mean_squared_error', cv=stratified_cv_iterator)

search_func.fit(second_order.fit_transform(X), y)
print ('Best alpha: %0.5f' % search_func.best_params_['alpha'])
print ('Best CV mean squared error: %0.3f' % np.abs(
        search_func.best_score_))

Out:  Best alpha: 0.00006
Best CV mean squared error: 12.235
```

From the viewpoint of performance, we obtained a slightly worse but comparable mean squared error value.

> You will have noticed that using the `Lasso` regularization takes more time (there are usually more iterations) than applying the ridge one. A good strategy for speeding up things is to apply the lasso only on a subset of the data (which should take less time), find out the best alpha, and then apply it directly to your complete sample to verify whether the performance results are consistent.

However, what is most interesting is evaluating what coefficients have been reduced to zero:

```
In: print ('Zero value coefficients: %i out of %i' % \
(np.sum(~(search_func.best_estimator_.coef_==0.0)),
len(search_func.best_estimator_.coef_)))

Out:  Zero value coefficients: 85 out of 105
```

Now, our second-degree polynomial expansion has been reduced to just 20 working variables, as if the model has been reduced by a recursive selection, with the advantage that you don't have to change the dataset structure; you just apply your data to the model and only the right variables will work out the prediction for you.

 If you are wondering what kind of regularization to use first, `ridge` or `lasso`, a good rule of thumb is to first run a linear regression without any regularization and check the distribution of the standardized coefficients. If there are many with similar values, then `ridge` is the best choice; if instead you notice that there are a few important coefficients and many lesser ones, using `lasso` is advisable to remove the unimportant ones. In any case, when you have more variables than observations, you should always use `lasso`.

Elastic net

Lasso can rapidly and without much hassle reduce the number of working variables in a prediction model, rendering it simpler and much more generalizable. Its strategy is simple: it aims to retain only the variables that contribute to the solution. Consequently, if, by chance, among your features you have a couple of strongly collinear variables, an L1 regularization will keep just one of them, on the basis of the characteristics of the data itself (noise and correlation with other variables contribute to the choice).

Such a characteristic anyway may prove undesirable because of the instability of the L1 solution (the noise and strength of correlations may change with the data) since having all the correlated variables in the model guarantees a more reliable model (especially if they all depend on a factor that is not included into the model). Thus, the alternative elastic net approach has been devised by combining the effects of L1 and L2 regularization.

In elastic net (Scikit-learn's `ElasticNet` class), you always have an `alpha` parameter that controls the impact of regularization on the determination of the model's coefficients, plus a `l1_ratio` parameter that helps weight the combination between the L1 and L2 parts of the regularization part of the cost function. When the parameter is `0.0`, there is no role for L1 so it is equivalent to a ridge. When it is set to `1.0`, you have a lasso regression. Intermediate values act by mixing the effects of both types of regularizations; thus, while some variables will still be reduced to zero value coefficients, collinear variables will be reduced to the same coefficient, allowing them all to be still present in the model formulation.

In the following example, we try solving our model with elastic net regularization:

```
In: from sklearn.linear_model import ElasticNet
elasticnet = ElasticNet(alpha=1.0, l1_ratio=0.15, normalize=True,
  max_iter=10**6, random_state=101)
  from sklearn.grid_search import RandomizedSearchCV
  from scipy.stats import expon
  np.random.seed(101)
  search_func=RandomizedSearchCV(estimator=elasticnet,
  param_distributions={'alpha':np.logspace(-5,2,100),
  'l1_ratio':np.arange(0.0, 1.01, 0.05)}, n_iter=30,
scoring='mean_squared_error', n_jobs=1, iid=False,
refit=True, cv=stratified_cv_iterator)
search_func.fit(second_order.fit_transform(X), y)
print ('Best alpha: %0.5f' %
search_func.best_params_['alpha'])
print ('Best l1_ratio: %0.5f' % \
  search_func.best_params_['l1_ratio'])
print ('Best CV mean squared error: %0.3f' % \
  np.abs(search_func.best_score_))

Out:  Best alpha: 0.00002
Best l1_ratio: 0.60000
Best CV mean squared error: 11.900
```

By introspecting the solution, we realize that this is achieved by excluding a larger number of variables than a pure L1 solution; however, the resulting performance is similar to a L2 solution:

```
In: print ('Zero value coefficients: %i out of %i' %
  (np.sum(~(search_func.best_estimator_.coef_==0.0)),
  len(search_func.best_estimator_.coef_)))

Out:   Zero value coefficients: 102 out of 105
```

Stability selection

As presented, L1-penalty offers the advantage of rendering your coefficients' estimates sparse, and effectively it acts as a variable selector since it tends to leave only essential variables in the model. On the other hand, the selection itself tends to be unstable when data changes and it requires a certain effort to correctly tune the C parameter to make the selection most effective. As we have seen while discussing elastic net, the peculiarity resides in the behavior of Lasso when there are two highly correlated variables; depending on the structure of the data (noise and correlation with other variables), L1 regularization will choose just one of the two.

In the field of studies related to bioinformatics (DNA, molecular studies), it is common to work with a large number of variables based on a few observations. Typically, such problems are denominated p >> n (features are much more numerous than cases) and they present the necessity to select what features to use for modeling. Because the variables are numerous and also are quite correlated among themselves, resorting to variable selection, whether by greedy selection or L1-penalty, can lead to more than one outcome taken from quite a large range of possible solutions. Two scholars, Nicolai Meinshausen and Peter Buhlmann, respectively from the University of Oxford and ETH Zurich, have come up with the idea of trying to leverage this instability and turn it into a surer selection.

Their idea is straightforward: since L1-penalty is influenced by the cases and variables present in the dataset to choose a certain variable over others in the case of multicollinearity, we can subsample the cases and the variables to involve and fit with them a L1-penalized model repetitively. Then, for each run, we can record the features that got a zero coefficient and the one that didn't. By pooling these multiple results, we can calculate a frequency statistic of how many times each feature got a non-zero value. In such a fashion, even if the results are unstable and uncertain, the most informative features will score a non-zero coefficient more often than less informative ones. In the end, a threshold can help to exactly retain the important variables and discard the unimportant ones and the collinear, but not so relevant, ones.

[The scoring can also be interpreted as a ranking of each variable's role in the model.]

Scikit-learn offers two implementations of stability selection: `RandomizedLogisticRegression` for classification tasks and `RandomizedLasso` as a regressor. They are both in the `linear_model` module.

They also both share the same key hyper-parameters:

- C : is the regularization parameter, by default set to 1.0. If you can manage to find a good C on all the data by cross-validation, put that figure in the parameter. Otherwise, start confidently using the default value; it is a good compromise.

- scaling : is the percentage of feature to be kept at every iteration, the default value of 0.5 is a good figure; lower the number if there are many redundant variables in your data.

- sample_fraction : is the percentage of observations to be kept; the default value of 0.75 should be decreased if you suspect outliers in your data (so they will less likely be drawn).

- n_resampling : the number of iterations; the more the better, but 200-300 resamples should bear good results.

Experimenting with the Madelon

From our past experimentations, stability selection does help to quickly fix any problem inherent to variable selection, even when dealing with sparse variables such as textual data rendered into indicator variables.

To demonstrate its effectiveness, we are going to apply it to the Madelon dataset, trying to get a better AUC score after stability selection:

```
In: from sklearn.cross_validation import cross_val_score
    from sklearn.linear_model import RandomizedLogisticRegression
    from sklearn.preprocessing import PolynomialFeatures
    from sklearn.pipeline import make_pipeline
    threshold = 0.03 # empirically found value
    stability_selection =
RandomizedLogisticRegression(n_resampling=300, n_jobs=1,
        random_state=101, scaling=0.15,
        sample_fraction=0.50, selection_threshold=threshold)
    interactions = PolynomialFeatures(degree=4,
interaction_only=True)
    model = make_pipeline(stability_selection, interactions, logit)
    model.fit(Xt,yt)
```

Since it is a classification problem, we are going to use the RandomizedLogisticRegression class, setting 300 resamples and subsampling 15% of variables and 50% of observations. As a threshold, we are going to retain all those features that appear significant in the model at least 3% of the time. Such settings are quite strict, but they are due to the presence of high redundancy in the dataset and extreme instability of L1 solutions.

Fitting the solution using a `make_pipeline` command allows us to create a sequence of actions to be first fitted and used on training data and then reapplied, using the same configuration, to the validation data. The idea is to first select the important and relevant features based on stability selection and then to create interactions (just multiplicative terms) using polynomial expansion to catch the non-linear components in the data with new derived features. If we were to create polynomial expansion without first selecting which variables we should use, then our dataset would exponentially grow in the number of variables and it could prove impossible even to store it in-memory.

`RandomizedLogisticRegression` acts more as a pre-processing filter than a predictive model: after fitting, though allowing us to have a glance at the produced scores, it won't allow any prediction on the basis of the host of created models, but it will allow us to transform any dataset similar to ours (the same number of columns), keeping only the columns whose score is above the threshold that we initially defined when we instantiated the class.

In our case, after having the resamples run, and it may take some time, we can try to figure out how many variables have been retained by the model:

```
In: print ('Number of features picked by stability selection: %i'
% \ np.sum(model.steps[0][1].all_scores_ >= threshold))

Out: Number of features picked by stability selection: 19
```

Here, 19 variables constitute a small set, which can be expanded into four-way interactions of the type var1 × var2 × var3 × var4, allowing us to better map the unknown transformations at the origin of the Madelon dataset.

```
In: from sklearn.metrics import roc_auc_score
print ('Area Under the Curve: %0.3f' % roc_auc_score(
         yv,model.predict_proba(Xv)[:,1]))

Out: Area Under the Curve: 0.885
```

A final test on the obtained probability estimates reveals to us that we reached an AUC value of 0.885, a fairly good improvement from the initial 0.602 baseline.

Summary

During this chapter, we have covered quite a lot of ground, finally exploring the most experimental and scientific part of the task of modeling linear regression or classification models.

Starting with the topic of generalization, we explained what can go wrong in a model and why it is always important to check the true performances of your work by train/test splits and by bootstraps and cross-validation (though we recommend using the latter more for validation work than general evaluation itself).

Model complexity as a source of variance in the estimate gave us the occasion to introduce variable selection, first by greedy selection of features, univariate or multivariate, then using regularization techniques, such as Ridge, Lasso and Elastic Net.

Finally, we demonstrated a powerful application of Lasso, called stability selection, which, in the light of our experience, we recommend you try for many feature selection problems.

In the next chapter, we will deal with the problem of incrementally growing datasets, proposing solutions that may work well even if your problem is that of datasets too large to easily and timely fit into the memory of your working computer.

Online and Batch Learning 7

In this chapter, you will be presented with best practices when it comes to training classifiers on big data. The new approach, exposed in the following pages, is both scalable and generic, making it perfect for datasets with a huge number of observations. Moreover, this approach can allow you to cope with streaming datasets—that is, datasets with observations transmitted on-the-fly and not all available at the same time. Furthermore, such an approach enhances precision, as more data is fed in during the training process.

With respect to the classic approach seen so far in the book, batch learning, this new approach is, not surprisingly, called online learning. The core of online learning is the *divide et impera* (divide and conquer) principle whereby each step of a mini-batch of the data serves as input to train and improve the classifier.

In this chapter, we will first focus on batch learning and its limitations, and then introduce online learning. Finally, we will supply an example of big data, showing the benefits of combining online learning and hashing tricks.

Batch learning

When the dataset is fully available at the beginning of a supervised task, and doesn't exceed the quantity of RAM on your machine, you can train the classifier or the regression using batch learning. As seen in previous chapters, during training the learner scans the full dataset. This also happens when **stochastic gradient descent** (SGD)-based methods are used (see *Chapter 2, Approaching Simple Linear Regression* and *Chapter 3, Multiple Regression in Action*). Let's now compare how much time is needed to train a linear regressor and relate its performance with the number of observations in the dataset (that is, the number of rows of the feature matrix X) and the number of features (that is, the number of columns of X). In this first experiment, we will use the plain vanilla `LinearRegression()` and `SGDRegressor()` classes provided by Scikit-learn, and we will store the actual time taken to fit a classifier, without any parallelization.

Let's first create a function to create fake datasets: it takes as parameters the number of training points and the number of features (plus, optionally, the noise variance), and returns normalized training and testing feature matrixes and labels. Note that all the features in the X matrix are numerical:

```
In:
import matplotlib.pyplot as plt
import matplotlib.pylab as pylab
%matplotlib inline

In:
from sklearn.preprocessing import StandardScaler
from sklearn.datasets.samples_generator import make_regression
import numpy as np

def generate_dataset(n_train, n_test, n_features, noise=0.1):
    X, y = make_regression(n_samples=int(n_train + n_test),
                           n_features=int(n_features),
                           noise=noise,
                           random_state=101)

    X_train = X[:n_train]
    X_test = X[n_train:]

    y_train = y[:n_train]
    y_test = y[n_train:]


    X_scaler = StandardScaler()
    X_train = X_scaler.fit_transform(X_train)
    X_test = X_scaler.transform(X_test)

    y_scaler = StandardScaler()
    y_train = y_scaler.fit_transform(y_train)
    y_test = y_scaler.transform(y_test)

    return X_train, X_test, y_train, y_test
```

Let's now store the time needed to train and test the learner in all the combinations of these configurations:

- Two classifiers: LinearRegression() and SGDRegressor()
- Number of observations: 1000, 10000, and 100000
- Number of features: 10, 50, 100, 500, and 1000

To average the results, each training operation is performed five times. The testing dataset always comprises 1000 observations:

```
In:
from sklearn.linear_model import LinearRegression, SGDRegressor
import time

In:

n_test = 1000

n_train_v = (1000, 10000, 100000)
n_features_v = (10, 50, 100, 500, 1000)
regr_v = {'LR': LinearRegression(), 'SGD':
SGDRegressor(random_state=101)}
results = {}

for regr_name, regr in regr_v.items():

    results[regr_name] = {}

    for n_train in n_train_v:
        for n_features in n_features_v:

            results[regr_name][(n_train, n_features)] = {'train':
[], 'pred': []}

            for n_repetition in range(5):

                X_train, X_test, y_train, y_test = \
                generate_dataset(n_train, n_test, n_features)

                tick = time.time()
                regr.fit(X_train, y_train)
                train_time = time.time() - tick

                pred = regr.predict(X_test)
                predict_time = time.time() - tick - train_time


                results[regr_name][(n_train,
n_features)]['train'].append(train_time)
                results[regr_name][(n_train,
n_features)]['pred'].append(predict_time)
```

Let's finally plot the results. In the following screenshot, the chart on the left shows the training time of the `LogisticRegressor` algorithm against the number of features, whereas the chart on the right displays the time against the number of observations:

```
In:
pylab.rcParams['figure.figsize'] = 12, 6
plt.subplot(1, 2, 1)

for n_train in n_train_v:
    X = n_features_v
    y = [np.mean(results['LR'][(n_train, n_features)]['train'])
        for n_features in n_features_v]
    plt.plot(X, y, label=str(n_train) + " train points")

plt.title('Training time VS num. features')
plt.xlabel('Num features')
plt.ylabel('Training time [s]')
plt.legend(loc=0)


plt.subplot(1, 2, 2)

for n_features in n_features_v:
    X = np.log10(n_train_v)
    y = [np.mean(results['LR'][(n_train, n_features)]['train'])
        for n_train in n_train_v]
    plt.plot(X, y, label=str(n_features) + " features")

plt.title('Training time VS num. training points')
plt.xlabel('Num training points [log10]')
plt.ylabel('Training time [s]')
plt.legend(loc=0)
plt.show()

Out:
```

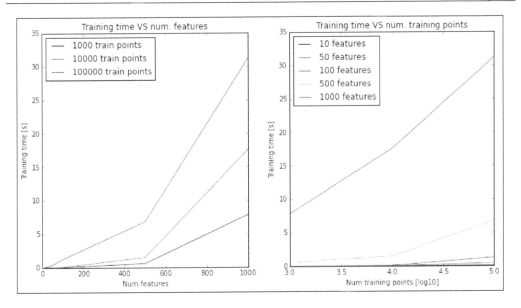

In the plots, you can see that the classifier is pretty good on small datasets, with a small number of features and observations. While dealing with the largest X matrix, 1,000 features and 100,000 observations (containing 100 million entries), the training time is just above 30 seconds: that's also the limit above which the regressor no longer scales.

Let's now see what happens with the testing time:

```
In:
plt.subplot(1, 2, 1)

for n_train in n_train_v:
    X = n_features_v
    y = [np.mean(results['LR'][(n_train, n_features)]['pred'])
        for n_features in n_features_v]

    plt.plot(X, y, label=str(n_train) + " train points")

plt.title('Prediction time VS num. features')
plt.xlabel('Num features')
plt.ylabel('Prediction time [s]')
plt.legend(loc=0)


plt.subplot(1, 2, 2)
```

```
for n_features in n_features_v:
    X = np.log10(n_train_v)
    y = [np.mean(results['LR'][(n_train, n_features)]['pred'])
        for n_train in n_train_v]

    plt.plot(X, y, label=str(n_features) + " features")

plt.title('Prediction time VS num. training points')
plt.xlabel('Num training points [log10]')
plt.ylabel('Prediction time [s]')
plt.legend(loc=0)
plt.show()
Out:
```

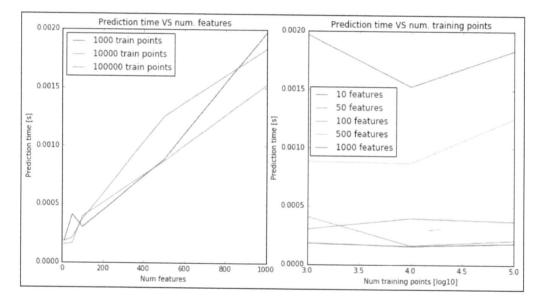

The testing time does scale as a linear function of the number of features, and it's independent of it. It seems that applying the linear approach is not very much of a problem on big data, fortunately.

Let's now see what happens with the SGD implementation of linear regression:

```
In:
plt.subplot(1, 2, 1)

for n_train in n_train_v:
    X = n_features_v
    y = [np.mean(results['SGD'][(n_train, n_features)]['train'])
        for n_features in n_features_v]
```

```
        plt.plot(X, y, label=str(n_train) + " train points")

plt.title('Training time VS num. features')
plt.xlabel('Num features')
plt.ylabel('Training time [s]')
plt.legend(loc=0)


plt.subplot(1, 2, 2)

for n_features in n_features_v:
    X = np.log10(n_train_v)
    y = [np.mean(results['SGD'][(n_train, n_features)]['train'])
        for n_train in n_train_v]
    plt.plot(X, y, label=str(n_features) + " features")

plt.title('Training time VS num. training points')
plt.xlabel('Num training points [log10]')
plt.ylabel('Training time [s]')
plt.legend(loc=0)
plt.show()
Out:
```

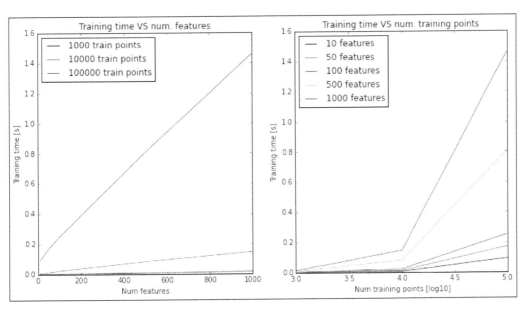

The results have drastically changed in comparison with the previous regressor: on the biggest matrix, this learner takes around 1.5 seconds. It also seems that the time needed to train an SGD regressor is linear with respect to the number of features and the number of training points. Let's now verify how it works in testing:

```
In:
plt.subplot(1, 2, 1)

for n_train in n_train_v:
    X = n_features_v
    y = [np.mean(results['SGD'][(n_train, n_features)]['pred'])
        for n_features in n_features_v]

    plt.plot(X, y, label=str(n_train) + " train points")

plt.title('Prediction time VS num. features')
plt.xlabel('Num features')
plt.ylabel('Prediction time [s]')
plt.legend(loc=0)


plt.subplot(1, 2, 2)

for n_features in n_features_v:
    X = np.log10(n_train_v)
    y = [np.mean(results['SGD'][(n_train, n_features)]['pred'])
        for n_train in n_train_v]

    plt.plot(X, y, label=str(n_features) + " features")

plt.title('Prediction time VS num. training points')
plt.xlabel('Num training points [log10]')
plt.ylabel('Prediction time [s]')
plt.legend(loc=0)
plt.show()
Out:
```

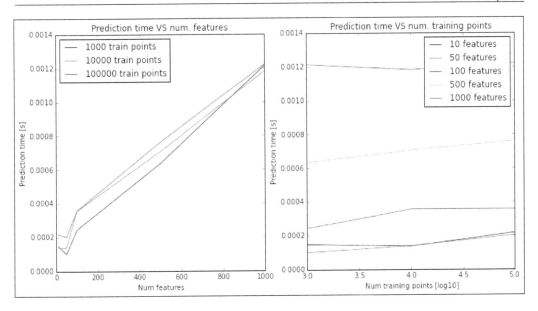

Applying the SGD-based learner on a test dataset takes about the same time as the other implementation. Here, again, there is really no problem when scaling the solution on big datasets.

Online mini-batch learning

From the previous section, we've learned an interesting lesson: for big data, always use SGD-based learners because they are faster, and they do scale.

Now, in this section, let's consider this regression dataset:

- Massive number of observations: 2M
- Large number of features: 100
- Noisy dataset

The X_train matrix is composed of 200 million elements, and may not completely fit in memory (on a machine with 4 GB RAM); the testing set is composed of 10,000 observations.

Let's first create the datasets, and print the memory footprint of the biggest one:

```
In:
# Let's generate a 1M dataset
X_train, X_test, y_train, y_test = generate_dataset(2000000,
10000, 100, 10.0)
print("Size of X_train is [GB]:", X_train.size * X_train[0,0].
itemsize/1E9)


Out:
Size of X_train is [GB]: 1.6
```

The X_train matrix is itself 1.6 GB of data; we can consider it as a starting point for big data. Let's now try to classify it using the best model we got from the previous section, SGDRegressor(). To access its performance, we use MAE, the Mean Absolute Error (as for error evaluation, the lower the better).

```
In:
from sklearn.metrics import mean_absolute_error

regr = SGDRegressor(random_state=101)
tick = time.time()
regr.fit(X_train, y_train)
print("With SGD, after", time.time() - tick ,"seconds")
pred = regr.predict(X_test)
print("the MAE is [log10]:", np.log10(mean_absolute_error(y_test,
pred)))


Out:
With SGD, after 5.958770098299116 seconds
the MAE is [log10]: -1.2422451189257
```

On our computer (equipped with Mac OS and 4 GB of RAM), this operation takes around 6 seconds, and the final MAE is $10^{-1.24}$.

Can we do better? Yes, with mini-batches and online learning. Before we see these in action, let's introduce how SGD works with mini-batches.

1. Split the X_train matrix in batches of N observations. Since we're using SGD, if possible it's better to shuffle the observations, as the method is strongly driven by the order of the input vectors. At this point, every mini-batch has N lines and M columns (where M is the number of features).

2. We train the learner using a mini-batch. SGD coefficients are initialized randomly, as shown previously.

3. We train the learner using another mini-batch. SGD coefficients are initialized as the output of the previous step (using the `partial_fit` method).

4. Repeat step 3 until you've used all the mini-batches. In each step, the coefficients of the SGD model are refined and modified according to the input.

This is clearly a smart approach, and it doesn't take too long to implement. You just need to set the initial values of each coefficient for every new batch and train the learner on the mini-batch.

Now, in terms of performance, what do we get using online learning?

- We have an incremental way to train the model. Since, at every step, we can test the model, we can stop at any point we think is good enough.

- We don't need to keep the whole `X_train` matrix in memory; we just need to keep the mini-batch in RAM. That also means that the consumed RAM is constant.

- We have a way to control the learning: we can have small mini-batches or big ones.

Let's see now how it performs, by changing the batch size (that is, the number of observations for each observation):

```
In:
def get_minibatch(X, y, batch_size):
    # We will shuffle consistently the training observations
    from sklearn.utils import resample
    X, y = resample(X, y, replace=False, random_state=101)
    n_cols = y.shape[0]
    for i in range(int(n_cols/batch_size)):
        yield (X[i*batch_size:(i+1)*batch_size, :],
y[i*batch_size:(i+1)*batch_size])

    if n_cols % batch_size > 0:
        res_rows = n_cols % batch_size
        yield (X[-res_rows:, :], y[-res_rows:])


plot_x = []
plot_y = []
plot_labels = []

for batch_size in (1000, 10000, 100000):
    regr = SGDRegressor(random_state=101)
```

```
        training_time = 0.0

        X = []
        y = []

        for dataset in get_minibatch(X_train, y_train, batch_size):
            tick = time.time()
            regr.partial_fit(dataset[0], dataset[1])
            training_time += (time.time() - tick)
            pred = regr.predict(X_test)
            X.append(training_time)
            y.append(np.log10(mean_absolute_error(y_test, pred)))

    print("Report: Mini-batch size", batch_size)
    print("First output after [s]:", X[0])
    print("First model MAE [log10]:", y[0])
    print("Total training time [s]:", X[-1])
    print("Final MAE [log10]: ", y[-1])
    print()

    plot_x.append(X)
    plot_y.append(y)
    plot_labels.append("Batch size: "+str(batch_size))
```

Out:

```
Report: Mini-batch size 1000
First output after [s]: 0.0007998943328857422
First model MAE [log10]: -0.942320304943
Total training time [s]: 1.3718714714050293
Final MAE [log10]:  -1.24036819201

Report: Mini-batch size 10000
First output after [s]: 0.007853984832763672
First model MAE [log10]: -1.23171862851
Total training time [s]: 1.308701992034912
Final MAE [log10]:  -1.24038903474

Report: Mini-batch size 100000
First output after [s]: 0.05989503860473633
First model MAE [log10]: -1.24053929732
Total training time [s]: 1.1995868682861328
Final MAE [log10]:  -1.24053790326
```

In the end, the final MAE is always the same; that is, batch learning and online learning eventually provide the same results when both are trained on the whole training set.

We also see that, by using a small mini-batch (1,000 observations), we have a working model after just 1 millisecond. Of course, it's not a perfect solution since its MAE is just $10^{-0.94}$, but still we now have a reasonable working model.

Now, let's compare timings to fully train the model. Using mini-batches, the total time is around 1.2 seconds; using the batch it was greater than 5 seconds. The MAEs are more or less equal — why such a difference in timings? Because the dataset didn't all fit in RAM and the system kept on swapping data with storage memory.

Let's now focus on mini-batch size: is smaller really always better? Actually, it will produce an output earlier, but it will take more time in total.

Here's a plot of the training time and the MAE of the learner, when trained with different mini-batch sizes:

```
In:
plt.subplot(1,2,1)
for i in range(len(plot_x)):
    plt.plot(plot_x[i], plot_y[i], label=plot_labels[i])
plt.title('Mini-batch learning')
plt.xlabel('Training time [s]')
plt.ylabel('MAE')
plt.legend(loc=0)

plt.subplot(1,2,2)
for i in range(len(plot_x)):
    plt.plot(plot_x[i], plot_y[i], label=plot_labels[i])
plt.title('Mini-batch learning: ZOOM 0-0.15s')
plt.xlabel('Training time [s]')
plt.ylabel('MAE')
plt.xlim([0, 0.15])
plt.legend(loc=0)

plt.show()
Out:
```

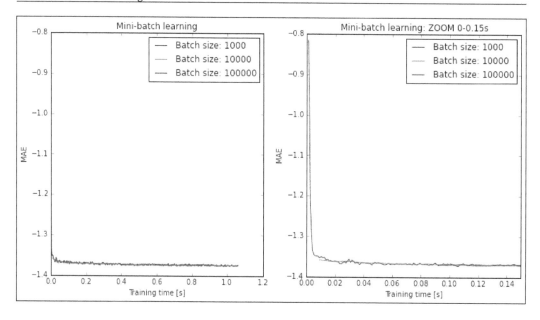

A real example

Let's now combine feature hashing (seen in *Chapter 5, Data Preparation*), batch-learning, and SGD. From what we've seen so far, this should be the best way to deal with big data because:

1. The number of features is constant (feature hashing).
2. The number of observations per batch is constant (batch learning).
3. It allows streaming datasets.
4. The algorithm is stochastic (SGD).

All these points together will ensure a few consequences:

1. We can very quickly have a model (after the first mini-batch) that is refined with time.
2. RAM consumption is constant (since every mini-batch has exactly the same size).
3. Ideally, we can deal with as many observation as we want.

In the real-world example, let's use a textual input: the Twenty Newsgroups dataset. This dataset contains 20,000 messages (textual content) extracted from 20 different newsgroups, each of them on a different topic. The webpage of the project is: https://archive.ics.uci.edu/ml/datasets/Twenty+Newsgroups.

The goal is to classify each document in one of the possible labels (it's a classification task). Let's first load it, and split it into train and test. To make it more real, we're going to remove headers, footers, and quoted e-mail from the dataset:

```
In:
from sklearn.datasets import fetch_20newsgroups
from sklearn.feature_extraction.text import HashingVectorizer

to_remove = ('headers', 'footers', 'quotes')

data_train = fetch_20newsgroups(subset='train', random_state=101,
                                remove=to_remove)

data_test = fetch_20newsgroups(subset='test', random_state=101,
                               remove=to_remove)


labels = data_train.target_names
targets = np.unique(data_train.target)
```

Let's now create a function that yields mini-batches of the dataset:

```
In:
def get_minibatch_docs(docs, targets, batch_size):
    n_docs = len(docs)
    for i in range(int(n_docs/batch_size)):
        yield (docs[i*batch_size:(i+1)*batch_size],
               targets[i*batch_size:(i+1)*batch_size])

    if n_docs % batch_size > 0:
        res_rows = n_docs % batch_size
        yield (docs[-res_rows:], targets[-res_rows:])
```

Now, the core task is simply to classify the document. We first apply feature hashing via the HashingVectorizer class, whose output feeds a SGDClassifier (another class with the partial_fit method). This fact will ensure an additional advantage: since the output of the HashingVectorizer is very sparse, a sparse representation is used, making the mini-batch size even more compact in memory

To understand what the best hash size is, we may try a full search with sizes of 1000, 5000, 10000, 50000, and 100000 and then measure the accuracy for each learner:

```
In:
from sklearn.linear_model import SGDClassifier
from sklearn.metrics import accuracy_score
```

```
import sys

minibatch_size = 1000
values_to_plot = {}

for hash_table_size in (1000, 5000, 10000, 50000, 100000):

    values_to_plot[hash_table_size] = {'time': [], 'score': []}

    vectorizer = HashingVectorizer(stop_words='english',
    non_negative=True, n_features=hash_table_size,
    ngram_range=(1, 1))

    X_test = vectorizer.transform(data_test.data)
    y_test = data_test.target

    clf = SGDClassifier(loss='log')
    timings = []

    for minibatch in get_minibatch_docs(data_train.data,
    data_train.target, minibatch_size):
        y_train = minibatch[1]

        tick = time.time()
        X_train = vectorizer.transform(minibatch[0])
        clf.partial_fit(X_train, y_train, targets)

        timings.append(time.time() - tick)

        pred = clf.predict(X_test)

        values_to_plot[hash_table_size]['score'].append(accuracy_score
(y_test, pred))

    values_to_plot[hash_table_size]['time'] = np.cumsum(timings)
```

Finally, we plot our results on a graph representing time and accuracy for each size of the hash size. The X signs on the graph are the instances (and related accuracy) when the classifier outputs a model:

```
In:
for k,v in sorted(values_to_plot.items()):
    plt.plot(v['time'], v['score'], 'x-', label='Hashsize size
'+str(k))
plt.title('Mini-batch learning: 20newsgroups')
```

```
plt.xlabel('Training time [s]')
plt.ylabel('Accuracy')
plt.legend(loc=0)

plt.show()
Out:
```

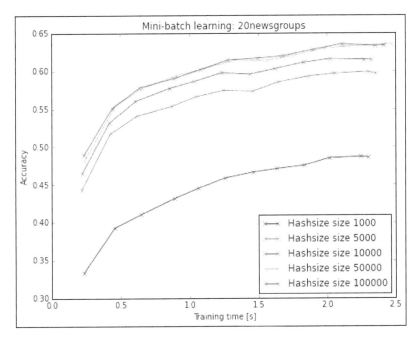

It appears from the obtained results that using a hash table bigger than 10,000 elements can allow us to achieve the best performance. In this exercise, the mini-batch size was fixed to 1,000 observations; this means that every mini-batch was a matrix of 10 M elements, represented in sparse way. It also means that, for every mini-batch, the memory used is up to 80 MB of RAM.

Streaming scenario without a test set

In many real cases, the test dataset is not available. What can we do? The best practice would be to:

1. Fetch the data until you reach a specific mini-batch size; let's say 10 observations.

2. Shuffle the observations, and store eight of them within the train set, and two in the test set (for an 80/20 validation).

3. Train the classifier on the train set and test on the test set.

4. Go back to step 1. With each mini-batch, the train set will increase by 10 observations and the test set by 2.

We have just described the classic method, used when data is consistent and the dataset is not very large. If the features change throughout the streaming, and you need to build a learner that has to adapt to rapid changes of feature statistics. then simply don't use a test set and follow this algorithm. In addition, this is the preferred way to learn from big data:

1. Fetch the data till you reach a mini-batch size; let's say 10 observations. Don't shuffle and train the learner with all the observations.

2. Wait till you fetch another mini-batch. Test the classifier on those observations.

3. Update the classifier with the mini-batch you received in the previous step.

4. Go back to step 2.

The good thing about this algorithm is that you don't have to keep anything but the model and the current mini-batch in memory; these are used first to test the learner, and then to update it.

Summary

In this chapter, we've introduced the concepts of batch and online learning, which are necessary to be able to process big datasets (big data) in a quick and scalable way.

In the next chapter, we will explore some advanced techniques of machine learning that will produce great results for some classes of well-known problems.

8
Advanced Regression Methods

In this chapter, we will introduce some advanced regression methods. Since many of them are very complex, we will skip most of the mathematical formulations, providing the readers instead with the ideas underneath the techniques and some practical advice, such as explaining when and when not to use the technique. We will illustrate:

- Least Angle Regression (LARS)
- Bayesian regression
- SGD classification with hinge loss (note that this is not a regressor, it's a classifier)
- Regression trees
- Ensemble of regressors (bagging and boosting)
- Gradient Boosting Regressor with Least Angle Deviation

Least Angle Regression

Although very similar to Lasso (seen in *Chapter 6, Achieving Generalization*), Least Angle Regression, or simply LARS, is a regression algorithm that, in a fast and smart way, selects the best features to use in the model, even though they're very closely correlated to each other. LARS is an evolution of the Forward Selection (also called Forward Stepwise Regression) algorithm and of the Forward Stagewise Regression algorithm.

Here is how the Forward Selection algorithm works, based on the hypothesis that all the variables, including the target one, have been previously normalized:

1. Of all the possible predictors for a problem, the one with the largest absolute correlation with the target variable y is selected (that is, the one with the most explanatory capability). Let's call it p_1.

2. All the other predictors are now projected onto p_1 Least Angle Regression, and the projection is removed, creating a vector of residuals orthogonal to p_1.

3. Step 1 is repeated on the residual vectors, and the most correlated predictor is again selected. Let's name it p^2 Apply subscript.

4. Step 2 is repeated, using p_2, creating a vector of residuals orthogonal to p_2 (and also p_1).

5. This process continues until the prediction is satisfying, or when the largest absolute correlation falls below a set threshold. After each iteration, a new predictor is added to the list of predictors, and the residual is orthogonal to all of them.

This method is not very popular because it has a serious limitation due to its extremely greedy approach; however, it's fairly quick. Let's now consider that we have a regression problem with two highly correlated variables. Forward Selection, on this dataset, will select the predictor on the basis of the first or the second variable, and then, since the residual will be very low, will reconsider the other variable in a far later step (eventually, never). This fact will lead to overfitting problems on the model. Wouldn't it be better if the two highly correlated variables were selected together, balancing the new predictor? That's practically the core idea of the Forward Stagewise Regression algorithm, where, in each step, the best predictor is partially added to the model. Let's provide the details here:

1. In the model, every feature has an associate weight of zero — that is, $w_i = 0$ for each feature i.

2. Of all the possible predictors for a problem, the one with the largest (absolute) correlation with the target variable y is partially added to the model — that is, in the model, the weight of w_i is increased by ε.

3. Repeat step 2, until the exploratory power is below a predefined threshold.

This method represents a great improvement on the Forward Selected because, in the case of correlated features, both of them will be in the final model with a similar weight. The result is very good, but the enormous number of iterations needed to create the model is the really big problem with this algorithm. Again, the method becomes impractical because of its running time.

The LARS algorithm instead operates as follows:

1. In the model, every feature has an associate weight of zero — that is, $w_i = 0$ for each feature i.

2. Of the possible predictors for a problem, the one with the largest (absolute) correlation with the target variable y is partially added to the model — that is, in the model, the weight of w_i is increased by ε.

3. Keep increasing w_i till any other predictor (let's say j) has as much correlation with the residual vector as the current predictor has.

4. Increase w_i and w_j simultaneously until another predictor has as much correlation with the residual vector as the current predictors have.

5. Keep adding predictors and weights until all the predictors are in the model or it meets another termination criterion, such as the number of iterations.

This solution is able to compose the best pieces of Forward Selection and Stagewise Regression, creating a solution that is stable, not so prone to overfitting, and fast. Before getting to the examples, you may wonder why it is named Least Angle Regression. The answer is very simple: if the features and output are represented as vectors in the Cartesian space, at every iteration LARS includes in the model the variable most correlated with the residual vector, which is the one that generates the least angle with the residual. Actually, the whole process can be expressed visually.

Visual showcase of LARS

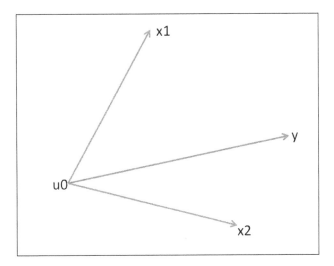

Here is the visual situation: two predictors (**x1** and **x2**), not necessarily orthogonal, and the target (**y**). Note that, at the beginning, the residual corresponds to the target. Our model starts at **u0** (where all the weights are *0*).

Then, since **x2** makes a smaller angle with the residual compared to **x1**, we start *walking* in the direction of **x2**, while we keep computing the residual vector. Now, a question: where should we stop?

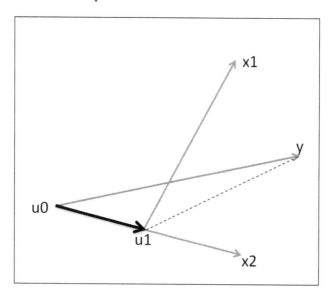

We should stop at **u1**, where the angle between the residual and **x1** is the same as the angle between the residual and **x2**. We then walk in the direction of the composition **x1** and **x2**, reaching **y**.

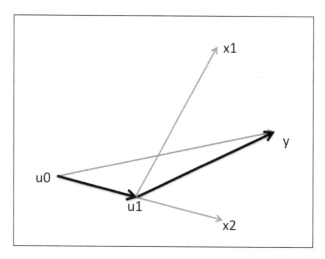

A code example

Let's now see LARS in action in Python on the Diabetic dataset, which consists of 10 numerical variables (age, sex, weight, blood pressure, and so on) measured on 442 patients, and an indication of disease progression after one year. First, we want to visualize the path of the weights of the coefficients. To do so, the `lars_path()` class comes to our help (especially if its training is verbose):

```
In:
%matplotlib inline
import matplotlib.pyplot as plt
import numpy as np

from sklearn import linear_model
from sklearn import datasets
from sklearn.preprocessing import StandardScaler

diabetes = datasets.load_diabetes()
X = StandardScaler().fit_transform(diabetes.data)
y = StandardScaler(with_mean=True, with_std=False) \
        .fit_transform(diabetes.target)

alphas, _, coefs = linear_model.lars_path(X, y, verbose=2)

xx = np.sum(np.abs(coefs.T), axis=1)
xx /= xx[-1]

plt.plot(xx, coefs.T)
ymin, ymax = plt.ylim()
plt.vlines(xx, ymin, ymax, linestyle='dashed')
plt.xlabel('|coef| / max|coef|')
plt.ylabel('Coefficients')
plt.axis('tight')
plt.show()

Out:
```

Step	Added	Dropped	Active set size	C
0	2		1	19960.733269
1	8		2	18696.7980058
2	3		3	9521.69759738
3	6		4	6645.07641798
4	1		5	2735.84447649
5	9		6	1866.54369652
6	4		7	1449.91074453
7	7		8	420.081823008
8	5		9	115.157274041
9	0		10	106.993857228

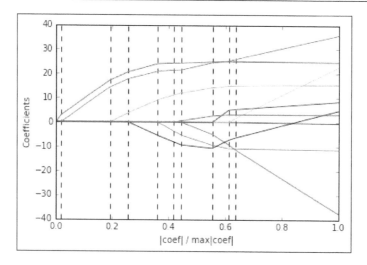

In the output table, you can see that the first feature inserted in the model is the number 2, followed by the number 8 and so on. In the image, instead, you can simultaneously see the values of the coefficients (colored lines) and the steps (dotted lines). Remember that, at every step, one coefficient becomes non-zero, and all the coefficients in the model are updated linearly. On the right side of the image, you can find the final values of the weights.

This is the graphical way to see the LARS coefficients; if we only need a regressor (exactly as we've seen in the previous chapters), we can just use the `Lars` class:

```
In:
regr = linear_model.Lars()

regr.fit(X, y)

print("Coefficients are:", regr.coef_)
Out:
Coefficients are:
[ -0.47623169 -11.40703082  24.72625713  15.42967916 -37.68035801
   22.67648701   4.80620008   8.422084    35.73471316   3.21661161]
```

As you may expect, the regressor object can be fitted with the method `.fit`, and its weights (coefficients) are exactly the ones shown in the previous screenshot. To get the quality of the model, in a similar fashion to the other regressors, you can use the method score. In respect of the training data, here's the scoring output:

```
In:
print("R2 score is", regr.score(X,y))
Out:
R2 score is 0.517749425413
```

LARS wrap up

Pros:

- The smart way in which coefficients are updated produces low overfitting
- The model is intuitive and easily interpretable
- The training is as fast as Forward Selection
- It is great when the number of features is comparable with, or greater than, the number of observations

Cons:

- It might not work very well when the number of features is very large — that is, where the number of features is far greater than the number of observations, since in such an occurrence it's very probable you'll find spurious correlations
- It won't work with very noisy features

Bayesian regression

Bayesian regression is similar to linear regression, as seen in *Chapter 3, Multiple Regression in Action*, but, instead of predicting a value, it predicts its probability distribution. Let's start with an example: given X, the training observation matrix, and y, the target vector, linear regression creates a model (that is a series of coefficients) that fits the line that has the minimal error with the training points. Then, when a new observation arrives, the model is applied to that point, and a predicted value is outputted. That's the only output from linear regression, and no conclusions can be made as to whether the prediction, for that specific point, is accurate or not. Let's take a very simple example in code: the observed phenomenon has only one feature, and the number of observations is just 10:

```
In:
from sklearn.datasets import make_classification
from sklearn.datasets import make_regression

X, y = make_regression(n_samples=10, n_features=1,
n_informative=1, noise=3, random_state=1)
```

Now, let's fit a *classic* linear regression model, and let's try to predict the regression value for a point outside the training support (in this simple example, we predict the value for a point whose x value is double the max of the training values):

```
In:
regr = linear_model.LinearRegression()
```

```
regr.fit(X, y)

test_x = 2*np.max(X)
pred_test_x = regr.predict(test_x)
pred_test_x
Out:
array([ 10.79983753])
```

Let's now plot the training points, the fitted line, and the predicted test point (on the extreme right of the image):

```
In:
plt.scatter(X, y)
x_bounds = np.array([1.2*np.min(X), 1.2*np.max(X)]).reshape(-1, 1)
plt.plot(x_bounds, regr.predict(x_bounds) , 'r-')
plt.plot(test_x, pred_test_x, 'g*')
plt.show()
Out:
```

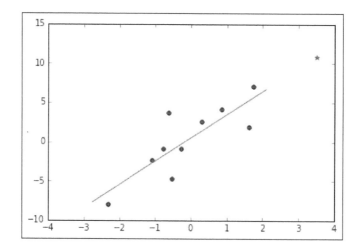

To have a probability density function of the predicted value, we should start from the beginning and change a hypothesis and some steps in the linear regressor. Since this is an advanced algorithm, the math involved is very heavy and we prefer to communicate the idea underlying the methods, instead of exposing pages and pages of math formulation.

First, we are only able to infer a distribution on the predicted value if every variable is modeled as a distribution. In fact, weights in this model are treated as random variables with a normal distribution, centered in zero (that is, a spherical Gaussian) and having an unknown variance (learnt from the data). The regularization imposed by this algorithm is very similar to the one set by Ridge regression.

The output of a prediction is a value (exactly as in linear regression) and a variance value. Using the value as the mean, and the variance as an actual variance, we can then represent the probability distribution of the output:

```
In:
regr = linear_model.BayesianRidge()
regr.fit(X, y)
Out:
BayesianRidge(alpha_1=1e-06, alpha_2=1e-06, compute_score=False,
              copy_X=True, fit_intercept=True, lambda_1=1e-06,
              lambda_2=1e-06, n_iter=300, normalize=False,
              tol=0.001, verbose=False)
In:
from matplotlib.mlab import normpdf

mean = regr.predict(test_x)
stddev = regr.alpha_
plt_x = np.linspace(mean-3*stddev, mean+3*stddev,100)
plt.plot(plt_x, normpdf(plt_x, mean, stddev))
plt.show()
Out:
```

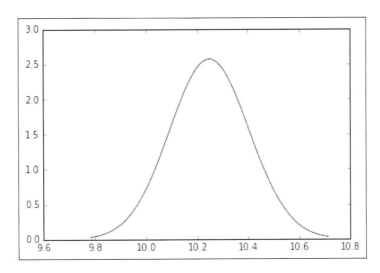

Bayesian regression wrap up

Pros:

- Robustness to Gaussian noise
- Great if the number of features is comparable to the number of observations

Cons:

- Time-consuming
- The hypotheses imposed on the variables are often far from real

SGD classification with hinge loss

In *Chapter 4, Logistic Regression* we explored a classifier based on a regressor, logistic regression. Its goal was to fit the best probabilistic function associated with the probability of one point to be classified with a label. Now, the core function of the algorithm considers all the training points of the dataset: what if it's only built on the boundary ones? That's exactly the case with the linear **Support Vector Machine** (SVM) classifier, where a linear decision plane is drawn by only considering the points close to the separation boundary itself.

Beyond working on the support vectors (the closest points to the boundary), SVM uses a new decision loss, called **hinge**. Here's its formulation:

$$loss(x) = max(0.1 - l \cdot w \cdot x)$$

Where t is the intended label of the point x and w the set of weights in the classifier. The hinge loss is also sometimes called **softmax**, because it's actually a clipped max. In this formula, just the boundary points (that is, the support vectors) are used.

In the first instance, this function, although convex, is non differentiable, so approaches based on stochastic gradient descent (SGD) are theoretically invalid. In practical terms, since it's a continuous function, it has a piecewise derivative. This leads to the fact that SGD can be actively used in this technique to derive a quick and approximate solution.

Here's an example in Python: let's use the `SGDClassifier` class (as seen in *Chapter 4, Logistic Regression*) with the `hinge` loss, applied on a dataset of `100` points drawn from `2` classes. With this piece of code, we're interested in seeing the decision boundary and the support vectors chosen by the classifier:

```
In:
from sklearn.linear_model import SGDClassifier

# we create 50 separable points
X, y = make_classification(n_samples=100, n_features=2,
                           n_informative=2, n_redundant=0,
                           n_clusters_per_class=1, class_sep=2,
```

```
                              random_state=101)

# fit the model
clf = SGDClassifier(loss="hinge", n_iter=500, random_state=101,
                    alpha=0.001)
clf.fit(X, y)

# plot the line, the points, and the nearest vectors to the plane
xx = np.linspace(np.min(X[:,0]), np.max(X[:,0]), 10)
yy = np.linspace(np.min(X[:,1]), np.max(X[:,1]), 10)

X1, X2 = np.meshgrid(xx, yy)
Z = np.empty(X1.shape)
for (i, j), val in np.ndenumerate(X1):
    x1 = val
    x2 = X2[i, j]
    p = clf.decision_function([[x1, x2]])
    Z[i, j] = p[0]
levels = [-1.0, 0.0, 1.0]
linestyles = ['dashed', 'solid', 'dashed']
plt.contour(X1, X2, Z, levels, colors='k', linestyles=linestyles)
plt.scatter(X[:, 0], X[:, 1], c=y, cmap=plt.cm.Paired)

plt.show()
```

Out:

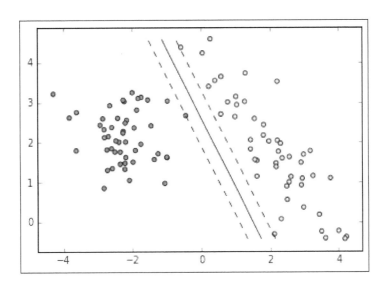

The image presents the points belonging to the two classes' points (the dots on the right and left) and the decision boundary (the solid line between the classes). In addition, it contains two dotted lines, which connect the support vectors for each class (that is, points on these lines are support vectors). The decision boundary is, simply, the line at the same distance between them.

Comparison with logistic regression

The logistic regression learner is intended to make use of all the input points of the training set, and emit a probability as output. SGD with hinge loss, instead, directly produces a label, and only uses the points on the boundary to improve the model. How are their performances? Let's make a test with an artificial dataset with 20 features (of them, 5 are informative, 5 redundant, and 10 random) and 10,000 observations. Then, we split the data into 70/30 as training set and test set and we train two SGD classifiers: one with the hinge loss function and the second with the logistic loss function. Finally, we compare the accuracy of their predictions on their test set:

```
In:
from sklearn.cross_validation import train_test_split
from sklearn.metrics import accuracy_score

X, y = make_classification(n_samples=10000, n_features=20,
                           n_informative=5, n_redundant=5,
                           n_clusters_per_class=2, class_sep=1,
                           random_state=101)


X_train, X_test, y_train, y_test =  train_test_split(
    X, y, test_size=0.3, random_state=101)

clf_1 = SGDClassifier(loss="hinge", random_state=101)
clf_1.fit(X_train, y_train)

clf_2 = SGDClassifier(loss="log", random_state=101)
clf_2.fit(X_train, y_train)

print('SVD             : ', accuracy_score(y_test,
clf_1.predict(X_test)))
print('Log. Regression: ', accuracy_score(y_test,
clf_2.predict(X_test)))
Out:
SVD             :   0.814333333333
Log. Regression:   0.756666666667
```

As a rule of thumb, SVM is generically more accurate than logistic regression, but its performance is not extraordinary. SVM, though, is slower during the training process; in fact, with regard to training times, logistic regression is more than 30% faster than SVM.

```
In:
%timeit clf_1.fit(X_train, y_train)
Out:
100 loops, best of 3: 3.16 ms per loop
In:
%timeit clf_2.fit(X_train, y_train)
Out:
100 loops, best of 3: 4.86 ms per loop
```

SVR

As for linear regressor/logistic regression, even SVM has a regression counterpart, called **Support Vector Regressor** (SVR). Its math formulation is very long and beyond the scope of this book. However, since it's very effective, we believe it is important to depict how it works in practice, as applied to the Boston dataset and compared with a linear regressor model:

```
In:
from sklearn.svm import SVR
from sklearn.linear_model import SGDRegressor
from sklearn.metrics import mean_absolute_error
from sklearn.datasets import load_boston


boston = load_boston()
X = StandardScaler().fit_transform(boston['data'])
y = boston['target']


X_train, X_test, y_train, y_test =  train_test_split(
    X, y, test_size=0.3, random_state=101)

regr_1 = SVR(kernel='linear')
regr_1.fit(X_train, y_train)

regr_2 = SGDRegressor(random_state=101)
regr_2.fit(X_train, y_train)
```

```
print('SVR              : ', mean_absolute_error(y_test,
regr_1.predict(X_test)))
print('Lin. Regression: ', mean_absolute_error(y_test,
regr_2.predict(X_test)))
Out:
SVR              :   3.67434988716
Lin. Regression:   3.7487663498
```

SVM wrap up

The pros are as follows:

- Can use SGD to speed up the processing
- Output is usually more accurate than logistic regression (since only boundary points are in the formula)

The cons are as follows:

- It works very well if the points of the two classes are linearly separable, although an extension for non-linearly separable classes is available. In this case, though complexity is very high, results are still usually great.
- As for logistic regression, it can be used for two-class problems.

Regression trees (CART)

A very common learner, recently used very much due to its speed, is the regression tree. It's a non-linear learner, can work with both categorical and numerical features, and can be used alternately for classification or regression; that's why it's often called **Classification and Regression Tree** (CART). Here, in this section, we will see how regression trees work.

A tree is composed of a series of nodes that split the branch into two children. Each branch, then, can go in another node, or remain a leaf with the predicted value (or class).

Starting from the root (that is, the whole dataset):

1. The best feature with which to split the dataset, *F1*, is identified as well as the best splitting value. If the feature is numerical, the splitting value is a threshold *T1*: in this case, the left child branch will be the set of observations where *F1* is below *T1*, and the right one is the set of observations where *F1* is greater than, or equal to, *T1*. If the feature is categorical, the splitting is done on a subset of levels *S1*: observations where the *F1* feature is one of these levels compose the left branch child, all the others compose the right branch child.

2. This operation is then run again (independently) for each branch, recursively, until there's no more chance to split.

3. When the splits are completed, a leaf is created. Leaves denote output values.

You can immediately see that making the prediction is immediate: you just need to traverse the tree from the root to the leaves and, in each node, check whether a feature is below (or not) a threshold or, alternatively, has a value inside (or outside) a set.

As a concluding remark, we discuss how to define the best feature to split. What about the best value or subset? Well, for regression trees, we use the criteria of the variance reduction: in each node, an extensive search is run among all features and among all values or levels in that feature. The combination that achieves the best possible variance in both the right branch and left branches, compared with the input set, is selected and marked as *best*.

Note that regression trees decide, for each node, the optimal split. Such a local optimization approach unfortunately leads to a suboptimal result. In addition, it is advisable that the regression tree should be pruned; that is, you should remove some leaves to prevent overfitting (for example, by setting a minimum threshold to the variance reduction measure). Such are the drawbacks of regression trees. On the other hand, they are somehow accurate and relatively quick to train and test.

In the code, regression trees are as easy as the other regressors:

```
In:
from sklearn.tree import DecisionTreeRegressor

regr = DecisionTreeRegressor(random_state=101)
regr.fit(X_train, y_train)

mean_absolute_error(y_test, regr.predict(X_test))
Out:
3.2842105263157895
```

Regression tree wrap up

Pros:

- They can model non-linear behaviors
- Great for categorical features and numerical features, without normalization
- Same approach for classification and regression
- Fast training, fast prediction time, and small memory fingerprint

Cons:

- Greedy algorithm: it doesn't optimize the full solution, just the best choice.

- It doesn't work very well when the number of features is significant.

- Leaves can be very specific. In this case, we need to "prune the tree", removing some nodes.

Bagging and boosting

Bagging and boosting are two techniques used to combine learners. These techniques are classified under the generic name of **ensembles** (or meta-algorithm) because the ultimate goal is actually to ensemble *weak* learners to create a more sophisticated, but more accurate, model. There is no formal definition of a weak learner, but ideally it's a fast, sometimes linear model that not necessarily produces excellent results (it suffices that they are just better than a random guess). The final ensemble is typically a non-linear learner whose performance increases with the number of weak learners in the model (note that the relation is strictly non-linear). Let's now see how they work.

Bagging

Bagging stands for **Bootstrap Aggregating**, and its ultimate goal is to reduce variance by averaging weak learners' results. Let's now see the code; we will explain how it works. As a dataset, we will reuse the Boston dataset (and its validation split) from the previous example:

```
In:
from sklearn.ensemble import BaggingRegressor
bagging = BaggingRegressor(SGDRegressor(), n_jobs=-1,
                          n_estimators=1000, random_state=101,
                          max_features=0.8)
bagging.fit(X_train, y_train)
mean_absolute_error(y_test, bagging.predict(X_test))
Out:
3.8345485952100629
```

The `BaggingRegressor` class, from the `submodule` ensemble of Scikit-learn, is the base class to create bagging regressors. It requires the weak learner (in the example, it's a `SGDRegressor`), the total number of regressors (1,000), and the maximum number of features to be used in each regressor (80% of the total number). Then, the bagging learner is trained as with the other learners seen so far, with the method fit. At this point, for each weak learner:

- 80% of the features composing the *X* train dataset are selected at random
- The weak learner is trained just on the selected features on a bootstrap with a replacement set of observations in the training set

At the end, the bagging model contains 1,000 trained `SGDRegressors`. When a prediction is requested from the ensemble, each of the 1,000 weak learners makes its prediction, then the results are averaged, producing the ensemble prediction.

Please note that both training and prediction operations are per-weak learner; therefore they can be parallelized on multiple CPUs (that's why `n_jobs` is `-1` in the example; that is, we use all the cores).

The final result, in terms of MAE, should be better than a single `SGDRegressor`; on the other hand, the model is about 1,000 times more complex.

Typically, ensembles are associated with decision or regression trees. In that case, the name of the regression ensemble changes to Random Forest Regressor (that is, a forest, composed of multiple trees). Since this technique is often used as the *default* bagging ensemble, there is an ad hoc class in Scikit-learn:

```
In:
from sklearn.ensemble import RandomForestRegressor

regr = RandomForestRegressor(n_estimators=100,
                             n_jobs=-1, random_state=101)
regr.fit(X_train, y_train)
mean_absolute_error(y_test, regr.predict(X_test))
Out:
2.6412236842105261
```

One additional feature of Random Forests is their ability to rank feature importance in the model (that is, they detect which features produce the highest variation of the predicted variable). Here's the code; always remember to normalize the feature matrix first (we've already done it in the previous section):

```
In:
sorted(zip(regr.feature_importances_, boston['feature_names']),
       key=lambda x: -x[0])
Out:
```

```
[(0.52639646470399315, 'LSTAT'),
 (0.27921428015177541, 'RM'),
 (0.054353831310065687, 'DIS'),
 (0.031820451224154722, 'CRIM'),
 (0.029793467094947356, 'NOX'),
 (0.021350472586185009, 'PTRATIO'),
 (0.015375071104791901, 'AGE'),
 (0.015233565046354791, 'TAX'),
 (0.01095820296701624, 'B'),
 (0.0075592385798185944, 'INDUS'),
 (0.0055375893522671962, 'RAD'),
 (0.001348634019939781, 'ZN'),
 (0.0010587318586900362, 'CHAS')]
```

The list is sorted from the most important feature to the least important (for this ensemble). If you change the weak learner, or any other parameter, this list may change.

Boosting

Boosting is a way to combine (ensemble) weak learners, primarily to reduce prediction bias. Instead of creating a pool of predictors, as in bagging, boosting produces a cascade of them, where each output is the input for the following learner. We'll start with an example, exactly as we've done in the previous sub-section:

```
In:
from sklearn.ensemble import AdaBoostRegressor
booster = AdaBoostRegressor(SGDRegressor(), random_state=101,
                            n_estimators=100, learning_rate=0.01)

booster.fit(X_train, y_train)
mean_absolute_error(y_test, booster.predict(X_test))
Out:
3.8621128094354349
```

The AdaBoostRegressor class, from the submodule ensemble of Scikit-learn, is the base class to create a Boosted Regressor. As for the bagging, it requires the weak learner (an SGDRegressor), the total number of regressors (100), and the learning rate (0.01). Starting from an unfitted ensemble, for each weak learner the training is:

- Given the training set, the cascade of already-fit learners produces a prediction

- The error between the actual values and the predicted ones, multiplied by the learning rate, is computed

- A new weak learner is trained on that error set, and inserted as the last stage in the cascade of already trained learners

At the end of the training stage, the ensemble contains 100 trained SGDRegressors organized in a cascade. When a prediction is requested from the ensemble, the final value is a recursive operation: starting from the last stage, the output value is the value predicted by the previous stage plus the learning rate multiplied by the prediction of the current stage.

The learning rate is similar to the one from the stochastic gradient descent. A smaller learning rate will require more steps to approach the results, but the granularity of the output will be better. A bigger rate will require fewer steps, but will probably approach a less accurate result.

Please note here that training and testing cannot be done independently on each weak learner, since to train a model you need the chain of outputs of the previous ones. This fact limits the CPU usage to only one, limiting the length of the cascade.

In the case of boosting with Decision/Regression Trees, the Scikit-learn package offers a pre-build class called GradientBoostingRegressor. A short code snippet should suffice to demonstrate how it works:

```
In:
from sklearn.ensemble import GradientBoostingRegressor

regr = GradientBoostingRegressor(n_estimators=500,
                                 learning_rate=0.01,
                                 random_state=101)
regr.fit(X_train, y_train)
mean_absolute_error(y_test, regr.predict(X_test))
Out:
2.6148878419996806
```

Even with Boosting, it is possible to rank feature importance. In fact, it's the very same method:

```
In:
sorted(zip(regr.feature_importances_, boston['feature_names']),
       key=lambda x: -x[0])
Out:
```

```
[(0.26442820639779868, 'LSTAT'),
 (0.21170609523931225, 'RM'),
 (0.11520512234965929, 'DIS'),
 (0.078532434845484278, 'TAX'),
 (0.075850985431776763, 'PTRATIO'),
 (0.0756604687541029, 'NOX'),
 (0.052097327327291075, 'B'),
 (0.041177393920216847, 'CRIM'),
 (0.034255068725583829, 'AGE'),
 (0.023541808250096587, 'INDUS'),
 (0.012189199051061582, 'CHAS'),
 (0.011705380397086919, 'RAD'),
 (0.0036505093105288107, 'ZN')]
```

Ensemble wrap up

The pros are as follows:

- Strong learners based on weak learners
- They enable stochastic learning
- The randomness of the process creates a robust solution

The cons are as follows:

- Training time is considerable, as well as the memory footprint
- The learning step (in the boosted ensemble) can be very tricky to properly set, similar to the update step (alpha) in the stochastic gradient descent

Gradient Boosting Regressor with LAD

More than a new technique, this is an ensemble of technologies already seen in this book, with a new loss function, the **Least Absolute Deviations** (LAD). With respect to the least square function, seen in the previous chapter, with LAD the L^1 norm of the error is computed.

Regressor learners based on LAD are typically robust but unstable, because of the multiple minima of the loss function (leading therefore to multiple best solutions). Alone, this loss function seems to bear little value, but paired with gradient boosting, it creates a very stable regressor, due to the fact that boosting overcomes LAD regression limitations. With the code, this is very simple to achieve:

```
In:
from sklearn.ensemble import GradientBoostingRegressor

regr = GradientBoostingRegressor('lad',
                                 n_estimators=500,
                                 learning_rate=0.1,
                                 random_state=101)
regr.fit(X_train, y_train)
mean_absolute_error(y_test, regr.predict(X_test))
Out:
2.6216986613160258
```

Remember to specify to use the `'lad'` loss, otherwise the default least square (L^2) is used. In addition, another loss function, huber, combines the least square loss and the least absolute deviation loss to create a loss function even more robust. To try it, just insert the string value `'huber'` instead of `'lad'` in the last run piece of code.

GBM with LAD wrap up

The pros are that it combines the strength of a boosted ensemble to the LAD loss, producing a very stable and robust learner and the cons are that training time is very high (exactly the same as training N consecutive LAD learners, one after the other).

Summary

This chapter concludes the long journey around regression methods we have taken throughout this book. We have seen how to deal with different kinds of regression modeling, how to pre-process data, and how to evaluate the results. In the present chapter, we glanced at some cutting-edge techniques. In the next, and last, chapter of the book, we apply regression in real-world examples and invite you to experiment with some concrete examples.

9
Real-world Applications for Regression Models

We have arrived at the concluding chapter of the book. In respect of the previous chapters, the present one is very practical in its essence, since it mostly contains lots of code and no math or other theoretical explanation. It comprises four practical examples of real-world data science problems solved using linear models. The ultimate goal is to demonstrate how to approach such problems and how to develop the reasoning behind their resolution, so that they can be used as blueprints for similar challenges you'll encounter.

For each problem, we will describe the question to be answered, provide a short description of the dataset, and decide the metric we strive to maximize (or the error we want to minimize). Then, throughout the code, we will provide ideas and intuitions that are key to successfully completing each one. In addition, when run, the code will produce verbose output from the modeling, in order to provide the reader with all the information needed to decide the next step. Due to space restrictions, output will be truncated so it just contains the key lines (the truncated lines are represented by [...] in the output) but, on your screen, you'll get the complete picture.

In this chapter, each section was provided with a separate IPython Notebook. They are different problems, and each of them is developed and presented independently.

Downloading the datasets

In this section of the book, we will download all the datasets that are going to be used in the examples in this chapter. We chose to store them in separate subdirectories of the same folder where the IPython Notebook is contained. Note that some of them are quite big (100+ MB).

 We would like to thank the maintainers and the creators of the UCI dataset archive. Thanks to such repositories, modeling and achieving experiment repeatability are much easier than before. The UCI archive is from Lichman, M. (2013). UCI Machine Learning Repository [http://archive.ics.uci.edu/ml]. Irvine, CA: University of California, School of Information and Computer Science.

For each dataset, we first download it, and then we present the first couple of lines. First, this will help demonstrate whether the file has been correctly downloaded, unpacked, and placed into the right location; second, it will show the structure of the file itself (header, fields, and so on):

```
In:
try:
    import urllib.request as urllib2
except:
    import urllib2
import requests, io, os
import zipfile, gzip

def download_from_UCI(UCI_url, dest):
    r = requests.get(UCI_url)
    filename = UCI_url.split('/')[-1]
    print ('Extracting in %s' %  dest)
    try:
        os.mkdir(dest)
    except:
        pass
    with open (os.path.join(dest, filename), 'wb') as fh:
        print ('\tdecompression %s' % filename)
        fh.write(r.content)


def unzip_from_UCI(UCI_url, dest):
    r = requests.get(UCI_url)
    z = zipfile.ZipFile(io.BytesIO(r.content))
    print ('Extracting in %s' %  dest)
```

```
    for name in z.namelist():
        print ('\tunzipping %s' % name)
        z.extract(name, path=dest)


def gzip_from_UCI(UCI_url, dest):
    response = urllib2.urlopen(UCI_url)
    compressed_file = io.BytesIO(response.read())
    decompressed_file = gzip.GzipFile(fileobj=compressed_file)
    filename = UCI_url.split('/')[-1][:-4]
    print ('Extracting in %s' % dest)
    try:
        os.mkdir(dest)
    except:
        pass
    with open( os.path.join(dest, filename), 'wb') as outfile:
        print ('\tgunzipping %s' % filename)
        cnt = decompressed_file.read()
        outfile.write(cnt)
```

Time series problem dataset

Dataset from: Brown, M. S., Pelosi, M. & Dirska, H. (2013). Dynamic-radius Species-conserving Genetic Algorithm for the Financial Forecasting of Dow Jones Index Stocks. Machine Learning and Data Mining in Pattern Recognition, 7988, 27-41.

```
In:
UCI_url = 'https://archive.ics.uci.edu/ml/machine-learning-
databases/00312/dow_jones_index.zip'
unzip_from_UCI(UCI_url, dest='./dji')
Out:
Extracting in ./dji
  unzipping dow_jones_index.data
  unzipping dow_jones_index.names
In:
! head -2 ./dji/dow_jones_index.data
Out:

quarter,stock,date,open,high,low,close,volume,percent_change_price,p
ercent_change_volume_over_last_wk,previous_weeks_volume,next_weeks_o
pen,next_weeks_close,percent_change_next_weeks_price,days_to_next_di
vidend,percent_return_next_dividend
1,AA,1/7/2011,$15.82,$16.72,$15.78,$16.42,239655616,3.79267,,,$16.71
,$15.97,-4.42849,26,0.182704
```

Regression problem dataset

Dataset from: Thierry Bertin-Mahieux, Daniel P.W. Ellis, Brian Whitman, and Paul Lamere. The Million Song Dataset. In Proceedings of the 12th International Society for Music Information Retrieval Conference (ISMIR), 2011.

```
In:
UCI_url = 'https://archive.ics.uci.edu/ml/machine-learning-
databases/00203/YearPredictionMSD.txt.zip'
unzip_from_UCI(UCI_url, dest='./msd')
Out:
Extracting in ./msd
  unzipping YearPredictionMSD.txt
In:
! head -n 2 ./msd/YearPredictionMSD.txt
Out:
```

```
2001,49.94357,21.47114,73.07750,8.74861,-17.40628,-13.09905,-25.0120
2,-12.23257,7.83089,-2.46783,3.32136,-2.31521,10.20556,611.10913,951
.08960,698.11428,408.98485,383.70912,326.51512,238.11327,251.42414,1
87.17351,100.42652,179.19498,-8.41558,-317.87038,95.86266,48.10259,-
95.66303,-18.06215,1.96984,34.42438,11.72670,1.36790,7.79444,-0.3699
4,-133.67852,-83.26165,-37.29765,73.04667,-37.36684,-3.13853,-24.215
31,-13.23066,15.93809,-18.60478,82.15479,240.57980,-10.29407,31.5843
1,-25.38187,-3.90772,13.29258,41.55060,-7.26272,-21.00863,105.50848,
64.29856,26.08481,-44.59110,-8.30657,7.93706,-10.73660,-95.44766,-82
.03307,-35.59194,4.69525,70.95626,28.09139,6.02015,-37.13767,-41.124
50,-8.40816,7.19877,-8.60176,-5.90857,-12.32437,14.68734,-54.32125,4
0.14786,13.01620,-54.40548,58.99367,15.37344,1.11144,-23.08793,68.40
795,-1.82223,-27.46348,2.26327
2001,48.73215,18.42930,70.32679,12.94636,-10.32437,-24.83777,8.76630
,-0.92019,18.76548,4.59210,2.21920,0.34006,44.38997,2056.93836,605.4
0696,457.41175,777.15347,415.64880,746.47775,366.45320,317.82946,273
.07917,141.75921,317.35269,19.48271,-65.25496,162.75145,135.00765,-9
6.28436,-86.87955,17.38087,45.90742,32.49908,-32.85429,45.10830,26.8
4939,-302.57328,-41.71932,-138.85034,202.18689,-33.44277,195.04749,-
16.93235,-1.09168,-25.38061,-12.19034,-125.94783,121.74212,136.67075
,41.18157,28.55107,1.52298,70.99515,-43.63073,-42.55014,129.82848,79
.95420,-87.14554,-45.75446,-65.82100,-43.90031,-19.45705,12.59163,-4
07.64130,42.91189,12.15850,-88.37882,42.25246,46.49209,-30.17747,45.
98495,130.47892,13.88281,-4.00055,17.85965,-18.32138,-87.99109,14.37
524,-22.70119,-58.81266,5.66812,-19.68073,33.04964,42.87836,-9.90378
,-32.22788,70.49388,12.04941,58.43453,26.92061
```

Multiclass classification problem dataset

Dataset from: Salvatore J. Stolfo, Wei Fan, Wenke Lee, Andreas Prodromidis, and Philip K. Chan. Cost-based Modeling and Evaluation for Data Mining With Application to Fraud and Intrusion Detection: Results from the JAM Project.

```
In:
UCI_url = 'https://archive.ics.uci.edu/ml/machine-learning-databases/
kddcup99-mld/kddcup.data.gz'
gzip_from_UCI(UCI_url, dest='./kdd')
Out:
Extracting in ./kdd
  gunzipping kddcup.dat
In:
!head -2 ./kdd/kddcup.dat
Out:
```

```
0,tcp,http,SF,215,45076,0,0,0,0,0,1,0,0,0,0,0,0,0,0,0,0,1,1,0.00,0.0
0,0.00,0.00,1.00,0.00,0.00,0,0,0.00,0.00,0.00,0.00,0.00,0.00,0.00,0.
00,normal.
0,tcp,http,SF,162,4528,0,0,0,0,0,1,0,0,0,0,0,0,0,0,0,0,2,2,0.00,0.00
,0.00,0.00,1.00,0.00,0.00,1,1,1.00,0.00,1.00,0.00,0.00,0.00,0.00,0.0
0,normal.
```

Ranking problem dataset

Creator/Donor: Jeffrey C. Schlimmer

```
In:
UCI_url = 'https://archive.ics.uci.edu/ml/machine-learning-databases/
autos/imports-85.data'
download_from_UCI(UCI_url, dest='./autos')
Out:
Extracting in ./autos
  decompression imports-85.data
In:
!head -2 ./autos/imports-85.data
Out:
```

```
3,?,alfa-romero,gas,std,two,convertible,rwd,front,88.60,168.80,64.10
,48.80,2548,dohc,four,130,mpfi,3.47,2.68,9.00,111,5000,21,27,13495
3,?,alfa-romero,gas,std,two,convertible,rwd,front,88.60,168.80,64.10
,48.80,2548,dohc,four,130,mpfi,3.47,2.68,9.00,111,5000,21,27,16500
```

A regression problem

Given some descriptors of a song, the goal of this problem is to predict the year when the song was produced. That's basically a regression problem, since the target variable to predict is a number in the range between 1922 and 2011.

For each song, in addition to the year of production, 90 attributes are provided. All of them are related to the timbre: 12 of them relate to the timbre average and 78 attributes describe the timbre's covariance; all the features are numerical (integer or floating point numbers).

The dataset is composed of more than half a million observations. As for the competition behind the dataset, the authors tried to achieve the best results using the first 463,715 observations as a training set and the remaining 51,630 for testing.

The metric used to evaluate the results is the **Mean Absolute Error** (**MAE**) between the predicted year and the real year of production for the songs composing the testing set. The goal is to minimize the error measure.

 The complete description of this problem and additional information (about the feature extraction phase) can be found at the website: `https://archive.ics.uci.edu/ml/datasets/YearPredictionMSD`

Now, let's start with some Python code. First of all, we load the dataset (remember, if that operation fails it means you should download the dataset by yourself before running the program in the previous section). Then, we split the training and testing parts according to the guidelines provided with the dataset. Finally, we print the size (in Megabytes) of the resulting DataFrame, in order to have an indication of the memory footprint of the dataset:

```
In:
import matplotlib.pyplot as plt
%matplotlib inline

import numpy as np
import pandas as pd

dataset = pd.read_csv('./msd/YearPredictionMSD.txt',
                      header=None).as_matrix()
In:
X_train = dataset[:463715, 1:]
y_train = np.asarray(dataset[:463715, 0])
```

```
X_test = dataset[463715:, 1:]
y_test = np.asarray(dataset[463715:, 0])
In:
print("Dataset is MB:", dataset.nbytes/1E6)
del dataset
Out:
Dataset is MB: 375.17116
```

Our dataset is not all that small, since it's almost 400 MB. We should, therefore, be very smart and use any appropriate trick to cope with it without running out of memory (and becoming heavily reliant on the swap file) or even crashing our operating system.

Let's now get a baseline for comparisons: we will use the plain vanilla linear regression (vanilla means that there's no additional flavor to it; as with plain ice cream, our model uses the standard hyper-parameters). We then print the training time (in seconds), the MAE in the train set, and the MAE in the test set:

```
In:
from sklearn.linear_model import LinearRegression, SGDRegressor
from sklearn.cross_validation import KFold
from sklearn.metrics import mean_absolute_error
import time
In:
regr = LinearRegression()

tic = time.clock()
regr.fit(X_train, y_train)
print("Training time [s]:", time.clock()-tic)

print("MAE train set:", mean_absolute_error(y_train,
                                 regr.predict(X_train)))

print("MAE test set:", mean_absolute_error(y_test,
                                 regr.predict(X_test)))
Out:
Training time [s]: 9.989145000000002
MAE train set: 6.79557016727
MAE test set: 6.80049646319
```

Using linear regression, we can achieve a MAE of 6.8 in around 10 seconds. In addition, the learner seems stable and robust since there is no difference between MAE in the train set and MAE in the test set (thanks to the generalization power of linear regression). Let's now try to do even better. We test a stochastic gradient descent variation, to see if we can achieve a better MAE more rapidly (eventually). We experiment with both a small and a high number of iterations:

```
In:
regr = SGDRegressor()

tic = time.clock()
regr.fit(X_train, y_train)
print("Training time [s]:", time.clock()-tic)

print("MAE train set:", mean_absolute_error(y_train,
                                    regr.predict(X_train)))

print("MAE test set:", mean_absolute_error(y_test,
                                    regr.predict(X_test)))
Out:
Training time [s]: 1.5492949999999972
MAE train set: 3.27482912145e+15
MAE test set: 3.30350427822e+15
In:
regr = SGDRegressor(n_iter=100)

tic = time.clock()
regr.fit(X_train, y_train)
print("Training time [s]:", time.clock()-tic)

print("MAE train set:", mean_absolute_error(y_train,
                                    regr.predict(X_train)))

print("MAE test set:", mean_absolute_error(y_test,
                                    regr.predict(X_test)))
Out:
Training time [s]: 24.713879
MAE train set: 2.12094618827e+15
MAE test set: 2.14161266897e+15
```

The results seem to suggest that SGD Regression is not appropriate for the shape of the dataset: getting better results may require much perseverance and take a very long time.

Now, we have two options: the first is to resort to an advanced classifier (such as an ensemble); otherwise, we can fine-tune the model with feature engineering. For this problem, let's go for the second choice, since the main goal of this book is to work on linear models. Readers are strongly advised to try the first approach as comparison.

Let's now try to use the polynomial expansion of the features, followed by a feature selection step. This ensures that we have all the features, built on top on the features of the problem, in order to select the best and run through a linear regressor.

Since we don't know a-priori which is the optimum number of features, let's treat that as a parameter and plot the MAE for the training and the testing set as a variable. Furthermore, since we're undertaking a regression task, feature selection should be targeting the best regression features; therefore the F-score for regression is used to rank and select the top K features.

We immediately encounter a problem: polynomial feature expansion creates so many additional features. Since we are operating on a quite big dataset, we might have to subsample the training set. Let's first count how many features are after the polynomial expansion:

```
In:
from sklearn.preprocessing import PolynomialFeatures
PolynomialFeatures().fit_transform(X_train[:10,:]).shape[1]
Out:
4186
```

With more than 4,000 features, we should select at least 10 times more observations, in order not to risk overfitting. We shuffle the dataset, and select one twelfth of it (so the number of observations is around 40,000). To manage that, we can use K-fold, and select just the indexes composing the test set of the first piece:

```
In:
from sklearn.pipeline import Pipeline
from sklearn import feature_selection
from sklearn.feature_selection import SelectKBest
import gc

folds = 12
train_idx = list(KFold(X_train.shape[0], folds, random_state=101,
shuffle=True))[0][1]

to_plot = []
```

```
for k_feat in range(50, 2001, 50):

    gc.collect()

    print('---------------------------')
    print("K = ", k_feat)

    poly = PolynomialFeatures()
    regr = LinearRegression()
    f_sel = SelectKBest(feature_selection.f_regression, k=k_feat)

    pipeline = Pipeline([('poly', poly), ('f_sel', f_sel),
('regr', regr)])

    tic = time.clock()
    pipeline.fit(X_train[train_idx], y_train[train_idx])
    print("Training time [s]:", time.clock()-tic)

    mae_train = mean_absolute_error(y_train[train_idx],
pipeline.predict(X_train[train_idx]))
    mae_test = mean_absolute_error(y_test, pipeline.predict(X_test))

    print("MAE train set:", mae_train)

    print("MAE test set:", mae_test)

    to_plot.append((k_feat, mae_train, mae_test))
Out:
...[output]...
In:
plt.plot([x[0] for x in to_plot], [x[1] for x in to_plot], 'b',
label='Train')
plt.plot([x[0] for x in to_plot], [x[2] for x in to_plot], 'r--',
label='Test')
plt.xlabel('Num. features selected')
plt.ylabel('MAE train/test')
plt.legend(loc=0)

plt.show()
Out:
```

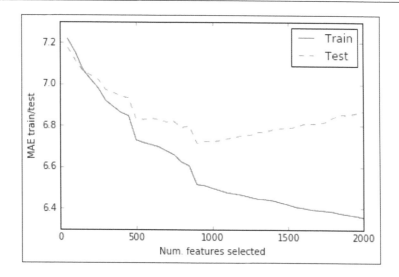

It seems that we have found the optimal value for K, the number of selected features, in K=900. At this point:

- The training MAE and the testing MAE diverge: if we are to use more than 900 features, we may have start overfitting.

- The testing MAE is at its minimum. The reading for the MAE in the test set is 6.70.

- This is the best tradeoff between performance and training time (23 seconds).

If you have a better machine (with 16 GB of RAM or more), you can re-run the last two cells, increasing the size of the training set (moving, for example, the number of folds from 12 to 8 or 4). The result should improve by some decimal places, although the training will be longer.

Testing a classifier instead of a regressor

As an open problem (we're not providing a solution), we could have solved this problem as a classification task, since the number of target variables is *just* 89 (which is higher than the majority of the classification problems, though). Following this path, you will encounter different kinds of problems (the MAE is wrongly defined on a classification problem). We encourage readers to have a go at this, and try to match the result we obtained with the regression learner; here is the first step:

```
In:
print(np.unique(np.ascontiguousarray(y_train)))
print(len(np.unique(np.ascontiguousarray(y_train))))
Out:
```

```
[ 1922.   1924.   1925.   1926.   1927.   1928.   1929.   1930.   1931.   1932.
  1933.   1934.   1935.   1936.   1937.   1938.   1939.   1940.   1941.   1942.
  1943.   1944.   1945.   1946.   1947.   1948.   1949.   1950.   1951.   1952.
  1953.   1954.   1955.   1956.   1957.   1958.   1959.   1960.   1961.   1962.
  1963.   1964.   1965.   1966.   1967.   1968.   1969.   1970.   1971.   1972.
  1973.   1974.   1975.   1976.   1977.   1978.   1979.   1980.   1981.   1982.
  1983.   1984.   1985.   1986.   1987.   1988.   1989.   1990.   1991.   1992.
  1993.   1994.   1995.   1996.   1997.   1998.   1999.   2000.   2001.   2002.
  2003.   2004.   2005.   2006.   2007.   2008.   2009.   2010.   2011.]
89
In:
from sklearn.linear_model import SGDClassifier
regr = SGDClassifier('log', random_state=101)

tic = time.clock()
regr.fit(X_train, y_train)
print("Training time [s]:", time.clock()-tic)

print("MAE train set:", mean_absolute_error(y_train,
                                   regr.predict(X_train)))

print("MAE test set:", mean_absolute_error(y_test,
                                   regr.predict(X_test)))
Out:
Training time [s]: 117.23069399999986
MAE train set: 7.88104546974
MAE test set: 7.7926593066
```

An imbalanced and multiclass classification problem

Given some descriptors of a sequence of packets, flowing to/from a host connected to the Internet, the goal of this problem is to detect whether that sequence signals a malicious attack or not. If it does, we should also classify the type of attack. That's a multiclass classification problem, since the possible labels are multiple ones.

For each observation, 42 features are revealed: please note that some of them are categorical, whereas others are numerical. The dataset is composed of almost 5 million observations (but in this exercise we're using just the first million, to avoid memory constraints), and the number of possible labels is 23. One of them represents a non-malicious situation (*normal*); all the others represent 22 different network attacks. Some attention should be paid to the fact that the frequencies of response classes are imbalanced: for some attacks there are multiple observations, for others just a few.

No instruction is given about how to split the train/test, or how to evaluate results. In this problem, we will adopt an exploratory goal: trying to reveal accurate information for all the labels. We warmly advise readers to take some further steps and tune the learner to maximize the precision of the detection, just for the malicious activities in the dataset.

 The full description of this problem can be found at the website: https://archive.ics.uci.edu/ml/datasets/ KDD+Cup+1999+Data.

First at all, let's load the data. The file doesn't contain the header; therefore we have to specify the column names while loading it with pandas:

```
In:
import matplotlib.pyplot as plt
%matplotlib inline
import matplotlib.pylab as pylab

import numpy as np
import pandas as pd

columns = ["duration", "protocol_type", "service",
           "flag", "src_bytes", "dst_bytes", "land",
           "wrong_fragment", "urgent", "hot", "num_failed_logins",
           "logged_in", "num_compromised", "root_shell",
           "su_attempted", "num_root", "num_file_creations",
           "num_shells", "num_access_files", "num_outbound_cmds",
           "is_host_login", "is_guest_login", "count", "srv_count",
           "serror_rate", "srv_serror_rate", "rerror_rate",
           "srv_rerror_rate", "same_srv_rate", "diff_srv_rate",
           "srv_diff_host_rate", "dst_host_count",
           "dst_host_srv_count", "dst_host_same_srv_rate",
           "dst_host_diff_srv_rate", "dst_host_same_src_port_rate",
           "dst_host_srv_diff_host_rate", "dst_host_serror_rate",
           "dst_host_srv_serror_rate", "dst_host_rerror_rate",
           "dst_host_srv_rerror_rate", "outcome"]

dataset = pd.read_csv('./kdd/kddcup.dat', names=columns,
nrows=1000000)
```

Let's now check the first few lines of the loaded dataset (in order to understand the overall shape of the dataset), its size (in terms of observations and features), and the types of features (to separate categorical from numerical ones):

```
In:
print(dataset.head())
```

```
Out:
...[head of the dataset] ...
In:
dataset.shape
Out:
(1000000, 42)
In:
dataset.dtypes
Out:
duration                       int64
protocol_type                 object
service                       object
flag                          object
src_bytes                      int64
dst_bytes                      int64
land                           int64
wrong_fragment                 int64
 urgent                        int64
hot                            int64
num_failed_logins              int64
logged_in                      int64
num_compromised                int64
root_shell                     int64
su_attempted                   int64
num_root                       int64
num_file_creations             int64
num_shells                     int64
num_access_files               int64
num_outbound_cmds              int64
is_host_login                  int64
is_guest_login                 int64
count                          int64
srv_count                      int64
serror_rate                  float64
srv_serror_rate              float64
rerror_rate                  float64
srv_rerror_rate              float64
same_srv_rate                float64
diff_srv_rate                float64
srv_diff_host_rate           float64
dst_host_count                 int64
dst_host_srv_count             int64
dst_host_same_srv_rate       float64
dst_host_diff_srv_rate       float64
dst_host_same_src_port_rate  float64
dst_host_srv_diff_host_rate  float64
dst_host_serror_rate         float64
```

```
dst_host_srv_serror_rate          float64
dst_host_rerror_rate              float64
dst_host_srv_rerror_rate          float64
outcome                            object
dtype: object
```

It seems we're operating on a very big dataset, since it has 1M rows and 42 columns, with some of them being categorical. Now, let's separate the target variable from the features, encoding the strings (containing attack names) with ordinal numbers. To do so, we can use the LabelEncoder object:

```
In:
sorted(dataset['outcome'].unique())
Out:
['back.', 'buffer_overflow.', 'ftp_write.', 'guess_passwd.',
'imap.', 'ipsweep.', 'land.', 'loadmodule.', 'multihop.',
'neptune.', 'nmap.', 'normal.', 'perl.', 'phf.', 'pod.',
'portsweep.', 'satan.', 'smurf.', 'teardrop.', 'warezmaster.']
In:
from sklearn.preprocessing import LabelEncoder

labels_enc = LabelEncoder()

labels = labels_enc.fit_transform(dataset['outcome'])
labels_map = labels_enc.classes_
Out:
array(['back.', 'buffer_overflow.', 'ftp_write.', 'guess_passwd.',
'imap.', 'ipsweep.', 'land.', 'loadmodule.', 'multihop.',
'neptune.', 'nmap.', 'normal.', 'perl.', 'phf.', 'pod.',
'portsweep.', 'satan.', 'smurf.', 'teardrop.', 'warezmaster.'],
dtype=object)
```

Targets, variables are now in a separate array, encoded as integers. Let's now remove the target column from the dataset, and one-hot encode all the categorical features. To do so, we can simply use the Pandas get_dummies function. The new shape of the dataset is therefore *larger*, because each level composing a categorical feature is now a binary feature:

```
In:
dataset.drop('outcome', axis=1, inplace=True)
In:
observations = pd.get_dummies(dataset, sparse=True)
del dataset
In:
observations.shape
Out:
(1000000, 118)
```

Since we have many available observations and many classes contain just a few samples, we can shuffle and split the dataset in two portions: one to be used in training, the other for testing:

```
In:
from sklearn.cross_validation import train_test_split

X_train, X_test, y_train, y_test = \
    train_test_split(observations.as_matrix(), labels,
                     train_size=0.5, random_state=101)

del observations
```

Given the exploratory nature of our task, let's now define a function to print the confusion matrix, normalized by the number of occurrences per each class:

```
In:
def plot_normalised_confusion_matrix(cm, labels_str,
title='Normalised confusion matrix', cmap=plt.cm.Blues):
    pylab.rcParams['figure.figsize'] = (6.0, 6.0)
    cm_normalized = cm.astype('float') / cm.sum(axis=1)[:,
np.newaxis]
    plt.imshow(cm_normalized, interpolation='nearest', cmap=cmap)
    plt.title(title)
    plt.colorbar()
    tick_marks = np.arange(len(labels_str))
    plt.xticks(tick_marks, labels_str, rotation=90)
    plt.yticks(tick_marks, labels_str)
    plt.tight_layout()
    plt.ylabel('True label')
    plt.xlabel('Predicted label')
    plt.show()
```

Let's now create a baseline for this task. We will use a simple SGDClassifier, with logistic loss, in this first step. For both training and test sets we will print the overall accuracy of the solution, the normalized confusion matrix, and the classification report (containing the precision, recall, F1-score, and support for each class).

```
In:
from sklearn.linear_model import SGDClassifier
from sklearn.metrics import classification_report, accuracy_score,
confusion_matrix

clf = SGDClassifier('log', random_state=101)
clf.fit(X_train, y_train)

y_train_pred = clf.predict(X_train)
y_test_pred = clf.predict(X_test)
```

```
print("TRAIN SET")
print("Accuracy:", accuracy_score(y_train, y_train_pred))

print("Confusion matrix:")
plot_normalised_confusion_matrix(confusion_matrix(y_train,
y_train_pred), labels_map)

print("Classification report:")
print(classification_report(y_train, y_train_pred,
target_names=labels_map))

print("TEST SET")
print("Accuracy:", accuracy_score(y_test, y_test_pred))

print("Confusion matrix:")
plot_normalised_confusion_matrix(confusion_matrix(y_test,
y_test_pred), labels_map)

print("Classification report:")
print(classification_report(y_test, y_test_pred,
target_names=labels_map))
```

```
Out:
TRAIN SET
Accuracy: 0.781702
Confusion matrix:
```

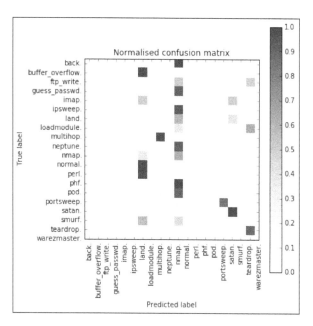

```
Classification report:
                 precision      recall    f1-score      support

          back.      0.00        0.00        0.00         1005
buffer_overflow.      0.00        0.00        0.00            1
      ftp_write.      0.00        0.00        0.00            2
   guess_passwd.      0.00        0.00        0.00           30
           imap.      0.00        0.00        0.00            2
        ipsweep.      0.00        0.00        0.00         3730
           land.      0.00        0.00        0.00           10
     loadmodule.      0.00        0.00        0.00            3
       multihop.      1.00        1.00        1.00       102522
        neptune.      0.06        0.00        0.00         1149
           nmap.      0.96        0.64        0.77       281101
         normal.      0.00        0.00        0.00            1
           perl.      0.00        0.00        0.00            2
            phf.      0.00        0.00        0.00           22
            pod.      0.00        0.00        0.00         1437
      portsweep.      1.00        0.88        0.93         2698
          satan.      0.99        0.99        0.99       106165
          smurf.      0.00        0.00        0.00          110
       teardrop.      0.00        0.90        0.01           10

    avg / total      0.96        0.78        0.85       500000

TEST SET
Accuracy: 0.781338
Confusion matrix:
```

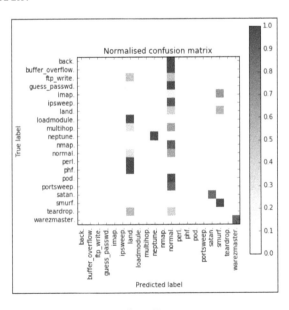

```
Classification report:
                  precision    recall   f1-score    support

          back.      0.00        0.00      0.00        997
buffer_overflow.      0.00        0.00      0.00          4
     ftp_write.      0.00        0.00      0.00          6
  guess_passwd.      0.00        0.00      0.00         23
          imap.      0.00        0.00      0.00         10
       ipsweep.      0.00        0.00      0.00       3849
          land.      0.00        0.00      0.00          7
    loadmodule.      0.00        0.00      0.00          2
      multihop.      0.00        0.00      0.00          3
       neptune.      1.00        1.00      1.00     102293
          nmap.      0.05        0.00      0.00       1167
        normal.      0.96        0.64      0.77     281286
          perl.      0.00        0.00      0.00          1
           phf.      0.00        0.00      0.00          1
           pod.      0.00        0.00      0.00         18
     portsweep.      0.00        0.00      0.00       1345
         satan.      1.00        0.88      0.94       2691
         smurf.      0.99        1.00      0.99     106198
      teardrop.      0.00        0.00      0.00         89
  warezmaster.      0.00        0.90      0.01         10

   avg / total      0.96        0.78      0.85     500000
```

Although the output is very long, some points are immediately visible in this baseline:

- Accuracy is low (0.80), but the classification is resilient to overfitting.
- Just two vertical lines dominate the confusion matrix. This indicates that the classifier fits only two classes during the training phase. Not surprisingly, they are the most populated ones.
- You can reach the same conclusion (that the class imbalance has influenced the results) by looking at the classification report: just a few classes have non-zero scores.

Such a problem is a very frequent one, and it happens when you try to fit a linear learner on a strongly imbalanced dataset. Let's now try to oversample small classes, and sub-sample the most popular ones. In the following function, we implemented a bootstrap algorithm with replacement, where each class gets, in the output data, at least min_samples_out observations and up to max_samples_out. This should force the learning algorithm to *take account of* all classes with a similar weight.

```
In:
import random
random.seed(101)

def sample_class_with_replacement(X, y, label, min_samples_out,
max_samples_out):
    rows = np.where(y==label)[0]

    if len(rows) == 0:
        raise Exception

    n_estraction = min(max(len(rows), min_samples_out),
max_samples_out)
    extracted = [random.choice(rows) for _ in range(n_estraction)]

    return extracted


train_idx = []

for label in np.unique(labels):
    try:
        idx = sample_class_with_replacement(X_train, y_train,
label, 500, 20000)
        train_idx.extend(idx)
    except:
        pass

X_train_sampled_balanced = X_train[train_idx, :]
y_train_sampled_balanced = y_train[train_idx]
```

Now, we can try to do better than the baseline, training out the learner on this modified (balanced) training set, and then applying it on the test set:

```
In:
from sklearn.linear_model import SGDClassifier
from sklearn.metrics import classification_report, accuracy_score
from sklearn.metrics import confusion_matrix

clf = SGDClassifier('log', random_state=101)
```

```
clf.fit(X_train_sampled_balanced, y_train_sampled_balanced)

y_train_pred = clf.predict(X_train_sampled_balanced)
y_test_pred = clf.predict(X_test)

print("TRAIN SET")
print("Accuracy:", accuracy_score(y_train_sampled_balanced,
y_train_pred))

print("Confusion matrix:")
plot_normalised_confusion_matrix(confusion_matrix(
        y_train_sampled_balanced, y_train_pred), labels_map)

print("Classification report:")
print(classification_report(y_train_sampled_balanced,
y_train_pred, target_names=labels_map))


print("TEST SET")
print("Accuracy:", accuracy_score(y_test, y_test_pred))

print("Confusion matrix:")
plot_normalised_confusion_matrix(confusion_matrix(y_test,
y_test_pred), labels_map)

print("Classification report:")
print(classification_report(y_test, y_test_pred,
target_names=labels_map))
Out:
TRAIN SET
Accuracy: 0.712668335121
[...]
TEST SET
Accuracy: 0.723616
[...]
```

The results suggest we're heading toward the right direction. The confusion matrix looks more diagonal (meaning that matches between rows and columns occur more on the diagonal), and the accuracy increases to 0.72 in the test set. Let's now try some values to achieve hyperparameter optimization, and boost the score to its max. For that, we run a grid-search cross-validation, using three folds:

```
In:
from sklearn.grid_search import GridSearchCV
```

```
parameters = {
    'loss': ('log', 'hinge'),
    'alpha': [0.1, 0.01, 0.001, 0.0001]
}

clfgs = GridSearchCV(SGDClassifier(random_state=101, n_jobs=1),
                     param_grid=parameters,
                     cv=3,
                     n_jobs=1,
                     scoring='accuracy'
                     )
clfgs.fit(X_train_sampled_balanced, y_train_sampled_balanced)
clf = clfgs.best_estimator_

print(clfgs.best_estimator_)

y_train_pred = clf.predict(X_train_sampled_balanced)
y_test_pred = clf.predict(X_test)

print("TRAIN SET")
print("Accuracy:", accuracy_score(y_train_sampled_balanced,
                                  y_train_pred))

print("Confusion matrix:")
plot_normalised_confusion_matrix(
    confusion_matrix(y_train_sampled_balanced, y_train_pred),
    labels_map)

print("Classification report:")
print(classification_report(
        y_train_sampled_balanced, y_train_pred,
        target_names=labels_map))

print("TEST SET")
print("Accuracy:", accuracy_score(y_test, y_test_pred))

print("Confusion matrix:")
plot_normalised_confusion_matrix(
    confusion_matrix(y_test, y_test_pred), labels_map)

print("Classification report:")
print(classification_report(
        y_test, y_test_pred, target_names=labels_map))

Out:
TRAIN SET
Accuracy: 0.695202531813
```

```
[...]
TEST SET
Accuracy: 0.706034
[...]
```

Although we run a grid-search cross-validation, the results look the same as in the previous experiment. We now try a different approach: since there are many output classes, let's try to use a `OneVsOne` strategy: instead of fitting one classifier per class, we fit a classifier for each pair of classes. That should result in a more accurate, although longer to train, model. Even here, each learner is cross-validated with a grid search and three folds:

```
In:
from sklearn.multiclass import OneVsOneClassifier
from sklearn.grid_search import GridSearchCV

parameters = {
    'estimator__loss': ('log', 'hinge'),
    'estimator__alpha': [1.0, 0.1, 0.01, 0.001, 0.0001, 0.00001]
}

clfgs =
GridSearchCV(OneVsOneClassifier(SGDClassifier(random_state=101,
n_jobs=1)),
                  param_grid=parameters,
                  cv=3,
                  n_jobs=1,
                  scoring='accuracy'
                  )
clfgs.fit(X_train_sampled_balanced, y_train_sampled_balanced)
clf = clfgs.best_estimator_

y_train_pred = clf.predict(X_train_sampled_balanced)
y_test_pred = clf.predict(X_test)

print("TRAIN SET")
print("Accuracy:", accuracy_score(y_train_sampled_balanced,
y_train_pred))

print("Confusion matrix:")
plot_normalised_confusion_matrix(confusion_matrix(y_train_sampled_
balanced, y_train_pred), labels_map)

print("Classification report:")
```

```
print(classification_report(y_train_sampled_balanced,
y_train_pred, target_names=labels_map))


print("TEST SET")
print("Accuracy:", accuracy_score(y_test, y_test_pred))

print("Confusion matrix:")
plot_normalised_confusion_matrix(confusion_matrix(y_test,
y_test_pred), labels_map)

print("Classification report:")
print(classification_report(y_test, y_test_pred,
target_names=labels_map))
Out:
TRAIN SET
Accuracy: 0.846250612429
[...]
TEST SET
Accuracy: 0.905708
[...]
```

The results are better, in both the training set and testing set. Let's now try a logistic regressor instead of SGDClassifier:

```
In:
from sklearn.linear_model import LogisticRegression

clf = OneVsOneClassifier(LogisticRegression(random_state=101,
n_jobs=1))
clf.fit(X_train_sampled_balanced, y_train_sampled_balanced)

y_train_pred = clf.predict(X_train_sampled_balanced)
y_test_pred = clf.predict(X_test)

print("TRAIN SET")
print("Accuracy:", accuracy_score(y_train_sampled_balanced,
                                  y_train_pred))

print("Confusion matrix:")
plot_normalised_confusion_matrix(
    confusion_matrix(y_train_sampled_balanced, y_train_pred),
    labels_map)

print("Classification report:")
print(classification_report(
```

```
        y_train_sampled_balanced, y_train_pred,
        target_names=labels_map))

print("TEST SET")
print("Accuracy:", accuracy_score(y_test, y_test_pred))

print("Confusion matrix:")
plot_normalised_confusion_matrix(
    confusion_matrix(y_test, y_test_pred), labels_map)

print("Classification report:")
print(classification_report(
        y_test, y_test_pred, target_names=labels_map))
```

Out:
TRAIN SET
Accuracy: 0.985712204876
Confusion matrix:

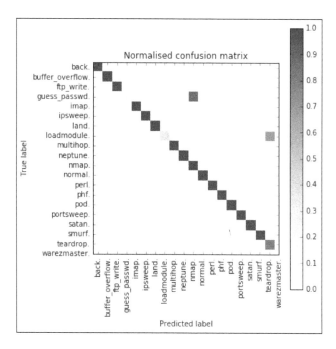

Classification report:

	precision	recall	f1-score	support
back.	1.00	0.98	0.99	1005
buffer_overflow.	1.00	1.00	1.00	500
ftp_write.	1.00	1.00	1.00	500

guess_passwd.	1.00	0.11	0.19	500
imap.	1.00	1.00	1.00	500
ipsweep.	1.00	0.99	1.00	3730
land.	1.00	1.00	1.00	500
loadmodule.	1.00	0.32	0.49	500
multihop.	1.00	1.00	1.00	20000
neptune.	0.91	1.00	0.95	1149
nmap.	0.97	1.00	0.98	20000
normal.	1.00	1.00	1.00	500
perl.	1.00	1.00	1.00	500
phf.	0.99	1.00	1.00	500
pod.	1.00	1.00	1.00	1437
portsweep.	0.98	1.00	0.99	2698
satan.	1.00	1.00	1.00	20000
smurf.	1.00	1.00	1.00	500
teardrop.	0.55	0.83	0.66	500
avg / total	0.99	0.99	0.98	75519

```
TEST SET
Accuracy: 0.996818
Confusion matrix:
```

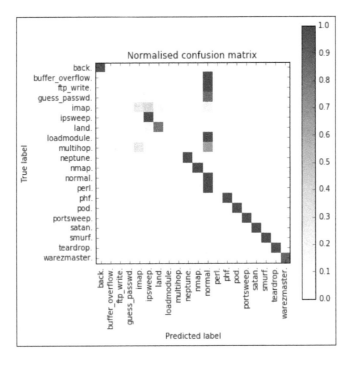

```
Classification report:
                  precision    recall   f1-score    support

         back.       1.00       0.98      0.99        997
buffer_overflow.      0.00       0.00      0.00          4
     ftp_write.       0.00       0.00      0.00          6
  guess_passwd.       1.00       0.13      0.23         23
         imap.        0.43       0.30      0.35         10
      ipsweep.        0.97       0.99      0.98       3849
         land.        0.38       0.86      0.52          7
   loadmodule.        0.00       0.00      0.00          2
     multihop.        0.00       0.00      0.00          3
      neptune.        1.00       1.00      1.00     102293
         nmap.        0.52       0.99      0.68       1167
       normal.        1.00       1.00      1.00     281286
         perl.        0.00       0.00      0.00          1
          phf.        0.17       1.00      0.29          1
          pod.        0.26       1.00      0.42         18
    portsweep.        0.96       0.99      0.98       1345
        satan.        0.96       1.00      0.98       2691
        smurf.        1.00       1.00      1.00     106198
     teardrop.        0.99       0.98      0.98         89
  warezmaster.        0.45       0.90      0.60         10

   avg / total        1.00       1.00      1.00     500000
```

The results look much better than the baseline and the previous solution. In fact:

1. The accuracy measured on the balanced training set is close to the one recorded on the test set. This ensures the generalization capabilities of the model.

2. The confusion matrix is *almost* diagonal. It means that all the classes have been included in the fitting (and the prediction) phase.

3. The precision/recall and F1 score are non-zero for many classes, even for those with little support.

At this point, we're satisfied with the solution. If you would like to dig further and test more model hypotheses on the full 5-million dataset, it's time now to move to non-linear classifiers. When doing so, please note in advance both the complexity and the running time required to get a prediction (after all, you're using a dataset containing more than 100 million values).

A ranking problem

Given some descriptors of a car and its price, the goal of this problem is to predict the degree to which the car is riskier than its price indicates. Actuaries in the insurance business call this process *symboling*, and the outcome is a rank: a value of +3 indicates the car is risky; -3 indicates that it's pretty safe (although the lowest value in the dataset is -2).

The description of the car includes its specifications in terms of various characteristics (brand, fuel type, body style, length, and so on). Moreover, you get its price and normalized loss in use as compared to other cars (this represents the average loss per car per year, normalized for all cars within a certain car segment).

There are 205 cars in the dataset, and the number of features is 25; some of them are categorical, and others are numerical. In addition, the dataset expressively states that there are some missing values, encoded using the string `"?"`.

Although it is not stated directly on the presentation page, the goal of our task is to minimize the *label ranking loss*, a measure that indicates how well we performed the ranking. This score works on probabilities, and a perfect rank gives a loss of zero. Using regression scores, such as MAE or MSE, has little relevance to this task, since the prediction must be an integer; also, a classification score such as `accuracy` makes no sense either, since it doesn't tell us how far we are from the perfect solution. Another score we will see in the code is **label ranking average precision** (**LRAP**). In this case, a perfect ranked output has a score of one (exactly like precision in the sense of classification). More information about the metrics is available on the Scikit-learn website: `http://scikit-learn.org/stable/modules/model_evaluation.html` or in the *Ranking Measures and Loss Functions in Learning to Rank* paper, presented in 2009 at the Advances in Neural Information Processing Systems Conference.

A full description of this problem can be found at: `https://archive.ics.uci.edu/ml/datasets/Automobile`.

First of all, let's load the data. The CSV file has no header; therefore we will manually set the column names. Also, since the author of the dataset has released the information, all the `"?"` strings will be handled as missing data—that is, Pandas `NaN` values:

```
In:
import matplotlib.pyplot as plt
%matplotlib inline
import matplotlib.pylab as pylab

import numpy as np
```

```
import pandas as pd

columns = ["symboling","normalized-losses","make","fuel-type",
           "aspiration","num-of-doors","body-style","drive-wheels",
           "engine-location","wheel-base","length","width","height",
           "curb-weight","engine-type","num-of-cylinders",
           "engine-size","fuel-system","bore","stroke",
           "compression-ratio","horsepower","peak-rpm","city-mpg",
           "highway-mpg","price"]

dataset = pd.read_csv('./autos/imports-85.data',
                      na_values="?", names=columns)
```

Although it doesn't guarantee everything is perfect, let's look at the first lines of the dataset. Here we're able to identify the missing data (containing NaN values) and understand which features are categorical and which numerical:

```
In:
print(dataset.head())
Out:
   symboling  normalized-losses         make fuel-type aspiration  \
0          3                NaN  alfa-romero       gas        std
1          3                NaN  alfa-romero       gas        std
2          1                NaN  alfa-romero       gas        std
3          2                164         audi       gas        std
4          2                164         audi       gas        std

   num-of-doors  body-style drive-wheels engine-location  wheel-base
...      \
0          two  convertible          rwd           front        88.6
...
1          two  convertible          rwd           front        88.6
...
2          two    hatchback          rwd           front        94.5
...
3         four        sedan          fwd           front        99.8
...
4         four        sedan          4wd           front        99.4
...

   engine-size fuel-system  bore  stroke compression-ratio horsepower
\
0          130        mpfi  3.47    2.68                 9        111
1          130        mpfi  3.47    2.68                 9        111
2          152        mpfi  2.68    3.47                 9        154
3          109        mpfi  3.19    3.40                10        102
```

4	136	mpfi 3.19	3.40	8	115

	peak-rpm	city-mpg	highway-mpg	price
0	5000	21	27	13495
1	5000	21	27	16500
2	5000	19	26	16500
3	5500	24	30	13950
4	5500	18	22	17450

```
[5 rows x 26 columns]
In:
dataset.dtypes
Out:
symboling              int64
normalized-losses    float64
make                  object
fuel-type             object
aspiration            object
num-of-doors          object
body-style            object
drive-wheels          object
engine-location       object
wheel-base           float64
length               float64
width                float64
height               float64
curb-weight            int64
engine-type           object
num-of-cylinders      object
engine-size            int64
fuel-system           object
bore                 float64
stroke               float64
compression-ratio    float64
horsepower           float64
peak-rpm             float64
city-mpg               int64
highway-mpg            int64
price                float64
dtype: object
```

It seems we have many categorical features. Here, we have to think carefully about what to do. The dataset contains only 205 observations; therefore transforming all the categorical features to dummy features is not a great idea (we may end up with more features than observations). Let's try to be very conservative with the number of features created. Carefully checking the features, we can use the following approach:

1. Some categorical features are actually (wordy) numerical: they contain numbers indicating a number. For them, we just need to map words to numbers. In this case, no additional features are created.

2. Some other categorical features are actually binary (two doors versus four doors, diesel versus gas, and so on). For them, we can map the two levels to different values (0 and 1). Even here, we don't need to create additional features.

3. All the remaining should be dummy-encoded.

This procedure is shown in the following cell. To create the first map, we simply use the map method provided by Pandas. For the second mapping, we use the LabelEncoder object provided by Scikit-learn; for the last one, we use the get_dummies function, as seen in the previous example:

```
In:
from sklearn.preprocessing import LabelEncoder


words_to_nums = {'two':2, 'three':3, 'four':4, 'five':5,
                 'six':6, 'eight':8, 'twelve':12}

columns_to_map = ['num-of-cylinders', 'num-of-doors']
columns_to_dummy = ['make', 'body-style', 'drive-wheels',
                    'engine-type', 'fuel-system']
columns_to_label_encode = ['fuel-type', 'aspiration',
                           'engine-location']

for col in columns_to_map:
    dataset[col] = dataset[col].map(pd.Series(words_to_nums))

for col in columns_to_label_encode:
    dataset[col] = LabelEncoder().fit_transform(dataset[col])

dataset = pd.get_dummies(dataset, columns=columns_to_dummy)

dataset.shape
Out:
(205,66)
```

Adopting this conservative approach, the final number of columns is 66 (previously it was 26). Now, let's extract the target value vector out of the DataFrame, and then map every NaN value to the median of the feature, creating the observation matrix.

Why did we use the median (instead of the mean)? Because the dataset is so small that we don't want to introduce new values:

```
In:
ranks = dataset['symboling'].as_matrix()
observations = dataset.drop('symboling', axis=1).as_matrix()
In:
from sklearn.preprocessing import Imputer
imp = Imputer(strategy="median", axis=0)
observations = imp.fit_transform(observations)
```

Now, it's time to split the observations into training and testing. Since the dataset is very small, we decided to have the testing set made up of 25% of the observations (around 51 samples). Also, we tried to achieve a testing set containing the same percentage of samples for each class. For this purpose, we've used the StratifiedKFold class.

```
In:
from sklearn.cross_validation import StratifiedKFold

kf = StratifiedKFold(ranks, 4, shuffle=True, random_state=101)
idxs = list(kf)[0]

X_train = observations[idxs[0], :]
X_test = observations[idxs[1], :]
y_train = ranks[idxs[0]]
y_test = ranks[idxs[1]]
```

The next step is creating two functions: the first should map classes to vectors of probability for each class (for example, class -2 becomes the vector [1.0, 0.0, 0.0, 0.0, 0.0, 0.0]; class +3 becomes the vector [0.0, 0.0, 0.0, 0.0, 0.0, 1.0], and so on). This step is required by the scoring function.

The second function we need is to check whether the classifier is trained on a dataset that includes all the classes (since we're operating on a training set composed of only 153 samples, and we will use cross validation, it's better to carefully check every step). To do so, we use a simple assert equality:

```
In:
def prediction_to_probas(class_pred):

    probas = []
```

```
    for el in class_pred:
        prob = [0.]*6
        prob[el+2] = 1.0
        probas.append(prob)
    return np.array(probas)

def check_estimator(estimator):
    assert sum(
        np.abs(clf.classes_ - np.array([-2, -1, 0, 1, 2, 3]))
    ) == 0
```

Now, it's time to classify. We will initially use a simple `LogisticRegression`. Since we have a multiclass problem, we can use more than one CPU in the training process. After training the classifier, we print the `Ranking loss` and the `Ranking avg precision score` to have a baseline for comparison purposes:

```
In:
from sklearn.linear_model import LogisticRegression

clf = LogisticRegression(random_state=101)
clf.fit(X_train, y_train)
check_estimator(clf)

y_test_proba = prediction_to_probas(y_test)
y_pred_proba = clf.predict_proba(X_test)
In:
from sklearn.metrics import label_ranking_average_precision_score
from sklearn.metrics import label_ranking_loss

print("Ranking loss:", label_ranking_loss(y_test_proba,
y_pred_proba))
print("Ranking avg precision:",
label_ranking_average_precision_score(y_test_proba, y_pred_proba))
Out:
Ranking loss: 0.0905660377358
Ranking avg precision: 0.822327044025
```

The baseline result is already not too bad. The `Ranking loss` is close to zero (and, in this case, the average label precision is close to 1). Now we try to improve the solution, using a grid-search cross-validation. Since we have very few samples in the training set, we have to use a boosted validation, where each fold may contain samples appearing in other folds. `StratifiedShuffleSplit` is the best option, ensuring as well that the validation set contains the same percentage of samples for each class. We will create five folds, each of them containing 70% of the training set as training, and the remaining 30 as testing.

The last thing we should create is a scoring function for the cross validation: Scikit-learn doesn't include any learn-to-rank scoring function out of the box in the `GridSearchCV` object, therefore we have to build it. We decide to build it as the label ranking loss multiplied by `-1`: since the goal of the grid search is to maximize the score, we have to invert it to find its minimum:

```
In:
from sklearn.grid_search import GridSearchCV
from sklearn.metrics import make_scorer
from sklearn.cross_validation import StratifiedShuffleSplit

def scorer(estimator, X, y):

    check_estimator(estimator)
    y_proba = prediction_to_probas(y)
    return -1*label_ranking_loss(y_proba,
estimator.predict_proba(X))

params = {'C': np.logspace(-1, 1, 10)}

cv = StratifiedShuffleSplit(y_train, random_state=101,

                          n_iter=5, train_size=0.70)
gs_cv = GridSearchCV(LogisticRegression(random_state=101),
                param_grid=params,
                n_jobs=1,
                cv=cv,
                scoring=scorer)

gs_cv.fit(X_train, y_train)
clf = gs_cv.best_estimator_

y_pred_proba = clf.predict_proba(X_test)

print("Ranking loss:",
    label_ranking_loss(y_test_proba, y_pred_proba))
print("Ranking avg precision:",
    label_ranking_average_precision_score(y_test_proba,
                                        y_pred_proba))
Out:
Ranking loss: 0.0716981132075
Ranking avg precision: 0.839622641509
```

With the hyper parameter optimization procedure, combined with the cross-validation, we've been able to improve the performance. Now, let's check how the confusion matrix looks for this solution:

```
In:
from sklearn.metrics import confusion_matrix

def plot_normalised_confusion_matrix(cm):
    labels_str = [str(n) for n in range(-2, 4)]
    pylab.rcParams['figure.figsize'] = (6.0, 6.0)
    cm_normalized = cm.astype('float') / cm.sum(axis=1)[:,
np.newaxis]
    plt.imshow(cm_normalized, interpolation='nearest',
cmap=plt.cm.Blues)
    plt.colorbar()
    tick_marks = np.arange(len(labels_str))
    plt.xticks(tick_marks, labels_str, rotation=90)
    plt.yticks(tick_marks, labels_str)
    plt.tight_layout()
    plt.ylabel('True label')
    plt.xlabel('Predicted label')
    plt.show()

plot_normalised_confusion_matrix(confusion_matrix(y_test,
clf.predict(X_test)), )
Out:
```

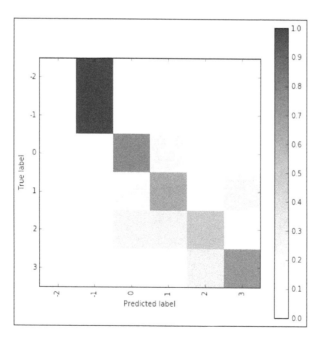

It looks pretty diagonal, except for the -2 class (where we have indeed very few samples). Overall, we consider a ranking loss lower than 0.1 to be an excellent result.

A time series problem

The last problem we're going to see in this chapter is about prediction in time. The standard name for these problems is time series analysis, since the prediction is made on descriptors extracted in the past; therefore, the outcome at the current time will become a feature for the prediction of the next point in time. In this exercise, we're using the closing values for several stocks composing the Dow Jones index in 2011.

Several features compose the dataset, but in this problem (to make a short and complete exercise) we're just using the closing values of each week for each of the 30 measured stocks, ordered in time. The dataset spans six months: we're using the first half of the dataset (corresponding to the first quarter of the year under observation, with 12 weeks) to train our algorithm, and the second half (containing the second quarter of the year, with 13 weeks) to test the predictions.

Moreover, since we don't expect readers to have a background in economics, we've tried to make things as simple as possible. In a real-life situation, such a prediction will be too simple to get money out of the market, but in this short example we've tried to keep the focus on the time series analysis, dropping all the other inputs and sources.

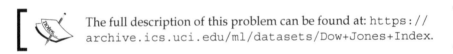

The full description of this problem can be found at: https://archive.ics.uci.edu/ml/datasets/Dow+Jones+Index.

According to the readme file distributed along with the dataset, there are no missing values; therefore, the loading operation is quite straightforward:

```
In:
import matplotlib.pyplot as plt
%matplotlib inline

import numpy as np
import pandas as pd


dataset = pd.read_csv('./dji/dow_jones_index.data')
```

Let's now try to decode the rows we're interested in (stock and close): it seems that the closing values are all strings, starting with $ and followed by the floating point value relative to the closing price. We should then select the correct columns and cast the closing price to the right data type:

```
In:
print(dataset.head())
Out:
     quarter stock     date      open     high      low    close
volume  \
0          1    AA  1/7/2011  $15.82   $16.72   $15.78   $16.42
239655616
1          1    AA  1/14/2011 $16.71   $16.71   $15.64   $15.97
242963398
2          1    AA  1/21/2011 $16.19   $16.38   $15.60   $15.79
138428495
3          1    AA  1/28/2011 $15.87   $16.63   $15.82   $16.13
151379173
4          1    AA  2/4/2011  $16.18   $17.39   $16.18   $17.14
154387761

    percent_change_price   percent_change_volume_over_last_wk  \
0               3.79267                                  NaN
1              -4.42849                             1.380223
2              -2.47066                           -43.024959
3               1.63831                             9.355500
4               5.93325                             1.987452

    previous_weeks_volume next_weeks_open next_weeks_close  \
0                     NaN          $16.71          $15.97
1               239655616         $16.19          $15.79
2               242963398         $15.87          $16.13
3               138428495         $16.18          $17.14
4               151379173         $17.33          $17.37

    percent_change_next_weeks_price  days_to_next_dividend  \
0                         -4.428490                     26
1                         -2.470660                     19
2                          1.638310                     12
3                          5.933250                      5
4                          0.230814                     97

    percent_return_next_dividend
0                       0.182704
1                       0.187852
```

```
2                          0.189994
3                          0.185989
4                          0.175029
In:
observations = {}

for el in dataset[['stock', 'close']].iterrows():

    stock = el[1].stock
    close = float(el[1].close.replace("$", ""))

    try:
        observations[stock].append(close)
    except KeyError:
        observations[stock] = [close]
```

Let's now create a feature vector for each stock. In the simplest instance, it's just a row containing the sorted closing prices for the 25 weeks:

```
In:
X = []
stock_names = sorted(observations.keys())

for stock in stock_names:
    X.append(observations[stock])


X = np.array(X)
```

Let's now build a baseline: we can try the regressor on the first 12 weeks, and then test it by recursively offsetting the data — that is, to predict the 13th week, we use the first 12 weeks; to predict the value at the 14th week, we use 12 weeks ending with the 13th one. And so on.

Note that, in this very simple approach, we build just a classifier for all the stocks, independently by their price, and we use both R^2 and MAE to score our learner for each week of analysis (a score for the 13th week, one for the 14th, and so on). Finally, we compute mean and variance of these scores:

```
In:
from sklearn.linear_model import LinearRegression
from sklearn.metrics import r2_score, mean_absolute_error

X_train = X[:, :12]
y_train = X[:, 12]

regr_1 = LinearRegression()
```

```
regr_1.fit(X_train, y_train)
In:
plot_vals = []

for offset in range(0, X.shape[1]-X_train.shape[1]):
    X_test = X[:, offset:12+offset]
    y_test = X[:, 12+offset]

    r2 = r2_score(y_test, regr_1.predict(X_test))
    mae = mean_absolute_error(y_test, regr_1.predict(X_test))

    print("offset=", offset, "r2_score=", r2)
    print("offset=", offset, "MAE      =", mae)

    plot_vals.append( (offset, r2, mae) )

print()
print("r2_score: mean=", np.mean([x[1] for x in plot_vals]),
"variance=", np.var([x[1] for x in plot_vals]))
print("mae_score: mean=", np.mean([x[2] for x in plot_vals]),
"variance=", np.var([x[2] for x in plot_vals]))
Out:
offset= 0 r2_score= 0.999813479679
offset= 0 MAE      = 0.384145971072
offset= 1 r2_score= 0.99504246854
offset= 1 MAE      = 1.602203752
offset= 2 r2_score= 0.995188278161
offset= 2 MAE      = 1.76248455475
offset= 3 r2_score= 0.998287091734
offset= 3 MAE      = 1.15856848271
offset= 4 r2_score= 0.997938802118
offset= 4 MAE      = 1.11955148717
offset= 5 r2_score= 0.985036566148
offset= 5 MAE      = 2.94239117688
offset= 6 r2_score= 0.991598279578
offset= 6 MAE      = 2.35632383083
offset= 7 r2_score= 0.995485519307
offset= 7 MAE      = 1.73191962456
offset= 8 r2_score= 0.992872581249
offset= 8 MAE      = 1.9828644662
offset= 9 r2_score= 0.990012202362
offset= 9 MAE      = 2.66825249081
offset= 10 r2_score= 0.996984329367
offset= 10 MAE      = 1.38682132207
offset= 11 r2_score= 0.999029861989
offset= 11 MAE      = 0.761720947323
offset= 12 r2_score= 0.996280599178
```

```
offset= 12 MAE      = 1.53124828142

r2_score: mean= 0.99489000457 variance= 1.5753065199e-05
mae_score: mean= 1.64526895291 variance= 0.487371842069
```

On the 13 testing weeks, the R^2 is 0.99 on average (with a variance of 0.0000157) and the MAE is 1.64 on average (with a variance of 0.48). That's the baseline; let's plot it:

```
In:
fig, ax1 = plt.subplots()
ax1.plot([x[0] for x in plot_vals], [x[1] for x in plot_vals],
'b-')
ax1.plot(plot_vals[0][0], plot_vals[0][1], 'bo')

ax1.set_xlabel('test week')
# Make the y-axis label and tick labels match the line color.
ax1.set_ylabel('r2_score', color='b')
for tl in ax1.get_yticklabels():
    tl.set_color('b')
ax1.set_ylim([0.9, 1.1])


ax2 = ax1.twinx()
ax2.plot([x[0] for x in plot_vals], [x[2] for x in plot_vals],
'r-')
ax2.plot(plot_vals[0][0], plot_vals[0][2], 'ro')
ax2.set_ylabel('mae score', color='r')
for tl in ax2.get_yticklabels():
    tl.set_color('r')
ax2.set_ylim([0, 3.3])

plt.xlim([-.1, 12.1])

plt.show()
Out:
```

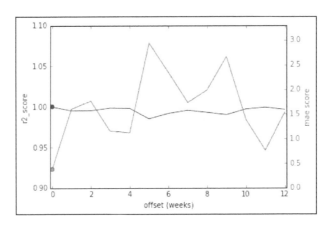

Are we sure that the value of 12 weeks ago is still a good predictor for the current week? Let's now try to improve our scores by decreasing the training weeks. As an additional advantage, we will also have more training data. Let's try using 5 (a little more than a month):

```
In:
training_len = 5

X_train_short = X[:, :training_len]
y_train_short = X[:, training_len]


for offset in range(1, 12-training_len):
    X_train_short = np.vstack( (X_train_short, X[:,
offset:training_len+offset]) )
    y_train_short = np.concatenate( (y_train_short, X[:,
training_len+offset]) )
In:
regr_2 = LinearRegression()
regr_2.fit(X_train_short, y_train_short)
In:
plot_vals = []

for offset in range(0, X.shape[1]-X_train.shape[1]):
    X_test = X[:, 12-training_len+offset:12+offset]
    y_test = X[:, 12+offset]

    r2 = r2_score(y_test, regr_2.predict(X_test))
    mae = mean_absolute_error(y_test, regr_2.predict(X_test))

    print("offset=", offset, "r2_score=", r2)
    print("offset=", offset, "MAE       =", mae)

    plot_vals.append( (offset, r2, mae) )

print()
print("r2_score: mean=", np.mean([x[1] for x in plot_vals]),
"variance=", np.var([x[1] for x in plot_vals]))
print("mae_score: mean=", np.mean([x[2] for x in plot_vals]),
"variance=", np.var([x[2] for x in plot_vals]))
Out:
offset= 0 r2_score= 0.998579501272
offset= 0 MAE       = 0.85687189133
offset= 1 r2_score= 0.999412004606
offset= 1 MAE       = 0.552138850961
```

```
offset= 2 r2_score= 0.998668959234
offset= 2 MAE     = 0.941052814674
offset= 3 r2_score= 0.998291291965
offset= 3 MAE     = 1.03476245234
offset= 4 r2_score= 0.997006831124
offset= 4 MAE     = 1.45857426198
offset= 5 r2_score= 0.996849578723
offset= 5 MAE     = 1.04394939395
offset= 6 r2_score= 0.998134003499
offset= 6 MAE     = 1.05938998285
offset= 7 r2_score= 0.998391605331
offset= 7 MAE     = 0.865007491822
offset= 8 r2_score= 0.999317752361
offset= 8 MAE     = 0.607975744054
offset= 9 r2_score= 0.996058731277
offset= 9 MAE     = 1.62548930127
offset= 10 r2_score= 0.997319345983
offset= 10 MAE     = 1.2305378204
offset= 11 r2_score= 0.999264102166
offset= 11 MAE     = 0.649407612032
offset= 12 r2_score= 0.998227164258
offset= 12 MAE     = 1.020568135


r2_score: mean= 0.998116990138 variance= 9.8330905525e-07
mae_score: mean= 0.995825057897 variance= 0.0908384278533
```

With this approach, both R^2 and MAE have improved, on average, and their variance is perceptibly lower:

```
In:
fig, ax1 = plt.subplots()
ax1.plot([x[0] for x in plot_vals], [x[1] for x in plot_vals],
'b-')
ax1.plot(plot_vals[0][0], plot_vals[0][1], 'bo')

ax1.set_xlabel('test week')
# Make the y-axis label and tick labels match the line color.
ax1.set_ylabel('r2_score', color='b')
for tl in ax1.get_yticklabels():
    tl.set_color('b')
ax1.set_ylim([0.95, 1.05])


ax2 = ax1.twinx()
```

```
ax2.plot([x[0] for x in plot_vals], [x[2] for x in plot_vals],
'r-')
ax2.plot(plot_vals[0][0], plot_vals[0][2], 'ro')
ax2.set_ylabel('mae score', color='r')
for tl in ax2.get_yticklabels():
    tl.set_color('r')
ax2.set_ylim([0, 2.2])

plt.xlim([-.1, 12.1])

plt.show()
Out:
```

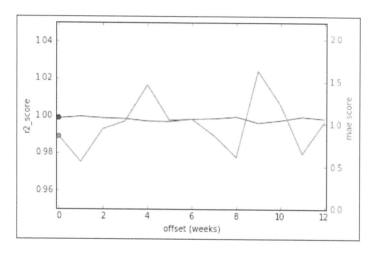

Since the approach seems to be working better, let's now try to grid-search the best training length, spanning from 1 to 12:

```
In:
training_lens = range(1,13)
models = {}


for training_len in training_lens:
    X_train_short = X[:, :training_len]
    y_train_short = X[:, training_len]

    for offset in range(1, 12-training_len):
        X_train_short = np.vstack( (X_train_short, X[:,
offset:training_len+offset]) )
        y_train_short = np.concatenate( (y_train_short, X[:,
training_len+offset]) )
```

```
    regr_x = LinearRegression()
    regr_x.fit(X_train_short, y_train_short)
    models[training_len] = regr_x

    plot_vals = []

    for offset in range(0, X.shape[1]-X_train.shape[1]):
        X_test = X[:, 12-training_len+offset:12+offset]
        y_test = X[:, 12+offset]

        r2 = r2_score(y_test, regr_x.predict(X_test))
        mae = mean_absolute_error(y_test, regr_x.predict(X_test))

        plot_vals.append( (offset, r2, mae) )

    fig, ax1 = plt.subplots()
    ax1.plot([x[0] for x in plot_vals], [x[1] for x in plot_vals],
'b-')
    ax1.plot(plot_vals[0][0], plot_vals[0][1], 'bo')

    ax1.set_xlabel('test week')
    # Make the y-axis label and tick labels match the line color.
    ax1.set_ylabel('r2_score', color='b')
    for tl in ax1.get_yticklabels():
        tl.set_color('b')
    ax1.set_ylim([0.95, 1.05])


    ax2 = ax1.twinx()
    ax2.plot([x[0] for x in plot_vals], [x[2] for x in plot_vals],
'r-')
    ax2.plot(plot_vals[0][0], plot_vals[0][2], 'ro')
    ax2.set_ylabel('mae score', color='r')
    for tl in ax2.get_yticklabels():
        tl.set_color('r')
    ax2.set_ylim([0, max([2.2, 1.1*np.max([x[2] for x in
plot_vals])])])

    plt.xlim([-.1, 12.1])

    plt.title("results with training_len={}".format(training_len))

    plt.show()
```

```
    print("r2_score: mean=", np.mean([x[1] for x in plot_vals]),
"variance=", np.var([x[1] for x in plot_vals]))
    print("mae_score: mean=", np.mean([x[2] for x in plot_vals]),
"variance=", np.var([x[2] for x in plot_vals]))
```

```
Out:
... [images are omitted] ...
results with training_len=1
r2_score: mean= 0.998224065712 variance= 1.00685934679e-06
mae_score: mean= 0.95962574798 variance= 0.0663013566722

results with training_len=2
r2_score: mean= 0.998198628321 variance= 9.17757825917e-07
mae_score: mean= 0.969741651259 variance= 0.0661101843822

results with training_len=3
r2_score: mean= 0.998223327997 variance= 8.57207677825e-07
mae_score: mean= 0.969261583196 variance= 0.0715715354908

results with training_len=4
r2_score: mean= 0.998223602314 variance= 7.91949263056e-07
mae_score: mean= 0.972853132744 variance= 0.0737436496017

results with training_len=5
r2_score: mean= 0.998116990138 variance= 9.8330905525e-07
mae_score: mean= 0.995825057897 variance= 0.0908384278533

results with training_len=6
r2_score: mean= 0.997953763986 variance= 1.14333232014e-06
mae_score: mean= 1.04107069762 variance= 0.100961792252

results with training_len=7
r2_score: mean= 0.997481850128 variance= 1.85277659214e-06
mae_score: mean= 1.19114613181 variance= 0.121982635728

results with training_len=8
r2_score: mean= 0.99715522262 variance= 3.27488548806e-06
mae_score: mean= 1.23998671525 variance= 0.173529737205

results with training_len=9
r2_score: mean= 0.995975415477 variance= 5.76973840581e-06
mae_score: mean= 1.48200981286 variance= 0.22134177338

results with training_len=10
```

```
r2_score: mean= 0.995828230003 variance= 4.92217626753e-06
mae_score: mean= 1.51007677609 variance= 0.209938740518

results with training_len=11
r2_score: mean= 0.994520917305 variance= 7.24129427869e-06
mae_score: mean= 1.78424593989 variance= 0.213259808552

results with training_len=12
r2_score: mean= 0.99489000457 variance= 1.5753065199e-05
mae_score: mean= 1.64526895291 variance= 0.487371842069
```

The best trade-off is with `training_len=3`.

Open questions

As you've seen, in this example we didn't normalize the data, using stocks with high and low prices together. This fact may confuse the learner, since the observations don't have the same center. With a bit of preprocessing, we may obtain better results, applying a per-stock normalization. Can you think what else could we do, and how could we test the algorithm?

Summary

In this chapter, we've explored four practical data science examples involving classifiers and regressors. We strongly encourage readers to read, understand, and try to add further steps, in order to boost performance.

Index

T

U

V

W

Z

Thank you for buying
Regression Analysis with Python

About Packt Publishing

Packt, pronounced 'packed', published its first book, *Mastering phpMyAdmin for Effective MySQL Management*, in April 2004, and subsequently continued to specialize in publishing highly focused books on specific technologies and solutions.

Our books and publications share the experiences of your fellow IT professionals in adapting and customizing today's systems, applications, and frameworks. Our solution-based books give you the knowledge and power to customize the software and technologies you're using to get the job done. Packt books are more specific and less general than the IT books you have seen in the past. Our unique business model allows us to bring you more focused information, giving you more of what you need to know, and less of what you don't.

Packt is a modern yet unique publishing company that focuses on producing quality, cutting-edge books for communities of developers, administrators, and newbies alike. For more information, please visit our website at www.packtpub.com.

About Packt Open Source

In 2010, Packt launched two new brands, Packt Open Source and Packt Enterprise, in order to continue its focus on specialization. This book is part of the Packt Open Source brand, home to books published on software built around open source licenses, and offering information to anybody from advanced developers to budding web designers. The Open Source brand also runs Packt's Open Source Royalty Scheme, by which Packt gives a royalty to each open source project about whose software a book is sold.

Writing for Packt

We welcome all inquiries from people who are interested in authoring. Book proposals should be sent to author@packtpub.com. If your book idea is still at an early stage and you would like to discuss it first before writing a formal book proposal, then please contact us; one of our commissioning editors will get in touch with you.

We're not just looking for published authors; if you have strong technical skills but no writing experience, our experienced editors can help you develop a writing career, or simply get some additional reward for your expertise.

Python Data Analysis

ISBN: 978-1-78355-335-8   Paperback: 348 pages

Learn how to apply powerful data analysis techniques with popular open source Python modules

1. Learn how to find, manipulate, and analyze data using Python.

2. Perform advanced, high performance linear algebra and mathematical calculations with clean and efficient Python code.

3. An easy-to-follow guide with realistic examples that are frequently used in real-world data analysis projects.

Learning Python Data Visualization

ISBN: 978-1-78355-333-4   Paperback: 212 pages

Master how to build dynamic HTML5-ready SVG charts using Python and the pygal library

1. A practical guide that helps you break into the world of data visualization with Python.

2. Understand the fundamentals of building charts in Python.

3. Packed with easy-to-understand tutorials for developers who are new to Python or charting in Python.

Please check **www.PacktPub.com** for information on our titles

Learning Python Design Patterns

ISBN: 978-1-78328-337-8   Paperback: 100 pages

A practical and fast-paced guide exploring Python design patterns

1. Explore the Model-View-Controller pattern and learn how to build a URL shortening service.

2. All design patterns use a real-world example that can be modified and applied in your software.

3. No unnecessary theory! The book consists of only the fundamental knowledge that you need to know.

Practical Data Science Cookbook

ISBN: 978-1-78398-024-6   Paperback: 396 pages

89 hands-on recipes to help you complete real-world data science projects in R and Python

1. The book is packed with simple and concise Python code examples to effectively demonstrate advanced concepts in action.

2. Explore concepts such as programming, data mining, data analysis, data visualization, and machine learning using Python.

3. Get up to speed on machine learning algorithms with the help of easy-to-follow, insightful recipes.

Please check **www.PacktPub.com** for information on our titles

CPSIA information can be obtained
at www.ICGtesting.com
Printed in the USA
LVHW022310260719
625586LV00004B/31/P